D0528665

UNIVERSITY OF
GLOUCE

Equal and Different

Male and Female in Church and Family

Michael Harper

Hodder & Stoughton

LONDON SYDNEY AUCKLAND

Typeset by Hewer Text Composition Services, Edinburgh
Printed and bound in Great Britain by
Cox & Wyman Ltd, Reading, Berks.

Hodder and Stoughton Ltd,
A division of Hodder Headline PLC
338 Euston Road
London NW1 3BH

To the memory of my father and mother,
from whom I discovered that 'dogs have four legs'

Contents

Foreword

By Larry Christenson and Joanne May

Pastor Larry Christenson

This book surprised me. Michael Harper and I have known each other for 30 years. We have worked together on ecumenical projects. We have ministered together on several continents. I thought we had talked about most things in which we shared a common interest. When I read the manuscript for this book, I encountered an interest, indeed a deep concern, of Michael's that we had *not* talked about over the years. I would not have guessed that he held the strong conviction about the ordination of women that he articulates in this book.

A paragraph in the Appendix, 'Personally speaking', sets the matter in perspective. It is one of the most telling statements in the book:

I am ashamed to say that the period 1976–88 for me was one of comparative indifference, certainly not strong feelings on either side of the women's ordination question. I have never thought women should be ordained, but equally never until the last few years felt strongly they should not. (pp. 212–13)

In other words, the position that Michael sets forth in this book is not simply the statement of a traditional belief or prejudice. It represents a *significant movement – from indifference to firm conviction*. And what has been the 'engine' of that movement?

A solid and sober study of the Word of God, enhanced by the testimony of church history, and a clear-eyed evaluation of ideologies and practices in contemporary life.

Here is a book – here is a man – whose understanding and conviction have been signally shaped by the authority of God's Word.

Almost at once, the reader will sense a great clarity of purpose. The formal statement of it comes towards the end of the book:

> we are concerned in this book with the objective truth, revealed by God through the Scriptures, and through the faithful handing down of the Church's understanding of them through many generations. (p. 207)

Precisely this has been lacking, both in the consideration of women's ordination, and of the broader issue of men's and women's roles in home and Church. The issue has been framed, *and policies have been formed*, by the fashionable rhetoric of secular culture. God's will and purpose, as revealed in Scripture, has been brushed over lightly.

Ironically, in the secular culture itself, the egalitarian rhetoric of feminism finds itself increasingly at cross purposes with the reality of what men and women experience in life. A substantial and growing body of empirical research finds that the egalitarian model does not produce the promised happy partnership between men and women.

Pastor Christenson is a Lutheran Pastor living in Minnesota, USA. He serves with Michael Harper on the Executive of the International Charismatic Consultation on World Evangelisation (ICCOWE); he is the author of many books including The Christian Family *which has sold over 2 million copies and been translated into eighteen languages.*

Dr Joanne May

When I started reading Michael Harper's book, women's ordination was not an issue of great personal interest or concern to me. I have changed! I believe that in Church leadership, as in family life, God has designed a system that works.

Michael's straightforward interpretation of Scripture is not only theologically accurate; it is sociologically authentic. He correctly links the ordination of women with the nature of family life on the one hand, and with feminism on the other.

It is important to note that feminists built their movement on rhetoric and theory that were, and continue to be, in direct conflict with well-designed, replicated research. Simultaneous with the beginning of feminism, a number of research studies measured marriages that were healthy and satisfying for both women and men. Without exception, these studies described the healthy families as having an authoritative style of leadership led by the father. The mother affirmed, or submitted to, the leadership of the father. As the father was affirmed in his leadership, he was then free to serve his wife and family, and the larger community as well. In other words, empirical research confirmed the biblical model of headship.

Submission and sacrifice, not the attainment of personal power, characterised this research model. A central finding in the research was that the moral development and the discipline of the children depended heavily on the father's leadership. Family relationships and the development of autonomy in the children came more from the mother. The functions of both parents proved extremely important, but they were different. When role reversals occurred, the results were often disastrous.

Feminists ignored this research and opted for an egalitarian model of family life. Their rhetoric promised a rosy new world of liberation and empowerment for women. Research models in the 1990s have shown that it does not work. It does not work because it rests on a false premise. At its heart stands the erroneous belief that personal power, through the mechanism of a score-keeping egalitarianism, is the road to happiness.

Michael's scholarly work has led me to consider possible links between feminism and the ordination of women. I reflected on the experience of some Protestant churches in the United States that began to ordain women in recent decades. It seems to me that we have seen a marked change in them. In mainline Protestant churches, adoption of feminism has become politically correct. One aspect of this has been a disproportionate emphasis on a leadership style that is distinctively female. It has quite likely influenced the role of the Church in the larger society.

The Church has been a responder to the ills of society. This is an important function, but aided by feminists, it has often become the only function. Something akin to a role reversal has taken place, not unlike role reversal in the family. The Church no longer leads in the discipline and moral development of society. It simply responds to the dysfunctions of a society in decay.

Research does not support the rhetoric of feminism that there is no difference in leadership style between men and women. The Church needs the heart of women to respond to the hurts of society. But it also needs the authority of ordained male leadership, if the Church is to exercise a positive influence in the world.

Dr May is Larry Christenson's sister, and lives in Excelsior, Minnesota. She is a Clinical Psychologist and Family Counsellor.

Appreciations

I would like to thank those who have helped me with the writing of this book. I am grateful to Pastor Larry Christenson and his sister, Dr Joanne May, a clinical psychologist, for their Foreword; our long and fruitful friendship with Larry and Nordis Christenson has meant so much to my wife Jeanne and to me. Larry's book *The Christian Family* was published in 1970. It is a classic defence of Christian family values.

I would add my thanks to Bishop Bertil Gartner, the former Bishop of Goteborg, Sweden. He is a man of great courage and integrity, who to the end of his episcopate resisted intense pressure to ordain women in Sweden. He has helped me with some of the sections where I have mentioned events in Sweden relative to this subject.

I would also like to thank David Pawson and Dr Roger Beckwith for looking at the biblical section. Many of their wise corrections and comments have been included in the book.

Jeanne and I appreciate our long friendship with Edward England, and his encouragements to continue writing. Also my thanks to Hodder & Stoughton; both of these relationships stretch back for over 30 years.

This book is dedicated to the memory of my father and mother. They convinced me from an early age that 'dogs have four legs', not five, and I shall be always grateful.

I would like to thank my wife Jeanne. I heard once that the wife of a well-known author was asked which book of his she liked the best. She replied that she did not know, because she hadn't read any of them. I have always joked that I can be sure to sell one copy of my books because my wife will buy it. Jeanne has shared fully in the preparatory reading, and the working out of each theme. Her comments and criticisms have been invaluable, especially on a subject we have both had to work out practically for many years.

Authors depend to a greater or less extent on the books of others. Many books have helped me, so it might be invidious to select any. However, I do want to mention particularly Dr Manfred Hauke's book *Women in the Priesthood?*, and his permission to quote from it. It deserves to be much better known and read.

Thanks be to God, for all his benefits. Through writing this book I have come to a greater trust than ever in the Lord Jesus Christ, who cared deeply for women, but also believed in and practised male headship in the Church and family. I have received fresh light on the subject, supremely through the Old and New Testaments, but also through our faithful ancestors, who have sought to be loyal to the biblical testimony. *Laus Deo*.

Michael Harper
Stanfords, October 1993

Chapter 1

Dogs have four legs

Does not the very nature of things teach you . . .?
(1 Cor. 11:14)

You may drive out nature with a pitchfork, yet she'll be constantly running back.
(Horace, *Ars Poetica* x. 24)

Dogs have four legs – at least, that is what I always thought until the General Synod of the Church of England in November 1992 voted that they have five. I am writing this book to reassure people that nature is right, because God created it. Dogs do have four legs, and I suspect a lot of other people think so.

I don't need to be told that female dogs also have four legs. It is not the sex of dogs that I have in mind, but the fact that all dogs, male and female, have four legs. I will not be surprised also if someone sends me a photograph of a dog with five legs (or more likely three). Possibly I will get postcards sent me from Italy with the famous six-legged Agip petroleum symbol on them. If I do, I will simply point out, without fear of contradiction, that such an animal is a genetic freak.

I shall show in this book that God has created gender, and put it within a sensible framework. When we keep it there, and follow the divine pattern, all will be well. We are not meant to tamper with the laws of nature. The cause of the ordination of women must show that it is consonant with nature (dogs have four legs), as well as Scripture and Tradition, and is not a freak (dogs have five legs), which is contrary to all three.

Let me list some of the dogs-have-four-legs gender specifics:

1. God has made men and women equally in his image.
2. God has given men the responsibility of headship, and women that of helper.
3. God's will is that marriage should be heterosexual.
4. Marriage is a life-long partnership between a man and a woman.
5. The father is the head of the family.
6. Children are to be desired, loved and cherished.
7. Parents, especially mothers, should give priority to their children in their early years.
8. Children are to be disciplined, and taught obedience, especially by their fathers.

And here are some of the dogs-have-five-legs gender specifics:

1. God has made women inferior to men.
2. God has made men and women equal in their roles.
3. God accepts same-sex marriages and relationships.
4. Divorce is acceptable whenever marriage fails, for whatever reason.
5. Neither the father nor the mother is the head of the family.
6. If children are not wanted, then through birth control we may prevent them being conceived, through abortion being born, and through childcare clinics being nurtured.
7. Our careers and leisure time are more important than our children.
8. Children are to be treated as equals.

I am listing here what is natural and unnatural. I am not judging individual circumstances. But a society that begins to treat as 'normal' or 'natural' what is the opposite is in grave danger. And that is the place we have come to, at least in the countries of the West.

Let me make it plain, this is *not* a book about a domestic squabble in the Church of England. The issues have far-ranging implications, not only for all Christians, but also for every living person on the face of the earth, whatever their colour or creed. All people are involved in gender, because everyone is either male or female. Also gender is now top priority on political as well as church agendas. The collapse of the family in Western society and the resulting rise in the cost of social benefits is a major matter for governments to handle. Add to that AIDS, the homosexual question, sexism, feminism, birth control, genetic engineering, abortion – to mention just a few – and you have a highly emotive catalogue of moral issues.

In fact gender is of *primary* concern to the world. The human race, at least in the Western world, is obsessively interested in it. To illustrate this, let's look at one randomly chosen issue of a tabloid newspaper. These items were all in the 1993 May Day edition of the *Daily Mail*:

- Sergeant Jose Zuniga is reported in trouble with the United States Army. A veteran of the Gulf War, he has publicly declared himself 'gay'. Should he continue, or should he leave?
- There is a report on a new TV series based on a novel by Jilly Cooper about the show-jumping world of 'saddles, sex and sensuality'. The heading says, 'riding is sexy for women'; why not for men?
- If riding is sexy for women, tipping obviously isn't. Another feature in this paper turns tipping into a gender issue, comparing men and women, and discovering that men tend to be more generous than women. We live and learn.
- Sex in the armed forces figures at least twice more. A photograph shows us the army's first front-line women helicopter pilots, and tells us that they beat eight male colleagues to get there.
- Another story is about 'a mother Wren in sex bias triumph'. Apparently the Royal Navy told her she had to choose between her job or her child when she became pregnant. Pretty reasonable, I would have thought. But the judge thought otherwise, and awarded her £7,770 damages against the Royal Navy for sex discrimination, and £2,000 for 'hurt feelings'. One is bound to ask what pregnant women are doing on active service, and what sort of a Royal Navy we now have when one of its members is awarded damages for hurt feelings. But today one is not meant to ask such questions.
- Problem families figure prominently in the papers these days, and this issue of the *Daily Mail* is no exception.

There is a report about one such family that has already cost the tax-payers in Britain £1 million. Sounds a very expensive problem. No wonder Western democracies are building up huge national debts fuelled by such expensive hand-outs.

- The major feature in this particular issue is given front page treatment. It is a distressing story about a gunman who shoots dead a baby and her mother. It appears the gunman is the father of this child, and the mother was living with another man. It raises the issue of patrimony, and the bias (sex discrimination?) that the courts of Britain have in favour of mothers rather than fathers.

All these stories are contained in one issue of a newspaper that has a mass circulation. Reading these stories, one would have to conclude that journalists are just as confused about the number of legs which dogs have as church people are! Although newspapers may be accused of many things, they at least know what their readers want, or they would be out of business tomorrow. I have mentioned a tabloid or popular paper; the so-called 'quality' newspapers have similar interests in gender, even if they might deal with them differently.

Gender these days is a growing preoccupation in Western politics, and I am not thinking of political sex scandals. In the American Presidential election campaign of 1992, it could be argued that Bill Clinton, who was elected by a small majority of the popular vote, got to the White House because he addressed these same matters. He, and his running mate Al Gore, made the homosexual and abortion issues major features of their election campaign, promising to change the laws relating to homosexuals in the armed forces (a promise largely reneged on), and to uphold the rights of women to choose to have an abortion whenever they wish. The President's wife Hillary is also the first declared feminist to be the First Lady in the White House. In July 1993, the British Conservative Party launched a major campaign to restore traditional family values, especially in the light of the alarming rise in single-parent families, with the resulting soaring bill for State support. Spear-heading this was Mr Tom Sackville, the Junior Health Minister, who said that marriage was not invented 'as some religious abstraction'. He went on to accuse church leaders of failing to give a firm moral lead. Gender is now firmly on the political agenda.

A theological *imbroglio*

It is hard to find an English word to describe the theological complexities of the subject of gender, especially as they relate to the ordination of women. So I have chosen an Italian one, which means literally 'a confused situation, usually involving a disagreement'. My computer dictionary defines it as 'a confused heap, a tangle'. It makes one wonder if the word was invented to describe Italian politics! We are going to need clear thinking, a strong nerve, a sense of history, and the conviction that truth is non-negotiable. We have to stick to our belief that dogs have four legs against all the pressures to persuade us that they have five.

Hans Küng was misguided in saying that the issue of the ordination of women is sociological rather than theological.[1] The issues about gender and the ordination of women are primarily *theological*, not sociological, and we must resist every effort to move the issue from the disciplines of theology to those of other sciences. It is a matter that affects much of what we believe. Father Thomas Hopko, the Dean of St Vladimir Orthodox Seminary in the United States, has written that the controversy 'shows what a person believes about *everything*'. It may well be as important a controversy in the twentieth century as Arianism was in the fourth century. Father Hopko goes on, 'I believe the very faith is at stake here'.[2] That is strong language coming from a theologian, but I believe he is right.

The most comprehensive book ever written on the ordination of women is *Women in the Priesthood?* by Manfred Hauke. The famous Catholic theologian, Hans Urs von Balthasar, has called this book 'definitive'. In it the author writes that the subject 'cannot be considered in isolation, since it involves a multitude of factors that makes it an exemplary focal point of theological contention . . . *The topic is connected in many ways with the organic totality of the religious life of the Church*' (italics mine).[3] Another Roman Catholic, Michael Novak, has written, 'one cannot yank the thread of sexual differentiation from the

Christian Faith without unravelling the whole. A weakening of the integrity of the mysteries of the Trinity, the Incarnation, the Church, Christian marriage and family life, and much else besides, must inevitably follow.'[4]

Let me enumerate some of the major Christian truths affected by these issues:

- The relationship between the Persons of the blessed Trinity.
- The Creator, the creation of men and women, and the natural laws governing their relationship to each other.
- The Incarnation and the authority of Christ.
- The authority of the Scriptures, how we interpret them, and whether they have the same authority today as they did when they were written.
- The Church, and its authority in matters of faith and morals.
- The ordained ministry in the Church.
- The Christian family, and the relationship between men and women, husbands and wives, parents and children.
- Sexuality, including unnatural same-sex relationships.

What we believe about the ordination of women relates to where we stand on these other matters. And what we believe or do not believe is a touchstone for members of all churches, not just Anglicans. Nor is it a matter of the competence or otherwise of women to be ordained. The question is not primarily whether they *can*, but whether they *should*.

As I have said, and want to stress again, *fundamentally the issue is theological*. The Church of England, like other Protestant churches, has constantly shifted its ground from theology to sociology, and then back to theology, as if they are interchangeable. It has also moved from ancient and well tried principles to superficial and ephemeral fashions of the moment. The tragic results speak for themselves.

We live at a time when there is a premium on truth of any kind. It is in short supply. Truthfulness does not have a high priority, not even theological truth. We have mentioned how some have tried to make this a sociological issue. Others have attempted to make it a psychological matter, seeing 'traditionalists' (those opposed to the ordination of women) as psychologically unbalanced. Many also judge it in terms of the experiences of the world. If the world can have women as prime ministers, airline pilots, surgeons, or judges, why not priests or presbyters? One must here point out that the Church is *not* the world. On the contrary, we should expect to be different; not for the sake of being different, but because of what God has revealed to us and done in us. Paul tells Christians in Romans 12:2, 'Do not conform any longer to the pattern of this world, but be transformed by the renewing of your mind.'

Gender issues are going to be a thorn in the flesh of the churches for many years to come. The Church of England is only a small part of the whole Anglican Communion, which is itself only a tiny part of the one Holy Catholic and Apostolic Church. Only 50% of the Anglican Communion has accepted the ordination of women; the debate will continue in the rest of the Anglican Communion for many years. Added to that, the two largest churches in the world, the Roman Catholic and the Eastern Orthodox, consider women priests/presbyters as invalid. The feminist cause is strongly organised in the Roman Catholic Church, especially in North America, and they have been encouraged by the decision of the Church of England. So the issue is very alive in that church. In other churches, like the House Churches, the question is by no means settled.

Painful and personal

There was much drama when the result of the voting in the General Synod in November 1992 was announced by the Archbishop of Canterbury. Some wept openly with joy, others sobbed with the pain of what had happened. Controversy in the Church is always distressing. It splits churches, fellowships, families and friends. The issue of the ordination of women has always been a delicate one. One has only to recall the feelings of many women, who have had to wait year after year for what they regarded as their calling and right to be priests or presbyters. They have felt judged and discriminated against, and belittled by the views of those who are against their being ordained.

We all feel deeply about this, not least because it is to do with our own personalities; it touches us at some of the deepest parts of our lives. Men and women have hurt each other, and often failed to understand and affirm the other's distinctive sexuality. To detail all of this would take up a lot of space.

Our background may affect our thinking, but this subject will always be painful. It has to be said that the opposition to the ordination of women has not always been based on good foundations. Some men are women haters. It easily becomes a power issue. There is also a kind of traditionalism that is another name for blind prejudice. Some of it is based on false ideas of leadership, desires to be exclusive and to achieve status. Some opposition is more inspired by human motives than divine.

At the same time it needs to be said that not all those in favour of the ordination of women are radical feminists, although some are. Some of my friends are amongst them, and some of the Christians I have come to admire most. One of the tragedies of the Reformation was that two great Christians like Sir Thomas More and Archbishop Thomas Cranmer were put to death within a few years of each other for opposite opinions.

When I finished writing this book I checked on the number of times I had used the words 'clear' or 'clearly'. I was surprised to discover there were 55 occurrences! It has been noticeable to me how both sides of disputes often use the word 'clearly' to describe a point, or say 'it is irrefutable' or some such words when referring to their arguments. I have now worked through this book to remove the word where it is inappropriate. If the arguments are 'clear', there is no need to say so. And if they are not clear, it is inappropriate to say they are. For instance, there is no need to say, '*Clearly* dogs have four legs.' Everyone knows they do.

There is a story about the American landscape artist James Whistler. A woman once remarked that a landscape reminded her of one of his paintings. 'Yes, madam,' he replied, 'nature is creeping up.' It is a consolation to know that if you drive out nature with a pitchfork, it will always run back!

Chapter 2

Words: usage and abusage

> 'It depends what you mean,' said Pooh Bear. 'I
> always mean what I say,' said Christopher Robin
> impatiently. 'Do you?' asked Pooh Bear. 'Well – I
> suppose I try to,' he added rather disconsolately,
> 'but people always seem to get cross with me, just
> the same.'
>
> (After A. A. Milne)

We must now look at some of the key, but sometimes misunderstood, words and phrases we shall be using in this book.

'Traditionalist'

The first is the word 'traditionalist'. Apparently on 11 November 1992 I became a 'traditionalist'. For those who know me, this is a bit of a joke, since for many years I have been anything but a traditionalist, in the normally accepted use of that term. I have been involved most of my life in pioneering a whole new and 'modern' approach to Church life – its worship, prayer, ministry and leadership. No one would describe what I have done as 'traditional'. Yet now apparently I am a traditionalist.

I received this title by proxy, because I would never have used the word to describe myself. All those who oppose the ordination of women are now labelled by the media in this way. However, it is a word that needs some explanation. Peter Gillquist, an Orthodox priest in the United States, calls this the 'T' word. 'Tradition' produces mixed responses in people. Some

are negative about it, because they believe tradition contradicts
the Bible, and they have their favourite text to prove it. Jesus
said, 'why do you break the command of God for the sake of
your tradition? . . . Thus you nullify the word of God for the
sake of your tradition' (Mt. 15:3,6). Paul also condemned this
kind of tradition in Colossians 2:8 when he referred to 'hollow
and deceptive philosophy which depends on human tradition
. . . rather than Christ'. *In that sense I am decidedly not a
traditionalist*. I suspect that the title conferred on us by others
may be intended in that bad sense. In other words that we
are standing in the way of progress, we are old-fashioned, and
hindering the life and ministry of the Church.

But in the Bible the word has a noble meaning as well. In
2 Thessalonians 2:15 Paul wrote, 'stand firm and hold to the
teachings [traditions] we passed on to you, whether by word of
mouth or by letter'. Again Paul a little later tells the Church to
'keep away from every brother . . . who does not live according
to the teaching [tradition] you received from us' (2 Thes. 3:6).
The NIV translators here reveal their prejudice against tradition.
Evangelicals tend to see 'tradition' as bad, 'teaching' as good.
But the same word (*paradosis*) is used in all these texts.

The word 'tradition' simply means 'handing over' or 'that
which is handed down'. My computer's thesaurus gives it a
contemporary ring with such alternatives as 'heritage', 'legacy',
'custom', 'culture', 'mores' and 'story'.

So, in the light of this, am I a 'traditionalist'? In the first sense of
the word I must thoroughly repudiate such a title. In the second
sense I am proud to be called it. So, in this book, I shall call
those who are against the ordination of women 'traditionalists',
even if some people use the word somewhat derogatorily.

'Feminist'

The *Oxford Paperback Dictionary* defines a 'feminist' as 'a
supporter of women's claims to be given rights equal to those
of men'. Since those in favour of the ordination of women
are supporting such claims, they can fairly be described as
'feminists'. No offence is intended. There are aspects of the
cause which should be agreed and supported by all Christians.

A feminist is one who believes in 'undifferentiated equality'. Feminists will differ widely as to how that may be achieved and where it is to be applied. For instance, much radical feminism sees the family as a hindrance to the equality it seeks. Christian feminists would not take this view.

It is, therefore, a fair way of describing those who believe that women as well as men should be ordained, on the grounds that they are equal. It is as adequate a title as calling those who see things differently as 'traditionalists'. As with 'tradition', there are honourable and dishonourable ways of seeing the word 'feminist'. Feminism in some of its aspects has a just cause. There has been and continues to be unjust sex discrimination in society, as there undoubtedly has been in the churches. No one would dispute that. But the way feminists address this injustice varies from witchcraft, communism, New Age and militant lesbianism, to eminent people including church leaders. It would be wrong to tar all feminists with the same brush, but Christian feminists base their arguments on much the same egalitarian principles as the most way-out feminist. Perhaps we should do a trade-off. If we agree to accept the title 'traditionalist', with all its possible misconceptions, I hope the other side will accept the title 'feminist' with all its potential misunderstandings.

'Subordination'

When moving into this subject one of the major problems that surfaces again and again is the identification in feminists' minds of subordination with inferiority. English words do change their meaning. The *Oxford Paperback Dictionary*, one of the newest to be produced, defines 'subordination' as 'of lesser importance or rank' or 'working under the control or authority of another person'. So the word can carry the general idea of 'inferiority' and 'control', and both are inappropriate to describe the husband/wife relationship in the home, or the man/woman relationship in the Church.

Submission is something that men as well as women are bound to accept, because in the Church and the world the network of checks and balances always ensures that this is so. Absolute dictators are few and far between. It needs to be remembered that men as well as women are in a relationship of submission to Jesus Christ as Lord. We need also to remember that as we submit to Christ, we do so to one who likewise submitted to his Father. In Hebrews we are told that Jesus' prayers were heard 'because of his reverent submission'. Also that 'although he was a son, he learned obedience from what he suffered' (Heb. 5:7–8). There is a divine quality in submission which is beautiful, and in the strongest contrast to the rebelliousness that characterises so much of our present society.

In 1 Peter 2:13 the apostle calls on Christians to 'submit yourselves to every authority instituted among men'. One of these 'institutions' is marriage, and addressing wives, he says, 'Wives, *in the same way* be submissive to your husbands' (1 Pet. 3:1). Wayne Grudem writes about this, 'in an age when submission to authority is frequently denigrated and thought to be degrading and dehumanizing Peter's words remind us that submission to rightful authority is beautiful and right in God's world'.[1] Peter says that such submission in God's sight is 'of great worth' (1 Pet. 3:4). To Edward Schumacher's famous phrase 'small is beautiful' we can add 'submission is beautiful'.

But there is a basic theological reason why the word 'subordination' is unsuitable to use. In the early centuries there were a number of heresies which taught the subordination of the Son to the Father, implying the Son's inferiority. The most dangerous of these was Arianism, but others also caused headaches in the Church of the first three centuries. These heresies have been grouped together and called 'Subordinationism'. They were condemned, in the case of Arianism, at the Council of Nicaea (AD 325), and, in the case of the Pneumatomachians, at the Council of Constantinople (AD 381).

As we shall see, the New Testament teaches that the Son was in a relationship of obedience to the Father throughout his life. He was not inferior in substance, but he was obedient 'unto death' (Phil. 2:8). Even at the return of Christ, it is said 'then shall the Son himself be made subject to the Father who put everything under him, so that God may be all in all' (1 Cor. 15:28). Whatever you may call this relationship, in its dynamic aspect it was not egalitarian. It is not surprising, therefore, to find a replication of this kind of relationship on earth between men and women, since both were created in the image of God. It is this concept of 'subordination' that we cannot avoid when writing about men and women as they relate to each other.

We shall, however, avoid using the *word* 'subordination', because it is offensive to women and potentially misleading in understanding the nature of Christ. It conjures up the wrong images of 'domination', 'inferiority', 'subservience' and 'control'. Instead we shall use the word 'submission'. For some this will be just as bad. I realise that feminists reject all such words as 'the very incarnation of evil, which has to be driven out'.[2] For them the relationship is always 'equal' and so any word implying otherwise is unacceptable. But it is the purpose of this book to show from the Old and New Testaments, as well as Church Tradition, that the truth lies in *both* the equality of the sexes and also in their relating in terms of headship and submission. So we have to use some word, and this one seems the best. In the *Oxford Paperback Dictionary* it is defined as 'submitting to power or authority, *willing to obey*'. That is as near as you can get to the way Paul describes the role of wives in the home and women in the Church.

'Patriarchy'

The term literally means the head of a family. We shall be using this term quite frequently. A patriarchy is a family or society in which authority is vested in males. The term 'patriarch' is used to describe the twelve descendants of Jacob (Acts 7:8). It is also a title used in the Orthodox Church to describe the heads of churches, for instance, the Ecumenical Patriarch of Constantinople.

'Hierarchy'

Here is another emotive word. It comes from the Greek word *hiereus* meaning a priest. So originally it was used almost exclusively in a religious sense to describe what the *Concise Oxford Dictionary* calls 'priestly government'. However, it is now used much more widely. The *Dictionary* says it means 'any graded organisation'. The more up-to-date *Oxford Paperback Dictionary* has 'a system with grades of status or authority ranking one above another in a series'. As such it is commonly accepted in the armed forces, where officers and other ranks have positions 'one above another'. The same is true of other organisations and professions, such as the civil service, the judiciary and businesses. We can thus talk about 'middle management' as those who rank in authority under top management, but above the lower echelons of a business organisation.

In other words, hierarchy has a perfectly normal and natural place in the description of relationships. We should not be surprised, for heaven also has its hierarchies. Chief of these is the Trinity itself, as we shall see in Chapter 17. The angels also are arranged in hierarchies. So if God created male and female in his image, it does not surprise us to find hierarchy in the relationships between them. We shall see how the whole concept of 'hierarchy', so deeply imbedded in all societies, came under threat from the French Revolution onwards. Its major enemy has been communism, with its war on inequalities, and its goal, the classless society. Feminism too has resented the word. Manfred Hauke writes, 'the duties of leadership in society and church are seen [by feminists] as second-level sexism, even though it is quite clearly recognised that a certain hierarchy in the human realm has its basis in the sovereign transcendence of God'.[3] The whole understanding and acceptance of hierarchy needs urgent reinstatement in our church and family life, as well as much wider and greater acceptance in our Western society.

'Ordination' and 'priesthood'

There are major difficulties also over the use of the word 'ordination' and the word 'priest'. Some question not only the ordination of women, but ordination itself. There will not be time in this book to look fully into this important matter, although it is certainly relevant. All one has time to say is that most churches do set apart people to hold appointments with a specific ministry of leadership. They are sometimes called 'ministers', 'pastors' or 'priests', but they are recognised by their church as holding office in it to lead the people of God. So far as the word 'priest' is concerned, I prefer the word 'presbyter', because it is the word used in the New Testament for an 'elder'. The other word in the New Testament is 'overseer' or 'bishop'. They are used interchangeably, and this is acknowledged in the Anglican Church, where the presbyter/priest is ordained by the bishop to be an extension of his own ministry. Presbyters or 'priests' are, if you like, local bishops. It makes no sense whatsoever to argue that women may become presbyters but not bishops. The two belong together. In this book I shall not be using the term 'ordination of women to the presbyterate/priesthood', which is too much of a mouthful. Instead I shall use the shortened form, 'the ordination of women'.

'Inclusive language'

Another area of controversy is 'inclusive language'. There are two major aspects to this. The first is the use of words like 'mankind' or 'forefather', which are offensive to some women. But we need to remember that the English word 'man' (mann) originally meant a person of either sex, and still means the same in the words 'human' and 'mankind'. So also the word 'woman' (wifmann) was a man who was a wife, hence female. So the word 'man', when used in the Bible, is 'inclusive', and so does not need to be changed in the way feminists insist. However, as a concession to them I have tried to avoid such words in this book. 'Mankind', for instance, appears in this book as 'humankind'. The other aspect is much more critical, the use of inclusive language for the divine titles. This is discussed in Chapter 17 of this book. I hope this clarifies the way in which I intend to use these words, and avoids unnecessary misunderstandings.

Pastoral concerns

If one is looking for a 'how-to-do-it' handbook, this is not it. The subject of this book does raise important pastoral matters, not least because it deals with the sensitive realm of authority and sexuality. But this book is mainly concerned with the theological principles, not how authority is to be exercised or how to handle sexual relationships. To cover adequately the pastoral aspects would have required another book. I would hasten to add that tackling the subject from the pastoral point of view without first undertaking the biblical and theological disciplines, is to put the cart before the horse. Now that family issues are more and more being raised, books on the pastoral dimension are being written. One of these, published just as I was finishing this book, and which I can recommend is *A Father's Place*, written by Mary Pytches.[4]

Gender issues and the world

This book, as the title suggests, is about sexual equality and order *in Church and family*. For the most part I do not deal with the issue of the role of men and women in society in general, apart from Chapter 12. I believe the Church has been wise since the First Century in not confusing what men and women do in the wider world with their roles in family life and the Church. The principles that the Church has consistently applied for nearly 2,000 years in Church and family have not been applied rigidly in the wider world. The Church could be accused of being inconsistent, but the matter is today largely academic. In the Middle Ages Church and State in Europe overlapped considerably. Today the two are widely separated in most parts of the world. Yet, as we shall see, even in those nations where sexual equality is part of their ideology (for instance, China, Cuba, etc.), very few women have ever risen to positions of authority in the State.

Now we need to look at the scriptural texts, which must ultimately form the basis of our understanding of this subject.

Part 1

The command of the Lord

What I am writing to you is the Lord's command. If
[anybody] ignores this, he himself will be ignored.
(1 Cor. 14: 37–38)

Chapter 3

A cord of three strands

A cord of three strands is not quickly broken.

(Ec. 4:12)

The first three chapters of Genesis are the benchmark for discovering what the Bible teaches on the gender issue. Both Jesus and Paul quote from these chapters when they are guiding the thoughts of their listeners and readers on this subject. So we must go there first. What I am proposing we do is to look at the texts, and at the same time ask a simple and practical question: 'Are the principles mentioned in these chapters observable as true in our world today?' For example, if I say, 'Dogs have four legs', you could argue with me, and prove to your satisfaction that in fact they have five. You are entitled to your opinion. But if I then take you to Crufts dog show in London and take you to see hundreds of the best pedigree dogs, and you then continue to insist that 'Dogs have five legs', I would have to conclude that either you were blind, and so not entitled to make such a statement, or sadly deluded.

So what we shall do is consider each chapter in turn and then look at the world around us, and our experience of life, and ask the question, 'Are the assertions made in these chapters verified by the facts of our human existence?' By looking at it this way we do not have to go into the question of whether the writer or writers were making historical or theological statements. To assert that dogs have four legs, we don't have to be a trained vet, or know how the legs function.

Genesis 1: the equality of men and women

Before we move on to the equality of the sexes, we need to
mention that Genesis 1 and 2 give ringing approval to sex itself.
This has to be stated because of the charge often levelled at the
Church that it is 'against sex', and also because of the degraded
exploitation and abuse of sex in our twentieth century. The
Church at times has disapproved even of the sexual act within
marriage. Augustine, for example, believed that sin was always
involved, and ascetic movements in the Church have sometimes
gone over the top in seeing abstention from sex an essential
element of personal holiness. Genesis says 'yes' to sex. There
is no doubt about that.

There are many *theories* about creation, and how it all
happened; but the *fact* of creation is beyond argument. Whether
God started it, or whether it was spontaneously generated is not
only a scientific question, but ultimately one of faith. The world
is there for all to see, touch and smell. The equality of men and
women is plainly stated, in the frequently quoted text, Genesis
1:27, *'God created man in his own image, in the image of God he
created him; male and female he created them.'* When Adam for
the first time saw the delectable sight of a woman, and greeted
the discovery with whoops of joy, he exclaimed, 'this is now
bone of my bones and flesh of my flesh' (Gn. 2:23). In other
words, he immediately realised that this was not a creature
like ET from outer space. She really was human like him, yet
different. Humankind's sexual adventures had begun.

These simple verses reveal two significant truths. First that
men and women are like God, they were created in his image.
And secondly, they are like each other, both totally human, or
to put it simply, both of the same species. It is no wonder that
feminists make much of Genesis 1, although they have their
problems with a lot of the rest of the Old Testament.

The crude basis of sexism is that women were created
inferior to men. Often this may be denied; but sexist men
act as if it were so, whether they concretely believe it or
not. They do this by acts of sex discrimination or sexual
harassment, when women are treated as if they are sex
objects or pets, or, what for women is often worse, with
condescension – like the 'dear lady' approach of that classic

chauvinist Sir Humphrey Appleby in the British TV series, *Yes, Prime Minister*.

The likeness of human beings to God is one of the most fundamental of theological statements. It carries with it immense comfort. There is not *in kind* a great gulf fixed between God and man. There are points of possible interception. There is overlap. But there are also great differences. In a sense God has made himself vulnerable by making us like him. It might have been safer for God to make human kind so different there would be no confusion or identity problems. The great danger, which has been the stuff of most heresies, is that we, as little gods ourselves, recreate God in our image. It is not hard to do; to read back our fallen humanity into the very nature of God.

Now men and women, the male and female components of the one 'man', are inherently created in unity and equality. One is not better than the other; or less human, or less potentially divine. When Paul in Galatians 3:28 wrote, 'there is neither male nor female', he was expressing this truth in another way. In terms of human life, men and women are equal. In terms of new spiritual life, they are also equal.

One of the good fruits of the feminist campaign of this century is that it has forced society, and men in particular, to accept the truth of sexual equality, as expressed in chapter 1 of Genesis. Although sex discrimination continues, Western society is now closer to agreeing, to use my illustration, that dogs after all have four legs and not five.

Genesis 2: men and women are different

Here we have more detail about the creation of male and female. They were not created at the same time, they were not created in the same way, and they were not created for the same purpose. Adam was created first, and then Eve. Adam was created from the dust of the ground, Eve from the side of Adam. Adam was put under the authority of God, and told what he could do and what he could not do. Eve was created to be Adam's companion and helper, and placed under his authority.

Here is where we run into disagreements. We usually do when authority is involved! God made it clear to Adam that there were 'noes' as well as 'yeses'. There were trees whose fruit he could pick at will, and there was one tree he could not eat from. Why was God so 'narrow-minded'? In Genesis 2 the question of how many legs a dog has does not have quite so easy an answer. But answers we must find, or else we shall have endless trouble, as Adam and Eve found to their cost (and ours) in chapter 3.

Let us look closely at the differences in Genesis 2 between male and female, and see what we can learn from them. First, woman came after man. Was she an after thought? There is no need to speculate, because we have already seen that the woman is equal to the man in value, potential and future glory. Yet Paul in 1 Timothy 2:13 gives the fact that Adam was formed first, and then Eve, as a reason why women may not teach or have authority over men.

Secondly, the woman was made from man, not, as Adam was, from the dust of the ground. If women object to coming *after* man in the created order, it is some compensation for them to know that they came from human flesh not dust. It is significant that Paul also uses this truth in affirming his statement in 1 Corinthians 11 that the man is the head of the woman (v. 8). It is possible that he has in mind the fact that the woman was created from Adam's side, not from his head. Thus she is called to be at his side, not in charge or sharing headship reciprocally. This account also points to the different roles of men and women. Man is formed from the earth, and so is given the task of subduing it. His God-given role relates more to *things* than people. The woman is formed from human flesh, because she is to be primarily concerned with *people* not things, and of course supremely in being mother to all humans, especially to the Son of God.

Thirdly, Eve was created to be Adam's companion and helper, a quite different role and function from that of her consort. Paul writes, 'neither was man created for woman, *but woman for man*' (1 Cor. 11:9). The man's role is not defined in terms of the woman's, but the woman's in terms of the man's. Women have no grounds for complaint, because the Hebrew word for 'helper' (*ezer*) is also applied in the Old Testament to God. Out of nineteen occurrences no less than fifteen apply to God, hardly suggesting a devaluation of women. To be a helper is a divine as well as a human task. The phrase literally means, 'a helper as his counterpart'. This is an affirmation of the woman, as having an equally dignified though different role. She is not to be the man's slave or drudge.

Genesis 2 does not explicitly say that Eve was to be submissive to Adam. But Paul deduces this from the evidence we have alluded to. Yet there is even stronger evidence, which makes this clearer. One of the clues to this is found in the mention of Adam naming not only his wife, but the whole of her sex (Gn. 2:23). Naming in Scripture is always an expression of authority (and incidentally is usually done by the father, not the mother). God brought the animals to Adam to be named, and he also brought Eve to him for the same purpose.

Now those who accept chapter 1 as the Creator's mandate, affirming the equality of the sexes, cannot dodge this second mandate, that the differences in the sexes go beyond the physical, and include the differing roles and ordering of the sexes. We must not tamper with this reality. Before we turn to the catastrophe of Genesis 3 we need to know that according to Claus Westermann, Genesis 2 'is unique in its high valuation of women among the creation myths of the whole of the Ancient Near East.'[1] Sadly, some feminists, though not all, have undertaken to dismiss the Old Testament, starting with Genesis 2. The treatment of women in the Old Testament certainly left room for improvement, (and the New Covenant ushered that in), but it was infinitely higher than that of the nations around them.

Genesis 3: the Fall

At first sight it would appear that Eve was to blame for the Fall of humanity. Paul does declare she was culpable. In 1 Timothy 2:14 he says, 'Adam was not the one deceived; it was the woman who was deceived and became a sinner.' Yet in his other epistles he places the blame fairly and squarely on Adam. 'As in Adam all die,' he writes (1 Cor. 15:22), and 'sin entered the world through one man . . . death reigned from Adam to the time of Moses . . .' (Rom. 5:12, 14). Of course they both sinned, but the major blame was Adam's.

As we have seen, Adam was given the responsibility to be the head in his relationship with Eve. It was to Adam that God gave his instructions about what fruit was permissible to eat (Gn. 2:16–17). It was Adam, not Eve, whom God called after the original sin in the garden, because he was the one primarily responsible for what had happened (Gn. 3:9).

When the serpent made its appearance, it seems that Adam was present, because later we are told that 'he was with her' (Gn. 3:6). Whereas God always addressed Adam not Eve, the serpent addressed Eve not Adam. Adam, far from intervening, just listened to the conversation. That was his sin. God was to accuse him when pronouncing him guilty, 'because you listened to your wife' (Gn. 3:17). He had been given the responsibility of caring for Eve, and seeing that God's orders were obeyed. He just said nothing, and let it all happen. A Swiss writer called Henri Frederic Amiel has said, 'Truth is violated by falsehood, but it is outraged by silence.' What was the original sin? *It was the woman taking over authority from the man, and the man saying and doing nothing to stop it*.

J. T. Walsh has done a helpful analysis of the four levels of authority before the Fall.[2] God is first, man next, then the woman, and finally the animals. In the fall this is inverted. The snake tells the woman what to do, the man follows the woman's example and instructions, and God's truth and word are totally ignored. Gordon Wenham has said, 'Eve listened to the serpent instead of Adam, and Adam listened to Eve instead of God'.[3] Then after the Fall God reinstates the hierarchy of authority. He puts the snake under the woman, the woman under the man, and all three under his divine authority.

But the man's sin is unmasked. He should have intervened in the meeting between the serpent and Eve, and not allowed her to take the forbidden fruit. Werner Neuer writes, 'the leadership position of the man makes him specially responsible for the transgression of the divine commandment'.[4] P. Brunner concludes, 'the fall is made final by the man's action. Only by the man's deed does the fall become ripe for judgement . . . it is true that Adam is deceived by Eve, but the fall is completed by Adam.'[5] Adam's enticement by Eve was no excuse. The buck of moral responsibility stopped with him.

One can begin to understand now why Jesus Christ, the

Apostles, the Church Fathers, and the Church generally never felt it right to entrust the office of teacher to women. One can also understand why men have been tempted to abdicate from their role of headship in the Church and in the family. In my estimation these are the key issues.

Judgement pronounced

God proceeds to pass judgement on the guilty parties, the snake, the woman and the man. The snake, or the symbol of Satan, is judged both as an animal (crawling on the belly and eating dust), and as a spiritual power (enmity between his kingdom and the human race and the crushing of his head). The woman will have pain in delivering children, and a husband to rule over her, while at the same time her desire will be for him. The man will have painful physical toil to cope with, many obstacles in the cultivation of the soil rather than the joys of tending an orchard. He will have to live 'by the sweat of his brow'.

Here is the clearest statement yet about the place of submission of the woman under the headship of the man. 'He will rule over you' is unambiguous. Some feminists have interpreted this as a curse which has been removed by the coming of Christ. It was a punishment for the sins of the Fall, which has now been removed by the Cross. This means, according to their argument, men and women are now equal again as in Genesis 1. There are several weaknesses in this argument. In the first place, none of the other curses were removed by the Cross. Women from that day to now still have pains in childbirth, and man still has, in most parts of the world, to cultivate the land by the sweat of his brow. But more cogent is the way Paul handles this. John Piper and Wayne Grudem write, 'Paul *never* appeals to the curse or the fall as an explanation for man's responsibility to lead; he always appeals to the acts of God before the fall' (1 Cor. 11:8–9; Eph. 5:31–32; 1 Tim. 2:13).[6] Genesis 2 has already indicated a role of submission for women, and that was *before* the Fall. How are we to interpret Genesis 3:14–19?

What does it mean that the man will rule over the woman? Whichever way we interpret it, there is no need for the woman to accept male oppression, any more than the man need accept the thorns and thistles which grow in his fields. Werner Neuer suggests that the Hebrew word 'rule' does not necessarily have a bad connotation.[7] The word *mashal* is also used in a good sense to describe God's rule, as in Isaiah 40:10 and Psalm 22:28. I believe he is right to say that there are only two possible ways of seeing it. Either it is a reaffirmation of the place given to the woman in Genesis 2. In other words, God is putting the woman back under the man, against whose authority she had rebelled. Or it is saying that women will now be oppressed by men, as a prophetic statement, without justifying it. If the latter is true, then certainly in Christ's teaching, and that of his Apostles, the 'oppression' aspect is done away in Christ, although, as we shall see, the submission aspect is retained. But it would, in the words of Manfred Hauke, 'be reading modern liberal ideas into the biblical text if one were to assume . . . any and every sort of subordination of women to men as a consequence of sin'.[8] Submission has already been established in Genesis 2.

The threefold cord

A favourite text for weddings is Ecclesiastes 4:12, 'Though one may be overpowered, two can defend themselves, a cord of three strands is not quickly broken.' I would suggest that we see the first three chapters of Genesis as strands which are not to be broken, but joined together. Genesis 1–3 reveal three strands of creation. The first strand is that God has created man and woman equally in his image. Neither man nor woman is more like God. Both masculinity and femininity are created by God, and both are good.

The second strand of creation established in these chapters is that God has given different roles to men and women. Neither role is superior or more important than the other. But they are different. Man is the head of the woman, who is his helper, and their roles in the family and in the Church are often, though not always, different.

The third strand of creation is that it is now 'fallen'. Men and women in themselves, and in their relationship to each other are flawed. Sex itself is still good; but both men and women have an innate tendency to sin. We are fallen creatures living in a fallen world.

The first strand of creation is affirmed by all except sexists. It is self-evident that men and women belong to the same species, and are equally human and equal in their potentiality to please God. They are both mortal, and both prone to sin.

The third strand ought also to be self-evident, but sometimes isn't. There are still many humanists, and some church leaders, who cling to belief in the innate goodness of people. To the contrary G. K. Chesterton wrote, 'the doctrine of original sin is the only philosophy empirically vindicated by 3,500 years of human history'. One of the greatest novelists of the twentieth century, and winner of the Nobel Prize for Literature, was William Golding. He died in 1993. He once wrote, 'man is a fallen being. He is gripped by original sin . . . I accept the theology and admit the triteness; but what is trite is true.'9 There may be those who would say all three conclusions I am affirming are 'trite'. If so, we can answer, 'Maybe trite, but certainly true.'

Having accepted the first and third strands, why reject the second? Like the others, it has been empirically vindicated. Steven Goldberg has written a book with the provocative title *The Inevitability of Patriarchy*.10 He writes as an anthropologist, not as a theologian. He concludes that all societies have always been patriarchal, and *always will be*. The first word in the title is provocative. In other words, humankind has always acknowledged in the family and in the cultural life of the tribe, that the man is the head, and the woman is placed under his authority. Dr John Fenwick, himself a zoology graduate, in a letter to the author has put it well, 'there is clearly a gender differentiation written into the universe, and it is silly to try and pretend otherwise in the area of ministerial leadership'.11

Listen carefully to what a *scientist* (Steven Goldberg) says: 'all anthropologists agree that there has never been a society which failed to associate hierarchical authority and leadership in these areas with men'.12 Today we see churches like King Canute standing on the shore-line commanding the tide to go back. It won't; what is sure is they will get their feet wet, and if they remain long enough they may even drown beneath the flood of nature's truth.

In his book *What will happen to God?* William Oddie gives a striking illustration of what I am saying.[13] When the *Titanic* sank in the North Atlantic in 1912 it was soon clear that there were not sufficient lifeboats for all those on board. So the captain ordered the women and children to fill the boats first. Most of the men accepted this, and helped these people onto the boats. But a few didn't, and one of the seamen in charge of a lifeboat found men pushing on ahead of the women. His name was Charles Lightoller, and he quickly brandished a revolver, threatening that he would shoot the men if they did not get off the boat.

In the inquest which was held after the disaster, the chairman, Senator Smith, asked Lightoller what made him do this. 'Was it the Captain's orders or the law of the sea?' he suggested. 'No,' said Lightoller, 'it was *the law of nature*.' He was right. The law of nature, created dynamically first in Adam and Eve, decrees that *men lay down their lives for women and children*, and women are submissive to men. Francis Bacon once wrote, 'Nature to be commanded must be obeyed.' No amount of theorising will change the fact that dogs have four legs.

Chapter 4

The primeval cry

Jesus said, 'When you pray, say: "Father . . ."'
(Lk. 11:2)

Paul describes the primeval cry in Romans 8:15, 'by the Spirit *we cry Abba, Father*'. This is not to denigrate the importance of our mothers. But when it comes to God, the cry that comes from deep within us is intimate, spontaneous and *patriarchal*. Paul says the same thing in Galatians 4:6, 'the Spirit calls out "Abba, Father"'. This is only a few verses after the words so beloved of feminists, 'there is neither male nor female' (Gal. 3:28). The heart-cry of the Christian is 'Father' because it was Christ's as well. Never was this more deeply expressed than in Gethsemane and on the Cross – 'Father, into your hands I commit my spirit' (Lk. 24:46).

The Old Testament is not good news for feminists, because it is so patriarchal. The word 'father', male headship, and female submission jump at you from almost every page. Radical feminists like Mary Daly simply write it all off (apart from Gn. 1). Her acknowledged mentor was Simone de Beauvoir, the author of *The Second Sex*, a book generally regarded as the 'Bible' of radical feminism. De Beauvoir sees Judaism and Christianity as a reaction against mother-goddess worship, and so through Paul 'the Jewish tradition, savagely anti-feminist, was affirmed'. As we shall see later, this splitting off of the Old Testament from the New was the grounds for one of the more dangerous heresies in the second century.

In the Old Testament God is revealed in male terms, not female. The people of God, by contrast, is usually in the female gender, most strikingly in Isaiah 66:11–12, although they of course comprise men as well as women. In Psalm 48:12–13 we are told to 'walk about Zion, go around *her*, count *her* towers, consider well *her* ramparts, view *her* citadels . . .' It has been pointed out that there are a few passages in which God is described in maternal symbolism. Actually, there are only two such texts, Isaiah 49:14–15 and 66:13. In these the prophet is not saying that God is 'Mother', only *like* a mother. Many metaphors are used to help us understand the nature of God. His strength is sometimes described in terms of a 'rock'. We do not deduce from this that God is rock. God's love for us is compared to that of a mother; in fact in Isaiah 49, his love is described as being greater and more constant than that of a mother for her child. Jesus also once expressed his compassion in terms of a mother hen gathering her chicks (Lk. 13:34), but Jesus' male gender has never been in doubt.

Hauke summarises his survey of these passages: 'God combines in himself every kind of creaturely value and does so in the most perfect way. Nevertheless the maternal symbolism has no independent value, but is, so to speak, a component part of the father symbol . . . *masculinity is inherently characteristic of the biblical image of God*.'[1] Or to put it another way, God is on a few occasions said to be *like a mother*; but he is revealed on many occasions, and supremely in the ministry of Jesus Christ, to *be* the Father. It is important to remember in this connection the words of Christ, 'call no man your father on earth, *for you have one Father, who is in heaven*' (Mt. 23:9). Jesus' sonship is not presented as analogous to the sons of earthly fathers. True fatherhood as well as true sonship is grounded in the New Testament understanding of God as the Father and Jesus Christ as his Son.[2]

In the Old Testament the father is the head of the family, and the male leadership of Israel and the Israelite nation is never in doubt. God is the 'God of Abraham, Isaac and Jacob' not of 'Sarah, Rebekah and Rachel'. Inheritance passed through the sons, and the twelve sons of Jacob became the twelve tribes of Israel, just as later the twelve apostles of Christ became the founding fathers of the Christian Church. The wives accepted the divine role of submission so hated by radical feminism. Sarah called her husband 'Lord', a fact quoted with approval by the apostle Peter (1 Pet. 3:6). It is important to know that the word 'Abram' means 'the father is exalted'. Gilbert Russell and Margaret Dewey describe this as 'a revolutionary declaration . . . signalling the crucial break with Great Mother religion'.[3]

Sometimes we see a recurrence of the rebellion of Eve in the garden, when she took over the headship, and when Adam meekly acquiesced. Both Sarah and Rebekah manipulated or deceived their husbands in the matters of Hagar and arranging for Jacob to take the birthright from his brother Esau. In both instances the weakness and carnality of the husbands was a strong contributing factor. But the headship of the man was never questioned by Sarah or Rebekah. The qualities expected in a godly woman in both the Old and New Testaments are meekness, submissiveness and gentleness. Feminists who object to such expectations would do well to reflect on the fact that exactly the same qualities are found perfectly exemplified in Jesus Christ, who was both meek, submissive and gentle, a model for both men and women, as he submitted his life totally to the Father (Jn. 5:30).

The leadership of the Patriarchs was followed by Moses the lawgiver, and one of the greatest leaders of all time, although called 'a very humble man, more humble than anyone else on the face of the earth' (Nu. 12:3). Then there were prophets and judges. This leadership was always male, with the one exception of Deborah. When Moses finds the going tough, he is advised by Jethro to delegate some of his authority to elders *all of whom were male*.

The judges seem to have been an interim arrangement, although even here all of them were men except Deborah. She is described as a prophetess (Jdg. 4:4). Throughout the Old and New Testaments we see that the prophetic ministry is one of those open to women as well as men. So this should not surprise us. When it came to war, Deborah gave the command of the army to Barak, although she did agree, under protest (Jdg. 4:8–9), to go with him into battle. Her principal role was to lead in the field of justice, to be a judge, a field in which women to this day have excelled. When Deborah praised God, she expressed joy that 'the princes in Israel' had taken the lead (Jdg. 5:2); in other words, the men, not the women. As David Pawson points out, 'Deborah's attitude was maternal . . . rather than matriarchal'.[4] On her own admission she was 'a mother in Israel' (Jdg. 5:7).

When Israel began to appoint kings, under the reluctant oversight of the prophet Samuel, male leadership was assured. While their neighbours had queens (for instance, Sheba and later Cleopatra of Egypt), Israel only had kings. The one exception was when there was no male regent or when the king was too young to reign. Thus it was a temporary arrangement, not a permanent one. The queen mother was usually given a place of honour, and sometimes acted in a consultative role (see, for example, Jer. 13:18).

Women have always been eligible for the ministry of prophecy. One of the most striking examples was Huldah (2 Ki. 22:14–20; 2 Ch. 34:22). Manfred Hauke pays her a fulsome compliment when he concludes, 'without her God-empowered contribution, the five books of Moses (the core of the Old Testament!) would probably not exist as we know them today. The King respectfully asks Huldah for her views on the matter, although such highly significant figures as Jeremiah and (probably) Zephaniah are numbered among her prophetic contemporaries.'[5]

Here we need to notice a distinction that is made, which carries over into the New Testament and the annals of the Church throughout its history, between a charismatic ministry, like prophecy, and an 'office' like a king, a priest or Levite, or an elder. Prophecy applies to a particular person and cannot be passed on by that person. In other words you cannot appoint prophets; their calling is only from God. But you certainly have to judge them, because the prophet can be a false one. By contrast 'office', although hopefully enhanced by charismatic blessings, is a human appointment, and maintains itself through history even without charismatic empowering.

Women in the Old Testament do have an important part to play, and there are several other notable examples. One of them is Miriam, the sister of Moses, who appears as a prophetess, and places herself on a level with her more famous brother (Ex. 15:20–21). Noadiah was a woman prophet who tried to intimidate Nehemiah (Ne. 6:14). Isaiah goes to a prophetess (Is. 8:3), although she may have been the wife of a prophet, and of course Joel's great prophecy, fulfilled at Pentecost, includes women as well as men in the ministry of prophecy. All this, as Hauke says, 'suffices to show that the sweeping thesis about the inferior position of women in the Old Testament religion cannot be sustained'.[6]

When we come to look at the position of women in relationship to the priesthood, we notice that all priests had to be male by divine law. The priesthood was of all ministries the most carefully guarded, and sometimes terrible judgement came on those who presumed to take the law into their own hands. When Uzzah tried to steady the sacred ark, he died instantly (2 Sa. 6:6). Also pride led to King Uzziah's downfall; he entered the temple to burn incense, and thus to become a priest illegally. When ordered by the legitimate priests to leave the sanctuary, he lost his temper, and immediately became leprous (2 Ch. 26:16–21).

It is not difficult to see the reason for all this. The temple was the symbol of the presence of God, supremely the Holy of Holies. It was the place where people met with God. All around Israel the nations had numerous female priests. This has been well documented in Mesopotamia, where they even acted in the service of male deities.[7] It was also true in Egypt. The Israelites' more immediate and threatening neighbours, the Canaanites, had priestesses in abundance, as has been proved by excavations at Ugarit. Hauke points out that the same word for priest is in the Phoenician language, which is closely related to Hebrew. It has a feminine form *khnt*, but in Hebrew *the feminine form is missing*.[8] Exactly the same is true of the Miniamin inscriptions from Sinai, there is no feminine equivalent in Hebrew. Priestesses were for pagans not for God's people, as C. S. Lewis pointed out in 1948 in his famous article, which we shall be referring to in Chapter 7.

The priests and Levites had two main functions in Israel. The first was to conduct the public worship of God, at the core of which were the various sacrifices and festivals. This was the very centre of the life of the community, because it was all directed towards the God of Israel, without whose presence and power the state could not exist. God was their total reason for existence. The priests and Levites also were the people's representatives before God. The High Priest, for example, when going into the Holy of Holies, represented all the people of God, not himself alone. But the priests and Levites also represented God to the people.

The other important function for the priest was *teaching*. In Israel the teaching was always done by men (Ho. 4:6; Mi. 3:11; Je. 18:18). We see in the Old Testament a shadow of the reality which came in Christ, who was both the teacher come from God (Jn. 3:2), and the High Priest to make a perfect sacrifice for us all (Heb. 7:26). The priests represent God to the people, teaching them his laws, and the people to God, making sacrifice on their behalf. Only men were eligible for such a ministry. In fact in the Old Testament not all men were eligible, only the descendants of Aaron from the tribe of Levi.

The equality of the sexes

We have so far been dealing with the differences between men and women in the Old Testament. We need to show how the equality expressed in Genesis 1, that both men and women are created in the image of God, was also seen in the life of Israel. There are many laws in which men and women are given equal status. One example given by Werner Neuer is that of striking or cursing one's father or mother.[9] In Jewish law both were a capital offence (Ex. 21:15, 17; Lv. 20:9). By contrast, in Babylonian law it only applied to the father. The high status of the married woman is celebrated in the famous and oft-quoted passage in Proverbs 31:10–31, although earlier in the same piece of writing the author warns his readers that sometimes women can be dangerous!

Personal experiences of God are enjoyed as much by women as men. The women take part with men in important national occasions like the return of the ark to Jerusalem (2 Sa. 6:5) and the worship recorded in Ezra (Ne. 8:2). Women could swear oaths in God's name (Ru. 1:17). The law basically applied to both sexes, although only men were its interpreters and teachers. One has only to look at the importance attached to Ruth and Rahab to see that women were not devalued. Rahab the harlot is included in the Epistle to the Hebrews' great roll of honour (Heb. 11:31), and both of them appear on that even greater roll of honour, the genealogy of the Lord Jesus Christ (Mt. 1:5).

It has, however, to be added that there was discrimination against women in the Old Testament; it was not all sweetness and light, even if the position of women was generally *way ahead of other nations at that time*. Legally, the man 'owned' his wife, who was regarded as her husband's possession.[10] But this must not be exaggerated in the light of the other freedoms which wives obviously enjoyed. They were full members of the Covenant, even though they were not circumcised. However, women were disadvantaged in laws relating to divorce and adultery. Only the man could divorce (Dt. 24:1). Also there was a double standard in that men were guilty of adultery if they consorted with a married or betrothed woman only. On the other hand women were guilty if they had sexual intercourse of any kind outside their marriage (Dt. 22:22–29). Women were also discriminated against in the laws of inheritance. Having said all this it needs to be remembered that women in Israel, according to J. Doller, 'had a status found among few other people'.[11]

The universal patriarchy in the Old Testament should not surprise us at all. It is a simple commentary on what we are told in Genesis 2, that men are called to be the *head* in the relationship with women, and women are called to be the *helper*. The truth of this is confirmed by the fact that Paul endorses this interpretation in 1 Corinthians and 1 Timothy. Another endorsement can be found in the study of anthropology. It seems that this is not only true of the Old and New Testaments, and the teaching of the majority of the churches until the twentieth century, but also of the whole history of humankind. We have already pointed out that our subject is as relevant to the readership of *The Times* as to those of the *Church Times*, to unbelievers as to Christians. The matter we are discussing affects the whole human race. Steven Goldberg goes even further. He believes, as the title of his book makes clear, that patriarchy is 'inevitable', that in fact it will never change.

Attempts have been made to show that there have been matriarchal societies in the past. Leaving aside mythical inventions like the Amazons, serious studies have tried to show that women-dominated societies have existed. Perhaps the most famous was a study done of the Iroquois Indians by Lewis Henry Morgan. This tribe ranged across a huge area of what is now the eastern part of the United States. The males in this society used to be away from home for long periods of time, roaming across the vast area of their homelands. Thus the women took charge while they were away. *But they did not continue to rule when their men returned.* In fact Morgan admits that the women were prohibited from ruling, and were considered 'servants'.[12] Hardly matriarchal. What is even more interesting is their present status. The Iroquois males can no longer roam, they are confined to their reservations. Evidence shows that in their new situation the tribe is definitely led and dominated by its males. They are patriarchal. The temporary rule of women when the menfolk are away has been the experience of other groups like the militaristic Spartans, who could hardly be called 'matriarchal'! It has also been a factor in the situations brought about by the two World Wars in the twentieth century, when large numbers of men have been away on active service.

Another anthropologist, Colin Turnbull, has cited the Mbuti Pygmies. But again, on closer examination the theory does not stand up. He admits that authority in the tribe is in the hands of the best hunter or elder male, and that in disputes and discussions women only serve as advisors. He also concedes that status is derived from hunting skills, and that the 'Molimo' ritual of crisis is reserved primarily for males. The well-known anthropologist Margaret Mead has often been quoted by radical feminists as demonstrating the reality of matriarchal societies, particularly the Tchambuli and the Mundugumor. She has publicly denied this and writes, 'men have always been the leaders in public affairs . . . and the final authorities at home . . .'[13]

One of the mistakes that is made is to fail to see that tasks and functions vary from culture to culture. In some societies men do what women do in others. That has nothing to do with dominance. For instance, in the United States, the medical profession has a high-status profile, and is dominated by men. In Russia it has a low status, and women doctors greatly outnumber men. The old Soviet Union is an interesting example of what I am saying. One of the main tenets of communism, firmly taught by Engels, was the equality of men and women. Lenin, after the Revolution in 1917, sought to put it into practice, but it never worked. The Soviet Union, and its successors, have been dominated by men. You only have to look at the old photos of the Politburo to see the truth of this. Even after World War 2, when the Russians lost an enormous number of men in battle, males still dominated most areas of the national life. Patriarchy is universal and inevitable.

Again, Steven Goldberg, in his book *The Inevitability of Patriarchy* is anxious to point out that he is not suggesting that one sex is superior to the other. 'It is as meaningless as to say that one society is superior to another.'[14] Men excel at lifting weights, women in singing the upper registers. He goes on to warn the feminist that if she believes 'that it is preferable to have her sex associated with authority and leadership rather than with the creation of life, then she is doomed to perpetual disappointment'.[15] You might just as well try to prove that the world is flat, or that dogs have five legs.

'Patriarchy is universal,' Goldberg writes. 'Most anthropologists consider the family, marriage and the taboo of incest universal . . . no real society could manage without them . . . there is not, nor has there ever been any society that even remotely failed to associate authority and leadership in suprafamilial areas with the male.'[16] Are the churches now seeking to 'buck the market'? Are they trying to overturn the course of nature? If so, it will have disastrous consequences.

In conclusion, we need to see that the exclusion of women from teaching, headship (elders), and priestly ministry in the Old Testament, was not the arbitrary decision of a God who wants to make women inferior, and to keep them in a place where they are dominated by men. As we have seen, it fits in with the pattern of societies everywhere in the world, and at all times in history. Another observable fact, pointed out by Goldberg, is that women equal or surpass men in all test areas *not related to dominance and abstract reasoning*.[17] Thus women come nowhere in those areas exemplified by philosophers like Aristotle, painters like Rubens, composers like Mozart, and one might add theologians like Augustine. The late Sir Kenneth Clark once said that 'the more mathematical/architectural a form or style of painting the greater the disparity between men and women who excel'. But on the performing side of art women often excel more than men. In the field of literature, Jane Austen, George Eliot and the Brontës can stand with the best male writers. In the area of crime fiction, Agatha Christie and

Dorothy Sayers will probably never be surpassed, at least by a man. But 'dominance and abstract reasoning' is the stuff of leadership and teaching, the very roles which Jesus Christ, the Apostles, and the Church Fathers denied to women. It is important for me to say that I do not use the word 'dominance' anywhere in this book to describe men's relationship to women, although Goldberg uses it constantly. Headship does not mean dominance, a word not used in the New Testament to describe such a relationship. Jesus did not 'dominate' his disciples. The sinful exercise of headship can sometimes involve domination, but it is un-Christlike behaviour. Yet headship does carry with it authority; when it is exercised it should be done in a Christian manner.

Here Goldberg makes a plea, which I would endorse:

> Men look to women for gentleness, kindness and love, for refuge from a world of pain and force, for safety from their own excesses. In every society a basic male motivation is the feeling that women and children must be protected. But the feminist cannot have it both ways: if she wishes to sacrifice all this, all that she will get in return is the right to meet men on male terms. She will lose.[18]

The feminist cause is doomed because the basis of it is contrary to nature, to the inevitability of patriarchy. Jesus Christ came to show the right way, the way of co-operation, not competition, the way of peace, not war, between the sexes. He did not come to change the created order, which includes the headship of men and the submission of women; but rather to transform it by his love and grace, so that what God created can be redeemed and function properly. If we don't find this way, then both men and women will be the losers, and the truth will be hidden from the world.

Chapter 5

Jesus, feminist or traditionalist?

'Haven't you read,' Jesus replied, 'that at the
beginning the Creator "made them male and
female"?'

(Mt. 19:4)

It is common to claim Jesus Christ as a supporter of causes
dear to our hearts, and not a few have claimed that he was
a feminist. I don't know anyone who has ever claimed that
he was a traditionalist! Christian feminists are right to see in
the life of Jesus Christ a deep compassion for women, and a
man who affirmed them by what he said and did. He treated
them with respect, and honoured them whenever he could. He
encouraged them to be part of his team, and ignored several
social taboos to show respect to them with words and actions
which would have been offensive to the narrow views of the
religious leaders of his day, who looked down on women, and
treated them as inferior.

Yet one also has to say that Jesus was a traditionalist,
accepting both the headship of men, and the submission of
women to them. Jesus did things of which no feminist would
approve. He appointed only male apostles. When he invited
only men to the Last Supper, it was contrary to even Jewish
practice. The Passover meal could be shared by the whole
family, men, women and children together, as indeed it had
been many years before when the Jews left Egypt in haste. As
we have seen Judaism was patriarchal through and through, and
Jesus himself said that he did not come as a law-breaker so far
as the Old Covenant was concerned. He had come *to fulfil it*.

Jesus confirmed the creation truth that men are called to be the head of their families. So it was natural for him to appoint twelve *men* to be the first heads of the new Christian community, the Church. They were to be the model for all future headship in the Church, and Peter, Paul, and the other apostles affirmed this through their teaching. This was all in spite of the fact that the women who followed Jesus often were more faithful, believing and dedicated than the men.

They showed their love by washing his feet, accompanying him to the Cross, and being the first to meet the risen Lord and be witnesses of his resurrection. You would have thought Jesus would have rewarded them, and at least had a couple in the apostolic band with the men. No, none of them were appointed, and none of them complained. Perhaps strangest of all, was the fact that he did not appoint his own mother Mary as an apostle. Not only did Jesus refrain from doing it, but the Church for the next 60 generations never questioned Jesus' judgement in the matter, in spite of the fact Mary was to be greatly honoured in some churches. They simply followed his example and only appointed men to positions of headship in the Church.

Much has been made of the statement of Jesus about authority and headship in Luke 22:25. The disciples had been arguing about who should be the greatest. So Jesus said, 'the kings of the Gentiles lord it over them; and those who exercise authority over them call themselves Benefactors. But you are not to be like that. Instead the greatest among you should be like the youngest, and the one who rules like the one who serves.' People try to deduce from this that Jesus is devaluing leadership, and that he wants us all to be on the same level, so to speak. In other words, it does not matter whether men lead women or women lead men. A closer look at the text will show that he is not saying anything of the kind. As the Son of God he exercised such a clear mandate of leadership and authority, that a Roman army officer compared Jesus' authority with his own (Lk. 7:8). Jesus is talking about the spirit of leadership, and leadership style, of which he himself was a perfect example. He refers to 'the one who rules', thus affirming that some do have rule; but he says that a person called to rule should see it as service, not as an opportunity to be 'the greatest' and to control people. Power is always dangerous, especially when one is put in a position of authority over people.

The restoration of Genesis 1

Jesus treated women with respect and men and women as equals. But this was not true of most of the society into which he was born. A hundred years after Jesus' coming, Rabbi Jehuda urged his fellow Jewish men to recite the oft-quoted prayer, 'Praised be God, that he did not create me as a *goy* [Gentile]! Praised, that he did not create me as a woman! Praised, that he did not create me as an ignorant person!' He was serious about it, although it is overlooked that Jewish women prayed a similar prayer affirming their own sexuality. Jesus came to fulfil, not by-pass the law, and part of that mission was to restore the teaching of Genesis 1, that women as well as men are created in the image of God, and are by no means inferior.

Women in Jesus' day were not required to learn the Torah, and in fact some Rabbis expressly forbade it. Rabbi Eliezer wrote (about 90 years after the death of Christ), 'may the words of the Torah be burnt before anyone delivers them up to women'. Conversing with a woman, even with one's own wife in public, was frowned upon, so one can imagine what a scandal it was when Jesus engaged in conversation with women who were strangers, even in public.[1] When guests came, the wife did not even share in the meal, or serve at the table. This is a Russian custom to this day. Some years ago I dined with a man whose wife was Russian. She not only remained in the kitchen, but after dinner gave me a reflexology treatment on my feet! The witness of a woman was not acceptable in court, which underlines what a revolution took place when Jesus witnessed first to women after his resurrection, and encouraged them to share what they had seen and heard with others.

Jesus showed no respect for these bizarre aspects of the Jewish culture, which had become a mockery of the truth. It deeply affronted him, and he went out of his way to treat women differently, however much it offended his peers. *But it needs to be stressed that he was not introducing a new feminist gospel.* He was simply restoring the sexual equality stated in Genesis 1.

He saw God as much in women as he did in men; and incidentally, as much in Gentiles as he did in Jews. Jesus actually said little or nothing verbally about sex discrimination. He said it all by his actions.

Jesus allowed himself to be handled by a practising prostitute (Lk. 7:37f.), and touched by a woman suffering from menstrual bleeding (Mk 5:24f.). He publicly commended her faith in spite of the fact she had technically broken the law. He publicly supports a woman caught in the act of adultery, though not of course defending her sin (Jn. 8:11). Jesus even set aside sabbath laws in order to heal a hunch-backed woman in the middle of a synagogue service (Lk. 13:10–17).

Against all the prevailing customs of the day, he welcomed women to travel with him and the disciples all the way to the Cross. Women were present at meals with him, and were allowed to serve him. He actually taught women like Mary, who sat at his feet. This was contrary to the convention of the day. He freely delivered them from demons, and healed them the same as men. He made no distinction between them. The Gospels also record the names of women quite as much as the men, thus indicating that Jesus was inaugurating the renewal of the sanctity of sex, and the recovery of a recognition of the dignity of women. To him they were equal with men.

Jesus showed a particular concern for mothers and for widows. When mothers wanted to bring their children to him, he rebuked the fussy, protective attitude of his disciples and welcomed them (Mk. 10:13–15). It was a poor widow whom he singled out for special praise (Lk. 21:3), and another whose son he raised from the dead (Lk. 7:11–17). It was reported that 'his heart went out to her'.

It is important also to notice that Jesus changed the rulebook as far as divorce was concerned, because of the obvious injustices committed against women by sexist attitudes. According to the Hillelites (the followers of Rabbi Hillel), a man could divorce his wife if she burnt his food, or if he met a prettier woman.[2] Jesus speaks of the absolute prohibition of divorce, tracing it back to the original will of God in Genesis (Mt. 5:31–32; 19:3–9). Thus Jesus strikes a blow for equal rights – justice for women as well as men. No wonder Elaine Storkey writes in her book, *What's Right with Feminism*, 'many feminists who have found it difficult to identify with the maleness of God as so often portrayed by the Church, discover in the Jesus of the Gospels a person whom they love and appreciate . . . Jesus never condescended to women and never ignored them.'[3]

David Pawson points out that Jesus was the only person who has ever chosen to be born.[4] His relationship with Mary is another affirmation of God's acceptance of women. I hope to deal with this sensitive aspect later, but in passing will now point out the interesting fact that the churches which most honour Mary (the Roman Catholic and the Orthodox) are most opposed to the ordination of women. This may well be a pointer in a direction not many are prepared to look at or even consider. Jesus never once spoke a denigrating word to women or about women. He never did anything unjust or contemptuous to them. No wonder women worldwide and through all the centuries have loved and served him with remarkable devotion.

The conserving of Genesis 2

There is, however, another side to the ministry of Jesus, he only appointed *male* apostles. This is a tough one for feminists, but is overlooked or excused on the basis of 'cultural constraints'. Had Jesus lived in our day, so these people say, he would have ordained women for sure. But then there is another traditionalist thing he did, he only invited men to the so-called 'Last Supper', and men were invited to share the Transfiguration with him. It is worth noting that in the parables, where leaders are mentioned, they are always male. Indeed no less than sixteen parables refer only to men, and of the four that refer to women (the yeast, the ten virgins, the lost coin and the persistent widow), the setting in all is domestic.

So we see that in the area of headship, Jesus follows the creation laws of Genesis 2. He is not reluctant sometimes to restrain women, when they might go further than they should. We see this at Cana when Jesus speaks firmly to his mother (Jn. 2:4), as also when she and his relatives came wanting to speak to him (Mt. 12:46–50). The Syro-Phoenician woman comes in for curt handling when she approaches him about her daughter (Mt. 15:21f.).

The presence of only the apostles at the Last Supper is most significant, not least because it was somewhat contrary to the Jewish practice. The Passover meal as we have said, even when it involved a pilgrimage to Jerusalem, was something of a family occasion, open to women and children as well as the men. Bishop Bertil Gartner, who was the last Swedish Lutheran bishop to refuse to ordain women, has written, 'this demarcation at the Last Supper must have a clearly defined meaning, namely that the apostles should deal with the mystery that was committed to them during the meal'.[5] It is possible that we have here, at the institution of the Holy Communion, the principle of the male celebrant. It might be that Jesus and the Early Church were wanting us to see something important here, because it was a departure from normal custom. Jesus' excluding women at the meal, and especially from the apostolic band, has never been seriously questioned by the Church until very recently. Those who do question it could be accusing Jesus of discrimination by implication, which is a serious charge. People usually excuse Jesus on the grounds that he was 'culturally conditioned'. So we need to turn to this matter next.

Jesus and culture

The best analysis I know of this important aspect of our subject is in Stephen Clark's book *Men and Women in Christ*.[6] The book covers the social aspects, and there are only a few pages on the ordination of women. He writes, 'a full treatment of the contemporary issue of ordination for women is outside the scope of this book'. It is the purpose of my book to show that the social and the theological are in fact intertwined, but the theological should determine the social, not the other way round. That is exactly what Stephen Clark does to good effect in his book, and it should be read by anyone who takes this aspect of the subject seriously.

The usual argument against regarding the maleness of the apostles as normative for all future generations, is that Jesus was conditioned by the culture of his day, and so had no alternative *in those days* but to appoint men. In other words the prevailing culture wouldn't have accepted anything else. In some ways it is a strange argument, because, as we have seen, Jesus was constantly affronting the culture of his day, not least in his behaviour towards women. Be that as it may, such an argument raises some important issues about Jesus Christ and how he was inspired, and how authoritative were his words and actions.

In the first place, Jesus was fully human. He was not some kind of androgynous creature, combining male and female. He was sexually male. He was also born into a particular culture, which he absorbed from his birth onwards, although later he was to be critical of some aspects of it, and would reject those features which did not accord with the Scriptures. In his humanity he was fully in touch with the Father, as well as fully inspired and empowered by the Holy Spirit.

Secondly, he was fully divine. He had existed with the Father and the Spirit from eternity. Because he had voluntarily accepted the weaknesses and limitations of the flesh, though not its sinfulness of which he was completely untainted, he was not, in his incarnate state, all-knowing. He did not know the details of nuclear physics, for example, although in heaven he had been involved with the Father in creating the world. So there were things hidden from him. But all he did know was true, not false. *All he taught, and what is recorded of his words, is free from error*.

Thirdly, he was in touch with his Father at all times, and his Father was outside time, and could see the end from the beginning. Although Jesus in his incarnate state could not always see into the future, and did not know, for example, the time of his return, *his Father did*, and had decided not to reveal it to his Son (Mt. 24:36). When Jesus chose the Twelve, Luke tells us that he first spent the night 'praying to God' (Lk. 6:12). So we know that it was the Father who revealed to the Son who should be appointed apostles, and that all of them should be men. Now the Father knew that the Church was from time to time going to be divided on this issue. Why did he not preempt future problems by including one or two women? It would have offended the Jews, but no more than the Cross did. It would have been welcomed by Gentiles, who were used to priestesses. The most reasonable answer is *'because God wanted there to be only male apostles'*. Jesus did the will of the

Father perfectly; in fact Jesus said 'I and the Father are one.' It could be argued that Jesus, as a person of the first century could not possibly have done anything else, and that he did not know that he was going by his decision to contribute towards denying women access to church headship for nearly 2,000 years. *But the Father knew, and Jesus did his Father's will perfectly, which had on this occasion been communicated to him.*

Some have said that the same argument would have prevented Gentiles from becoming apostles, bishops and presbyters, for there were no Gentile members of the apostolic company at that time. But Jesus had virtually no contact with any Gentiles, although he commanded his disciples to go and preach the Gospel to them. In any case, he had been sent, as he himself said, only to the 'lost sheep of Israel' (Mt. 15:24). There are plenty of references in both the Old and New Testaments to the Gospel being for all humankind. Jesus himself knew that after his death the Gospel was going to be preached all over the world, as he told his disciples. Thus in less than a generation there were Gentiles like Titus and Timothy holding the office of bishop, and in Antioch, Ignatius. Such appointments have never been contested. On the other hand, the idea of women bishops or presbyters has always been challenged from the second century onwards.

There is obviously some significance in the fact that Jesus chose, with the Father's guidance, *twelve* and not ten or fourteen men. Some, like Lukas Vischer, see the number only in terms of a fulfilment of the past (comparable with the twelve patriarchs), rather than a model for the future, and thus he can reject the importance of their maleness.[7] But there are clear hints that the apostles have a future role in the judgement also. We note this in Matthew 19:28 and Luke 22:30. The mention of the 24 elders in Revelation is perhaps another indication of this, with its symbolism of the twelve patriarchs and the twelve apostles.

Above all other factors, we need to see that the culture that Jesus imbibed from his mother's milk onwards, *was the culture of the Old Testament*. That is mostly what he heard and saw from a tender age. He never travelled further than his own country, except when as a baby Mary and Joseph took him into Egypt. Jesus said of the Old Testament, 'Scripture cannot be broken' (Jn. 10:25). Jesus often quoted from the Old Testament, and he affirmed both the truth of the equality of men and women (Gn. 1), and that of their different roles and functions (Gn. 2). He quoted from *both* chapters, but more important he demonstrated *both* throughout his life, by his love and acceptance of women, and by his giving a special role of headship only to men. Jesus, to quote the title of Steven Goldberg's book, believed and practised the 'inevitability of patriarchy'. Patriarchy was rooted in the Old Testament, the only 'Bible' Jesus knew, and its roots spread through the life and ministry of Jesus to the Church of the New Covenant. How the apostles accepted that teaching, and how they interpreted it in the light of concrete situations in the Church, we will see in the next three chapters.

Chapter 6

Joint heirs

> You are all sons of God through faith in Christ
> Jesus, for all of you who were baptised into Christ
> have been clothed with Christ. There is neither
> Jew nor Greek, slave nor free, male nor female,
> for you are all one in Christ Jesus. If you belong
> to Christ, then you are Abraham's seed, and heirs
> according to the promise.
>
> (Gal. 3:26–29)

> When the day of Pentecost came, they were all
> together in one place . . . All of them were filled
> with the Holy Spirit and began to speak in other
> tongues as the Spirit enabled them.
>
> (Acts 2:1,4)

David Pawson calls Galatians 3:28 'the Magna Carta' of the
Christian feminist cause. Paul Jewett, who takes a completely
different position from David, calls it 'the Magna Carta of
humanity'.[1] So we are on to something important. However,
we need to look at *all* of what Paul wrote here, not just the
key phrase 'neither male nor female', because we can only
understand it in the full context in which these words were
written.

The phrase 'neither male nor female' is quoted more than any
other in the promotion of feminist theology. It is usually lifted
out of the passage, without reference to the context. When the
Archbishop of Canterbury was questioned about the subject of
the ordination of women in the *Readers Digest*,[2] he quoted this

phrase in favour of it. We shall see later that it has been the favourite scripture from the second century onward to justify the ordaining of women.

Mary Daly, a radical Christian feminist, quotes Galatians 3:28 with enthusiasm, but does not think much of the rest of Paul. 'The most striking anti-feminist passages are, of course in the Pauline texts,' she writes; and she rails against 'the irresponsible use of these texts'.[3] One might not be surprised at this treatment of the scriptures from a former nun. But surely not from an Evangelical. The late Paul Jewett, an American Evangelical who was teaching at Fuller Seminary when he wrote the book *Man as Male and Female*, published in 1975, does the same thing, though without the radicalism of Mary Daly. He acknowledges that Paul 'appears to teach female subordination in certain passages . . .'[4] He goes on, 'to resolve this difficulty, one must recognise the human as well as the divine quality of scripture'. What he means is that when Paul wrote Galatians 3:28 he was inspired by God, but in the other passages he was only writing in a human way, namely 1 Corinthians 11:3–16; 14:33–38; 1 Timothy 2:11–14.

But a fair question is, By what criteria are we to judge what is 'human' in the apostle Paul's teaching and what is 'divine'? And what right do we have to set one part of Paul against another when it disagrees with our main thesis, which, in this case, is to eliminate the teaching of female submission? Is it our job to find out when Paul was 'in the Spirit'? Should we be distinguishing between when he was inspired by the new imperative of Christian liberation and wrote Galatians 3:28, and when he sadly lapsed back into his old Rabbinic misogyny and wrote about what women could not do in the Church? So, according to Paul Jewett, Galatians 3:28 is 'sound' and to be accepted, 1 Corinthians 11 and 14, and 1 Timothy 2 are to be rejected because Paul has lapsed into his pre-liberated state.

There are certain things Galatians 3:28 does not teach. Paul is not declaring the abolition of sexual differences. Nor is he saying that male and female no longer matter because we are in Christ. The subjects he is addressing are baptism, unity, and who inherits the promise to Abraham, not office and equality. There is no sexual differentiation whatsoever between men and women in baptism. Neither are there race or economic distinctions. Women as well as men are heirs with Christ, and receive the fullness of that inheritance equally with men. Women are as much loved, forgiven and graced as men and will be judged as strictly as them. In Christ they have the same full salvation as men, and judging by what has happened in Church history, there will be a lot more women than men in heaven, and they will be a lot nearer the throne. Men had better get used to that fact!

This passage is about *unity* not equality. Today these words are constantly confused. Many people see no difference between them, as if equality is unity, because it is thought to be the best way to it. The Bible says virtually nothing about equality, and Jesus did not pray for it. He prayed (and died) instead *that we might be one*, not that we might be equal (Jn. 17:21). In any case, equality is not the way to unity. *The miracle of Christian unity is that God brings together people who are naturally unequal, and welds them together in harmony with a love, which because it comes from God, transcends all natural inequalities.*

To deduce from this text that women can be ordained as well as men is a feat of cerebral gymnastics. The text, the context, and the whole letter have nothing whatever to do with the matter of headship and office in the Church. If Paul were asked today if there was any text he regretted writing, I think he might be tempted to reply, 'Galatians 3:28'. Few of his texts have been as misused as this one, or hitched to the wagon of so much heresy.

The analogy of slavery

One of the major ways in which people try to impose this view on the text is by drawing an analogy with the other distinctions mentioned in this passage, Jew and Greek, slave and free. F. F. Bruce was one of those who tried to do this.[5] He argued that if headship may be given to Gentiles and to slaves in the Church, why not to women? Others argue that since racial distinctions are now unacceptable, and particularly slavery has been abolished, we should also do away with the male/female distinction and so ordain women. It is all plausible, in spite of the fact that it contradicts what Paul says on this matter elsewhere, *when he is writing about it in the context of headship and ministry in the Church*. We shall look at these passages in the next chapter.

The historical parallel with the abolition of slavery is an attractive argument, because it fits in with the feminist rhetoric of their 'slavery' down the centuries, and with liberation theology. We shall be seeing in Chapter 15 that the World Council of Churches has made this association of ideas for years, as did Karl Marx and Engels in the tenets of communism. People like Archbishop Desmond Tutu see female liberation as linked to the message of racial emancipation, and this is one of the reasons why the decision to ordain women was comparatively easily agreed by the Church of the Province of Southern Africa. It is perfectly true that women, particularly in some Third-World situations, are sometimes oppressed by an adverse culture, especially when it has not yet been touched by Christian love. But it is a false argument to apply this to the ordination of women.

In the first place, slavery is not part of the order of creation. It was never ordained by God, and indeed it is obviously contrary to the will of God. We are created to be free, and to develop a variety of relationships of which marriage is the most important, but not to be the property of any person. Male headship, on the other hand, as we have already seen, *was created by God*. We shall see in the next chapter that it was affirmed by the Early Church and by many centuries of Christian experience. Roger Beckwith has put it well: 'what man has created, man can abolish [i.e. slavery], but he cannot abolish what God has created [i.e. headship]'.[6]

Roger Beckwith argues that the Bible gives many indications that slavery is an undesirable practice and conflicts with the principles of love laid down in both the Old and New Testaments. For instance, Paul lists 'slave traders' with murderers, adulterers and perverts as 'lawbreakers and rebels' (1 Tim. 1:10). The Old Covenant laws relating to slavery were liberal by the standards of the day. To sell oneself into slavery was regarded as an extreme measure (Lv. 25:39, 47), and if he was an Israelite he had to be released after a strictly limited period (Ex. 21:2f.; Lv. 25:40–46). He could volunteer to remain a slave, but could not be forced to (Ex. 21:5f.). Paul also encouraged slaves to accept their freedom if this was an option (1 Cor. 7:21–23).

Ultimately, in Western society slavery was to be abolished;

it was Christians who exerted most of the pressure for this to happen. But this would only be a correct parallel to the 'male/female' issue if the Christian Church and the family were to be abolished also. Of course, radical feminism has worked hard for this to happen, seeing as it does the Church and the family as the last residual remains of patriarchy in the Western world. But since the Church and the family remain and can never be abolished, neither can the principles of headship and submission which go with them.

Bishop Kallistos Ware puts it well:

> unlike the differentiation between Jew and Greek, or between slave and free, which reflect man's fallen state and are due to social convention, *not to nature*, the differentiation between male and female is an aspect of humanity's natural state *before* the Fall. The life of grace in the Church is not bound by social conventions or the conditions produced by the Fall; but it does conform to the order of nature, in the sense of unfallen nature as created by God. Thus the distinction between male and female is not abolished in the Church.[7]

The freedom of Pentecost

If Galatians 3:28 reveals the freedom women have to be children of God, and to share fully in the joys of Christian living, while accepting too the demands and duties that go with it, then the day of Pentecost bestowed on women the blessing of the Holy Spirit in as great a measure as it did upon men. The prophet Joel said that 'your sons and daughters will prophesy . . . even on my servants, both men and women, I will pour out my Spirit in those days' (Joel 2:28–29). This prophecy was fulfilled at Pentecost. Luke tells us that those in the upper room that morning included not only the apostles, but 'the women and Mary the mother of Jesus . . .' (Acts 1:14). All these women, including the Virgin Mary, were filled with the Holy Spirit and received the gift of tongues. No distinction whatsoever is made between men and women in the gifts and ministries of the Holy Spirit.

Acts and the letters of the New Testament are evidence that women played an important part in the life and ministry of the

Church; but there is no evidence that a single woman held office as a presbyter or bishop. Phoebe is mentioned by Paul as being a deaconess, and is singled out for particular honour (Rom. 16:1–2). Her ministry, consistent with Genesis 2, was that of a *helper*, not a head. Paul thanks her, 'for she has been a great *help* to me'. Priscilla, the wife of Aquila, always linked with her husband, obviously had a powerful ministry in partnership with him. There is no record of an unmarried woman being involved in a travelling ministry, except of the sort described in Luke 8:1–3.

Some have suggested that Junias (Rom. 16:7) was a female apostle. This is scraping the barrel! The name in Greek can be either masculine or feminine. Paul says that Junias and Andronicus 'have been in prison with me'. It is hardly likely that a woman would have shared a prison cell with Paul. But even if Junias were a woman (perhaps Junias and Andronicus were another married team, like Priscilla and Aquila), the word 'apostle' is used in several senses in the New Testament, sometimes as a simple delegate (as in 2 Cor. 8:23; Phil. 2:25). John Chrysostom thought she may have been a woman, but did not perceive her as the equivalent of a Peter or a Paul, with a teaching and leading ministry. Manfred Hauke regards the view that she was a woman as 'in the category of a modern myth'.[8] It is interesting that in the Orthodox tradition, some women have been called *Isapostolis* or 'equal to the apostles', without the Church, of course, making them priests. Examples of this are Mary Magdalene, Thekla, Helena (mother of the Emperor Constantine), and Nina, the missionary who converted Georgia.[9]

It is important to understand the distinction which the New Testament makes between the *charisms* of the Holy Spirit, which are given to all Christians, our birthright in Pentecost, and the *charisms* of office such as elders or bishops, which are given only to certain individuals. The ministries which bestow authority (in the teaching and overseeing office) were only given to men in the Church from Jesus Christ onwards. You do not appoint people to the spiritual gifts, nor can you command the moment. God does that. You certainly have to discern and oversee the gifts. It would be dangerous to confer an authority *per se* on the gifts, and those who bring them.

Gifts can sometimes be counterfeit. But the Church has always appointed people to the office of bishop or elder, after discerning that they are called and equipped by God. The *charisms* of office are as much the work and inspiration of the Holy Spirit, as the gifts bestowed by the same Spirit. As Cardinal Suenens has put it, 'we must never dissociate the institutional church from the charismatic church – these are but two aspects of a single reality'.[10]

Having been involved in the Charismatic Renewal for over 30 years, and given most of my time to its progress and development, I can understand how important all this is to the ministry of women. *Women have come into their own as never before in this movement of the Holy Spirit.* The feminine nature excels in ministries such as healing, prayer, deliverance, prophecy, and evangelism. My wife Jeanne and I became involved in the Charismatic Renewal during its beginnings in the early 1960s. I was at the time a staunch Evangelical, and a curate at All Souls, Langham Place. I was one of the early members of the Eclectic Society, set up by John Stott to gather like-minded clergy together. The wives were excluded from the meetings. The Holy Spirit showed me at once that he did not intend women to be treated thus as second-class citizens. As the Fountain Trust ministry developed, women played an important part, and the meetings, even of clergy, were always open to women as well as men.

The Holy Spirit showed at Pentecost that there was to be no gender *apartheid* so far as the gifts of the Spirit were concerned, just as in the home of Cornelius he was to demonstrate that there was to be no race barrier either. The Holy Spirit opens up for women an enormous range of ministries suitable for their particular gifts. In the book *Recovering Biblical Manhood and Womanhood*, John Piper, one of the editors, compiles a list of ministries in the Church open to women.[11] There are no less than 21 categories, with another 83 sub-categories. This is from an Evangelical perspective. I could add important charismatic ministries that are not contained in these lists, and others could well do the same. After all, there are so many areas of ministry where men are much less effective than women, especially the intuitive and caring ministries such as intercession and counselling.

It is important also to mention the importance which the Orthodox Church attaches to the wives of priests. In the Greek Church the priest is called *presbyteros* or *pappas*, and his wife *presbytera* or *pappadia*. In the Russian Church the priest is 'little father' (*vatushka*), and his wife 'little mother' (*matushka*).[12]

When we look at the Pentecostals and Charismatics, we see confusion about the differences between the charismatic and the institutional, and a tendency to ignore or devalue the institutional. As we shall see later, this was the basic error of another charismatic movement in the second century, the Montanists, who later started ordaining women to headship in the Church.

The Pentecostal historian, Vinson Synan, in an article in *Ministries Today*,[13] believes that it was the Evangelical revivals of the eighteenth and nineteenth centuries that first opened the way for women to be ordained. Charles Finney allowed women to speak in public meetings, and when founding Oberlin College made it the first co-educational college in America. The first woman to be ordained in America, albeit illegally, and almost certainly the first in the world, was Antoinette Brown, a former student of Finney's. This was in 1853 in the Congregational Church in South Butler, New York. It is worth observing that this was about a century before the first main-line Protestant church did the same – the Danish Lutheran Church in the 1950s.

Synan points out that in many spiritual movements (like the Charismatic Renewal) women are accepted *in the early stages*, but later men are preferred when such movements begin to be institutionalised. I agree with Vinson Synan, provided one does not see the process in a negative sense. The charismatic element can so easily become unbalanced in the euphoria of the moment; later more wisdom prevails, and the two elements come back into balance.

The Pentecostal Movement, which burst into prominence about the turn of the twentieth century, enhanced the place of women in ministry, as the Holy Spirit always does. Regarding the other side of the coin, that is the matter of 'office' in the Church, Pentecostals seem to have been less sensitive to the Holy Spirit. He is after all the Spirit of truth, as well as of power. Perhaps the weakness of Pentecostals is they have seldom addressed the theological issues at stake here. And maybe Vinson Synan is right that many of them regarded the rapture as imminent, so there was no time to be lost. Every Spirit-filled person, male and female, needed to be recruited. Katie Campbell of Virginia justified her ministry by noting, 'a woman brought sin into the world; they ought to help to take it out again'!

The most famous of Pentecostal women leaders was Aimee Semple McPherson, who founded the International Church of the Foursquare Gospel in 1923. She built the massive Angelus Temple in Los Angeles, and had a high-profile ministry until her death in 1944. This Church is still one of the leading Pentecostal denominations in America, although it has to be said that it is now largely led by men. Another leading preacher was Kathryn Kuhlman. She never started a denomination, and her ministry was healing, not teaching. When I attended her meetings, she sometimes did some teaching. I always noticed that those who knew her best would discreetly bow their heads at this point and pray that she would stop. It was awful! But when she began to pray for the sick, the anointing of the Spirit was invariably there.

Charismatics are divided on this issue, as are Evangelicals. Many Protestants have accepted the trends in their churches, and charismatic Episcopalians have not raised a whimper during the long and protracted struggle on this issue in the United States. Many Charismatics in Britain are comparatively indifferent to the ordination of women issue; evangelism and renewal are their priorities, and having seen women in action with a charismatic ministry, they are not fussed about their becoming 'priests'. As I shall show later, it has also to be seen against a general backcloth of theological indifferentism, to which experience-orientated movements are often prone. Whether a thing works or not becomes more important than whether it is biblically and theologically correct. If things work, Charismatics don't want to raise awkward issues about whether it squares with the Bible or the traditions of the Church. This is a short-sighted approach, as we shall see.

As Synan points out, the trend in the Pentecostal churches, after initial enthusiasm for women as pastors, tails off, and today 'fewer women are serving as pastors in these churches than ever before'. What is happening in the United States is matched elsewhere. Large numbers of women are being trained for a ministry they will never have. This is one of the prices we are paying for Christian feminist influence. The 'theory' is that women can fulfil exactly the same ministry as men. In practice most church people prefer men as their leaders. They will be accused of sex discrimination. I suspect, however, that the majority of Christians know at heart that dogs have four legs, and training them to have five makes no difference.

Chapter 7

No other practice

> If anyone wants to be contentious about this, we
> have no other practice – nor do the churches of God.
> (1 Cor. 11:16)

> The order established in creation cannot be broken
> in the church, nor can it imperil the man or the
> woman in their self-fulfilment under God.
> (Karl Barth)

It has sometimes been suggested that Paul's statements about what women could or could not do in Corinth amounted to what politicians (after half the British cabinet have resigned) call 'a little local difficulty'! Nothing could be further from the truth. When Paul writes to the Corinthians about the man being the head of the woman, and asserts later that women should be in submission, he says this is the practice and rule-book for all the churches of God everywhere (1 Cor. 11:16; 14:33). If you say, as some do, that Paul must have been culturally conditioned, you are bound to notice that Paul invokes the law (1 Cor. 14:34), God's creative acts (1 Tim. 2:13), and the command of the Lord Jesus Christ himself (1 Cor. 14:37). You can't go higher than that!

The famous fictional detective Sherlock Holmes was often exasperated when he arrived at the scene of a recent crime, to find all the clues obliterated by the boots of the local police. I have felt a bit like him, coming again to these well trodden texts, looking for new clues. But we must go over the ground again. I think I have found some more clues, and there are probably many people who haven't been over this ground before anyway. We will look at the main scriptures one by one.

1 Corinthians 11:3

Sometimes when I read this letter of Paul's, I am tempted to thank God that the church in Corinth was so immature, and that it got so many things badly wrong. For if it had been as exemplary as some of the other churches, we would know very little about the Lord's Supper or Eucharist, the gifts of the Holy Spirit, or the resurrection of Christ. It is because there were disorders in the Eucharist, malfunctioning spiritual gifts, and doubts about the resurrection that Paul gives us teaching, of which, at least in the first two areas, there is very little elsewhere in the New Testament.

To this we can also add, 'Thank God for the feminists in Corinth.' They provoked Paul to make important and definitive statements, which are as relevant today in our dispute with modern feminism, as they were in the first century. In his other letters, apart from 1 Timothy, Paul does not raise the subject. We can presume that the other churches were good 'traditionalists'.

There is another arresting clue to the problem Paul was facing with the women in Corinth. We have seen that he writes to the Galatians that in Christ 'there is neither Jew nor Greek, slave nor free, male nor female . . .' (Gal. 3:28). This letter was probably written five years or so before the letter to the Corinthians. In 1 Corinthians 12:13, he writes exactly the same words, *but omits the phrase 'male nor female'*. We may well ask the question 'Why?' Perhaps he suspected that the feminists in Corinth would handle it the same way their successors have done.

We have already pointed out that this is not a statement for one individual church or only one particular situation. Paul states, 'we have no other practice – *nor do the churches of God*'. You might as well say that the Eucharist, problems about which he next addresses, was only a local Corinthian custom, whereas we know it was a command of the Lord, and something which was central to the life of the Church.

What is Paul saying in 1 Corinthians 11:3? He is making the point that there is order in the Trinity, order in creation, and order in the Church, and the Corinthian women should not be contentious about it. Karl Barth describes it as 'a commandment which for all eternity directs the man and the woman *to their proper place*, and forbids all attempts to violate the ordinance that governs the relationship of the sexes'.[1] This verse is the key to the rest of the passage. He is speaking about three relationships, each of which has a person who is 'head' and a person who is in submission to that head. The first is that between Christ and men, the second between men and women, and the third between the Father and Christ. In these the heads are Christ, the man and the Father again. Those who are in submission are men (to Christ), women (to men) and Christ (to the Father).

In this passage the Greek word universally translated 'head' is *kephale*. Its main meaning in the Greek New Testament is literally the physical head, but its root meaning is the end or the extremity; thus the head of the body is the top extremity of our physical bodies. It is also employed to describe the extremity of a building, or the capstone (Lk. 20:17; Acts 4:11; 1 Pet. 2:7). It is also used metaphorically, as here, to mean 'one who has authority over'. Paul uses this word, in this sense, on a number of occasions. Jesus is designated the 'head over all things' (Eph. 1:22); 'the head of the church' (Eph. 4:15; 5:23); 'the head of the body' (Col. 1:18); and 'the head of all principality and power' (Col. 2:10). Peter also calls Christ 'the head of the corner' (1 Pet. 2:7). As we shall see, the same word is used to describe the husband in his relationship to his wife (Eph. 5:23).

Feminists obviously find this teaching hard going. Elaine Storkey relegates a discussion of it to an appendix in her book (*What's Right with Feminism*). However, eventually, after 2,000 years, an obscure English scholar (Stephen Bedale) in 1954 came to the rescue by suggesting an alternative translation of *kephale*. He proposed that this word could also be translated 'source'. It is true that 'source' could fit some of these texts, although, as we shall see, in most cases it does not make theological sense of them at all. But to establish such a translation it has to be demonstrated that this is a normal or usual use of the word in the Greek language. For that, the evidence is patently weak. It is somewhat like the two statements, 'Dogs have four legs' and

'Cats have four legs', both of which are true. But then to say, 'Dogs are cats' is not true.

There are two ways of determining whether this is a possible translation. One is to examine Greek literature and find out if there are any examples where the word *kephale* can properly be translated 'source'. The other, and more persuasive, is to look at its use in the Greek translation of the Old Testament, or the Septuagint, as it is called.

Wayne Grudem, an American scholar, has done an exhaustive study in this area. Out of 2,336 uses of the word in Greek literature, he has found only two that can possibly be translated 'source'. One is in Herodotus (4.91), and the other in the *Orphic fragment* (21a). The first refers to a part of a river, although it could be translated 'head' as well as 'source', and the other is an obscure reference to Zeus, which could mean either 'authority' or 'source'. So you have 2,334 clear references to two doubtful ones where it could mean 'source', odds of 1,167 to one! We then notice that both these writings come from the fifth century BC. Not very convincing.

When we come to the Septuagint, the evidence actually is non-existent. Of the occasions when the word *kephale* is used to translate Hebrew words, twelve times it translates 'authority over', and there is not a single instance when it means 'source'.

When we see Paul's metaphorical use of the word, we discover that it can only mean 'authority over' when referring to Christ. For instance, it says in this verse 3, 'the head of Christ is God'. This must mean 'authority over'. If instead you translated it 'source' you would be affirming the Arian heresy, which made the Father the source of the Son. That would never do! In the passages in Ephesians and Colossians the meaning is surely clear, that Christ has authority over the Church, he is its supreme Governor. If we translated Colossians 2:10 as 'source', we would make Christ the source of all evil! It is true that Paul in Colossians 1:16 speaks of Christ as the creator of 'all powers, rulers, and authorities'. But that was in the past and in their unfallen state. Colossians 2:10 refers to Christ's present position, and ours in him. He certainly is not the source of evil, but its master.

This novel way of translating *kephale* has no foundation what-soever, and yet feminists claim it sometimes without comment. Elaine Storkey writes about the '*frequent* metaphorical use of *kephale* as beginning, origin or source'.[2] When there is not a single clear example of such a rendering, the word 'frequent' is wholly inappropriate. Karl Barth's comments on this verse are important. He writes, 'there is real subordination, there can be no avoiding this fact. The chief statement of Paul (1 Corinthians 11) is *unambiguous*. There is an express irreversible order in the man/woman relationship.'[3] To believe otherwise is to strain the use of language. As Hercule Poirot, Agatha Christie's Belgian detective, once said, 'I do not like to distort facts to support a theory.' We need to see what the Scriptures say in this matter, not what we wish they said to support undifferentiated equality.

The rest of 1 Corinthians 11

It is verse 3 which is the key to the rest of Paul's discourse. It seems that it was the custom in Corinth for women to wear veils, partly to symbolise their position of submission to their husbands, as a sign of authority, and also because unveiled women were usually regarded as prostitutes. It is certainly not the custom today to wear veils in Western countries. Women are not obliged to do so. But that does not release them from what the veils symbolised in Corinth, that wives are to accept the authority of their husbands. They are not to offend society, when its scruples are justifiable, nor use their freedom in Christ to reject their divinely ordained 'order' in the Church and their family.

Having traced out the divine ordering of the sexes, Paul writes that this 'order' does not make men and women independent of each other. Far from it, they both need each other. In one sense men are more dependent on women than women on men, because all men are 'born of woman'.

To sum up, Paul is anxious to protect the women from losing their 'glory'. In their new-found freedom in Christ, they were moving away from their place of submission alongside men. This is paradoxically their loss, *because they lose their authority as women*. He continues the same theme a little later in this letter.

1 Corinthians 14:33b–38

We have seen the importance Paul attaches to this. It was not a mere 'local difficulty'. Paul is here using his full powers to deal with a major problem in the church at Corinth. As already mentioned, his words are of application to all churches, not just Corinth ('all the congregations of the saints', v. 33b). He appeals also to the Old Testament's authority ('as the Law says', v. 34). To cap it all he goes to the length of invoking the command of the Lord Jesus Christ himself. It is his command (v. 37). A stern penalty also will be incurred if these words are ignored (v. 38).

Paul here commands women 'to be silent in the churches' (v. 34). He does not allow them to speak. The Law commands them to be in submission. The temptation in our so-called 'liberated' society is to trivialise these words, to dismiss them as hopelessly inappropriate for our day, and as flagrant discrimination against women. Some see it as clear evidence that Paul was a woman hater.

There seem to be two interpretations we have to dismiss as inappropriate. The first is that Paul is here totally prohibiting women from contributing anything vocally in a church service. It seems Paul does not have this in mind. If we turn back one page we see that he expects women to have the priestly ministry of prayer (in church and aloud) and that of prophecy (1 Cor. 11:5). Both prayer and prophecy, vital ministries, were open to women in the Old Testament, as we have seen. It is hardly likely that Paul would have reversed this and prohibited them in the New.

The second interpretation, which we must reject also, is that Paul is here preventing women from chatting in church, or as we would say 'fellowshipping'. Surely Paul would not have pulled out all the stops, invoking the Law and the authority of Christ himself, for such a mundane matter as women conversing during a church service. It should be added that, in my experience, men are as bad if not worse than women in this matter, and one does not suppose that the churches have changed much in this respect since the first century.

Manfred Hauke stresses the importance of the statement of Paul, that it is 'the Lord's command'.[4] We know that Paul did have access to statements of Jesus Christ which are not in the Gospels. One can be found in Acts 20:35, when in Paul's talk to the Ephesian elders he quotes Christ's words, 'it is more blessed to give than to receive'. We do not know exactly what Christ said about behaviour in church, or when he said it, or even whether it was before or after his death and resurrection. All we can be certain of is that 'the command' that Paul refers to cannot have been anything trivial.

It is true that Paul tells the women to ask their husbands any questions they may have at home. Jewish custom did not normally approve of women speaking in public. Maybe more important than that is the statement, 'did the Word of God originate with you?' (1 Cor. 14:36). The implication here is that these women were *teaching* in church, something which was prohibited under the Law of Moses. If they did not understand what was being taught they should ask their husbands at home, *not* counter or supplement it with their own. Above all they should not be the teachers in the congregation. If asking questions in church is prohibited, teaching is prohibited *a fortiori*. This is consistent with Paul's other statement in 1 Timothy 2, which we will turn to next.

When we look at 1 Corinthians 14:38 we can gauge more fully the enormity of what Paul is saying. If a person ignores this teaching, he says, 'he himself will be ignored'. Manfred Hauke writes that disobedience of this command 'would place one's eternal salvation in jeopardy'.[5] You can't say anything more serious than that. It seems there are two possible interpretations, depending on who is doing the ignoring. Is it God, or is it the apostle?

Teignmouth Shore paraphrases it, 'a person who cannot recognise such an evident and simple truth must be of a perverse kind and so should be ignored' (by the apostle and others).[6] The other possibility is much more serious. It could mean that if a person does not know this truth he does not know God or God does not know him. Our word 'agnostic' comes from this Greek word. It is used frequently by Paul (as in 1 Cor. 15:34) to denote the state of mind of an unbeliever. So Hauke might be right that one's salvation could be at stake here. Leon Morris thinks the 'disregarding', as Moffatt translates it, could refer to the day of judgement.[7]

This passage, therefore, ends with a most solemn warning, whichever way we interpret it. It would be dangerous for anyone to take it lightly, or attempt to apply this teaching only to the church in Corinth, or the times of the apostles. The command of the Lord remains to this day and must be obeyed in every church situation.

1 Timothy 2:11–14

Unlike 1 Corinthians, this letter of Paul's was written to a person, not a church. Timothy was in charge of the church in Ephesus, and this letter, 2 Timothy and Titus have been rightly called the 'pastoral epistles', for pastoral concerns dominate them.

We have to remember that the divisions into chapters and verses came in the fourth century, so that there was no break in Paul's letter between the second and third chapters. This establishes the context of his remarks, which is to do with 'order' in the Church. In 1 Timothy 2:11–14 he deals with the ministry of women as it relates to teaching and headship. These ministries were not open to women. Then in 1 Timothy 3:1–13 he specifies the qualifications needed for the appointment of overseers (bishops) and deacons. What he says is consistent with what he has just said, and, as we shall see, he assumes that such appointments will be male and not female.

We need to pause for a moment and reflect on the situation which faced Timothy in Ephesus at this time. It is well known, and indeed there is a record of it in Acts, that Ephesian society was dominated by the temple to the goddess Artemis, one of the wonders of the world. Ephesus was the economic, political and religious centre of Asia Minor. The position of women was particularly well developed. Women had a stronger and more accepted position in this city than any other in the Roman Empire. Women had professional positions; there were, for example, a large number of women medical doctors. They also took a lead in the political arena. It has been written, 'the full observation of civil rights is found at its most developed in the Asia Minor of the imperial age'.[8]

But that was not all. Women were prominent teachers in the schools of the philosophers, and lectured their students regularly. More important for our study, female leadership dominated the religious scene. The cult of Cybele, in which a mother god was the central focus, was operating in Ephesus, with priestesses performing the central rites. Also present in Ephesus were the priestesses of Demeter, and the cult of Isis, which made equal rights for women part of its message. Another cult present was that of Dionysus, where men and women had equal rights in the services. A tradition has it that Bishop Timothy was killed by the Dionysians when he took a public stand against their orgies. But the most prominent cult was that of Artemis (see Acts 19:23f.), *where priestesses had a higher position than the priests*.

With such a background it can be seen that the Ephesians were hardly culturally hostile to women in leadership, as priestesses, or as teachers. In fact the whole Greek and Roman world of that time was awash with priestesses. In Crete *men*, not women, were banned from the priesthood.

Paul wants to warn Timothy, with such a feminist background, to see to it that women did not teach in the Church, nor hold a position (like that of a bishop or presbyter) in which they would take authority over men. It needs to be emphasised that Paul bases what he has to say about the ministry of women on the Old Testament Scriptures. It was not a local rule for Ephesus, it was a matter of established truth because it is based on the creation narrative in Genesis. Paul declares that 'Adam was formed first, then Eve', thus quoting Genesis 2:7. He goes on to recall that Adam was not deceived (that was not his sin), but Eve was and thereby sinned. Paul's appeal is to the chapter about sexual order (Gn. 2), not the one about sexual equality (Gn. 1). This is because the context is about order, not equality. In Galatians 3:28 it is the other way round.

It should not surprise us that Paul, having specifically ruled out women from the teaching office, and from a position of authority in the Church, should endorse this immediately afterwards in his statement about the qualities expected of a leader. If women may not teach or have authority over men, they can hardly be made overseers or bishops in the Church. This is so obvious there is no need for Paul to say specifically 'women need not apply'. He says that an overseer must be 'the *husband* of but one wife', not 'the *wife* of but one husband', thus assuming the male gender for the overseer. He also has to be someone who 'manages his own family well', and that refers, in the patriarchal context in which it was written, to the father, not the mother. Ephesus was full of priestesses, but the Church was only to have men in the places of authority, and the leadership of the services. Ephesus had many women in teaching positions, but in the Church women were not permitted to teach.

In writing in this way to Timothy, Paul was being consistent with the teaching and practice of the Old Testament, where women could neither be religious teachers nor priests; and with that of Jesus, who only appointed male apostles. This same consistent thread was to continue throughout the Church, through the teaching of the Church Fathers, the Schoolmen of the Middle Ages, the Reformers, and on until the last 40 years. Only in the case of heretics and some of the nonconformist groups was there to be any disagreement. It is a long and formidable chain of witnesses.

One of the most interesting witnesses to this was C. S. Lewis. He died over 30 years ago, yet his books sell more today than they did when he was alive. C. S. Lewis was for half his life a convinced pagan. In our Western world there are many pagans. But the vast majority of them are pagans by default. C. S. Lewis, however, *was a pagan by conviction*. Lewis conducted a life-long correspondence with a man who lived in Northern Ireland called Arthur Greeves. In 1979 the letters were published. In one of them he tells of the time he had with an Oxford don called Henry Dyson and the famous Tolkien. This was a major factor which led to his conversion. 'In pagan stories I was prepared to feel the myth as profound and suggestive of meanings beyond my grasp . . . The story of Christ is simply a true myth, a myth working on us in the same way as the others, but with this tremendous difference, *it really happened*.'[9]

Lewis was so saturated in pagan mythology that he knew what it was to be a pagan, and he knew the difference when he became a Christian in 1931. Many years later when he moved from Oxford to Cambridge, he said in his inaugural address, 'it took me as long to acquire inhibitions as others (they say) have taken to get rid of them. That is why I often find myself at such cross-purposes with the modern world: I have been a converted Pagan living among apostate Puritans.'[10] Lewis only wrote one article about the ordination of women, and that is less than six pages long. It was written in 1948 when the issue was surfacing because of a strong move in Denmark and Sweden to ordain women in their State Lutheran Churches. 'To ordain women,' C. S. Lewis wrote, 'we should be embarked on a different religion. Goddesses have, of course, been worshipped: many religions have had priestesses. But they are religions quite different in character from Christianity.'[11] Lewis was not like most of us, of which I would include myself, who have never been convinced pagans. He knew exactly how pagans think. He knew the pagan atmosphere first hand. He said to himself, 'This is pagan, not Christian.' His instinct was clear; priestesses belong to paganism not Christianity. We can trust his instinct in this matter.

In all that we have so far seen there is a consistent pattern flowing from the creation narrative in Genesis 1–3. Men and women are joint heirs of the Kingdom of God, and are to share in partnership with each other in the ministry of the Holy Spirit. For both men and women a new potential for faithful work and witness opened up with the coming of Jesus Christ, and the gift of the Holy Spirit. Men and women in Christ are truly one and equal.

At the same time Jesus Christ did not come to abrogate the divinely created distinctions between male and female, which are wider than the physical differences. In Genesis 2 God gave to Adam and to men ever since, the responsible role of 'head' in sexual relationships in the home and in the religious life of his people. To Eve he gave the role of 'helper'. The two roles are not interchangeable, nor are they a product of cultural conditioning. The whole of history bears testimony to this reality.

The centrality of the teaching office

The whole Bible witnesses to the fact that God has revealed himself to men and women. Also that he appoints amongst his people those who are responsible to pass on the teaching from generation to generation. They are required to be faithful, neither adding nor subtracting from what God has revealed, whether it is the Law in the Old Testament, or the teachings of Jesus and the apostles in the New. 'Hear . . . the laws I am about to teach you. Follow them so that you may live,' says Moses. 'Do not add to what I command you and do not subtract from it . . . teach these things to your children, and to their children after them' (Dt. 4:1, 2, 9). Often in the first five books of the Bible there is stress on the importance of correct and faithfully transmitted teaching.

The theme runs on through the Psalms, especially Psalm 119, where the cry 'teach me your decrees' is a frequent refrain (v. 124). It was the priests who were given the privilege and the responsibility of teaching the people. Ezekiel declares 'they are to teach my people the difference between the holy and the common and show them how to distinguish between the unclean and the clean' (Ezk. 44:23). Jesus followed the same pattern by gathering a small group of disciples around himself and teaching them, with a view to their teaching others. In Acts 2:42 we are told, 'they devoted themselves to the apostles' teaching . . .' Immediately after his ascension, and the coming of the Holy Spirit at Pentecost, the apostles began to pass on what their Master had taught them. Later the apostles appointed presbyters or elders to do the same. They were to teach 'what is in accord with sound doctrine' (Tit. 2:1). To Timothy Paul writes, 'command and teach these things . . . be diligent in these matters; give yourself wholly to them . . . watch your life and doctrine carefully' (1 Tim. 4:11, 15). Paul says about bishops that they must be 'able to teach' (1 Tim. 3:2). In 2 Timothy 2:2 Paul urges Timothy to pass on his teaching to 'reliable men, who will also be qualified to teach others'.

As we have noticed in both the Old and New Testament the teaching office was not given to women, and Paul categorically says, 'I do not permit a woman to teach' (1 Tim. 2:12). This is underlined both by the position of women, who are in submission to men, and by the heavy line that Paul takes in 1 Corinthians 14:33–38, when he raises this prohibition to dominical status. It is a 'command of the Lord'. But the key is not where women teach, who they teach, nor even what they teach. If they are giving false teaching, that can be corrected. It is the *position* they hold when they teach. They may not hold a position of authority in the Church so far as teaching is concerned. They may not be presbyters or bishops, who are the guardians of the truth, those who are entrusted with the responsibility of passing on the apostolic deposit, maintaining truth in the Church, and correcting error.

In practice does that mean that women cannot teach at all? Clearly no, because mothers have a particular responsibility to teach their children, and Paul says of the older women that they are 'to teach what is good . . . and train the younger women' (Tit. 2:3–4). In other words, women have the vital calling and responsibility of teaching women and children. As we have seen, women can prophesy and pray in church, and that does sometimes have a didactic element. But women may not hold a position of authority in the Church so far as teaching is concerned.

I now write frankly. A church which appoints and sustains in office bishops and clergy who deny the Virgin Birth and the bodily Resurrection has lost all credibility in the eyes of God and men. *The argument about whether or not women can be bishops and presbyters becomes merely academic, if the Church trivialises the truth by giving the teaching office to bishops and clergy, who in more faithful periods of the Church were called by the old-fashioned and unfashionable word, heretics.* There was a time when the apostle John fled from a bath-house when he heard that the heretic Cerinthus was in the building too. Eusebius reports the apostle as saying, 'let us flee, lest even the bath-house fall in; for within is Cerinthus, the enemy of the truth'.[12] The same apostle says that if anyone does not bring the teaching of Christ, 'do not take him into your house or welcome him. Anyone who welcomes him shares in his wicked work' (2 Jn. 10–11). Such stern instructions are ignored today, and false teachers are welcomed in the churches without so much as a rebuke. These are hard words that have to be said.

In conclusion, it needs to be stated categorically that the teaching office in the Church of England and all Protestant churches barely exists. There is little discipline in churches (other than the Roman Catholic and Orthodox) in matters of faith and morals. This speaks of gross unfaithfulness to the apostolic teaching passed on faithfully and often at great sacrifice by over 60 generations of our Christian ancestors. A Church that believes that heretical presbyters and bishops may teach in the Church, has no integrity, whatever it may say about women presbyters and bishops. Such a Church is under the judgement of God.

Chapter 8

God's order for the family

So I bow in prayer before the Father. Every family
in heaven and on earth gets its true name from him.
(Eph. 3:14–15, New Century Version)

In this book there is a special emphasis on the family. In this chapter we shall be looking at the biblical framework of the human family, husbands, wives and children. The family in the West is under grave threat, and that is a major reason why I have given it such a strong focus in this book. The trouble when one does this is that unmarried men and women, or singles as they are now called, are left out.

The biblical teaching about men and women and their roles in the Church is the same for singles as for married couples. But it needs to be made clear that singles are as truly called to be single as couples are to be married. So this book is written as much for them as for married people. In the book *Recovering Biblical Manhood and Womanhood*, John Piper, one of the editors, writes a special foreword for singles, and he shares eight biblical truths, which are special for them:[1]

1. Marriage, as we know it in this age, is not the final destiny of any human.
2. Jesus Christ, the most fully human person who ever lived, was not married.
3. The Bible celebrates celibacy because it gives extraordinary opportunity for single-minded investment in ministry for Christ (1 Cor. 7:32).
4. The apostle Paul and a lot of great missionaries after him

have renounced marriage for the sake of the Kingdom of God.

5. The apostle Paul calls singleness a gift from God (1 Cor. 7:7).

6. Jesus promises that forsaking family for the sake of the Kingdom will be repaid with a new family, the Church (Mk. 10:29).

7. God is sovereign over who gets married and who doesn't. And he can be trusted to do what is good for those who hope in him.

8. Mature manhood and womanhood are not dependent on being married.

Of course, singles are full members of the Church family, and can be part of an extended human family. As we read the New Testament we can see a close connection between the Church and the family. The Church is the family of God, and the Christian family is a paradigm of the Church. We have seen that in the Old Testament the people of God, called the Israel of God, is usually 'female' in her relationship to God, who reveals himself as 'Father'. Similarly the Church in the New Testament is described as the 'Bride of Christ', and Christ is pictured as the Bridegroom.

The Church as family

There are other examples in the New Testament where we see the writers, particularly Paul, viewing the Church family and the human family together. In other words, the relationships are similar. In Ephesians 3:14 Paul speaks of God the Father, 'from whom his whole family [literally fatherhood] in heaven and earth derives its name'. The Greek words are *pasa patria*, which, according to Francis Foulkes, cannot be translated 'the whole family', since 'the article would be required for this'. He goes on, 'It means strictly "lineage", "pedigree" (on the father's side) or more often a "tribe" or even "nation" . . . in effect the apostle is saying, think of any "father-headed group" *in heaven and earth*, each one is named from Him. From Him it derives its existence and its concept and experience of fatherhood.'[2] Again we see the link between the father as the head of the human family, and God as the Father of all families.

There are two other occasions when Paul refers to the Church as a family. In Ephesians 2:19, 'you are no longer foreigners and aliens, but fellow citizens with God's people *and members of God's household*'. An even more striking example is just after Paul has outlined the qualifications for overseers and deacons in the church, he refers to 'God's household, which is the Church of the living God, the pillar and foundation of the truth' (1 Tim. 3:15). Throughout the Old Testament, and by implication in the New, the human household, what we today call the 'extended family', is always headed by the father, never by the mother, unless the father was absent, either because of business, or death.

This relationship between the Church and marriage becomes much more explicit in Paul's famous teaching in Ephesians 5:22–33 about the marriage relationship between husbands and wives, which he compares with the relationship between Christ and the Church. For wives the particular focus is on submission, for the husband on self-sacrificial love. And Paul parallels this with the relationship that the believer has with Christ. The focus for the believer is on submission, whereas the focus of Christ is on his love for us, whereby he 'gave himself up for us' (v. 25), and his feeding and caring for the Church (v. 29). It is noteworthy here too that the Church is described by Paul as female, as the object of Christ's love. The verb used to describe the wife's role in relationship to her husband in verse 24 is *hupotasso*, which is clear in its meaning. It is to be *under* authority, or to arrange, set or appoint *under*. We know what that means in our following of Christ, and it should be equally unambiguous in the husband/wife relationship, which is entirely consistent with everything Paul has written in 1 Corinthians and 1 Timothy.

It needs also to be pointed out that Paul again uses the word 'head' (*kephale*) to describe the position of the husband in the marriage relationship as well as Christ and his position of authority over the Church. We have already shown how we must dismiss the idea that *kephale* should be translated 'source'. In this passage it is impossible to translate it thus, because Paul complements the theme of 'headship' with *hupotasso*, which can only mean, as we have seen, to be 'under' someone.

Some have resorted to ingenious arguments to avoid the force of what Paul is saying here. The chief one is to refer to the introductory remarks of Paul (v. 21), 'submit to one another out of reverence for Christ'. It is argued from this verse that Paul must be referring to reciprocity. Husbands are to submit to their wives, as well as wives to their husbands. Marriage should be an equal relationship.

If it is interpreted this way, to be consistent, one must apply it to the other relationships mentioned here as well. Thus parents are to submit to their children, and masters to their slaves. And indeed, most foolish of all, Christ is to submit to us. But that makes nonsense of what Paul is saying. Can you imagine, for example, a Managing Director submitting to and obeying his secretary! No, Paul is establishing here a framework of relationships which is essential if there is not to be anarchy in the home and in the work-place. That there sometimes is anarchy is not because verse 24 is being followed, but because 5:22–6:9 are being ignored. The call to mutual submission is a link phrase, referring back to the need for mutual respect in Christian worship, and forward to a general outlining of the place of submission in the basic human relationships to be mentioned. To make more of it than that is to distort and undermine what Paul is saying.

It needs also to be remembered that exactly the same relationships are dealt with in an identical way in Colossians 3:18–25, an earlier letter of Paul's than Ephesians, and one which is similar in content. In that letter there is no mention of mutual submission. In fact, the statement is even clearer than in Ephesians. In calling upon wives to submit to their husbands, the verb used is *hupotasso*. If one is still not convinced, the same statement is made in Titus 2:5, where the verb used is once more unambiguously *hupotasso*. Even if you take the line that Paul is a hardshell misogynist, there is another apostolic witness. Peter writes, 'wives in the same way be submissive [*hupotasso*] to your husbands (1 Pet. 3:1). Peter actually goes further than Paul; for later he draws attention to and commends the example of Sarah, Abraham's wife, 'who called him her master' (1 Pet. 3:5–6). The word he uses here for 'master' is *kurios*, which is the most common and arguably the most important title in the New Testament for our Lord Jesus Christ. That is a hard one for the Christian feminists when they press for undifferentiated equality between husbands and wives!

In the 1 Peter 3 passage it is sometimes argued that this only refers to mixed marriages, where the husband is not a Christian. It is true Peter does talk about 'winning over the husbands without words' (v. 2). But if you look at the reciprocal duty of husbands, it is clear that Christian husbands are in mind also. They are to treat their wives 'as heirs *with you* of the gracious gift of life' (v. 7). Peter also, in referring to the husbands, says, 'if any of them do not believe . . .' (v. 1), which implies that some did and some didn't.

We notice in this passage that Peter refers to wives as 'the weaker partner' (v. 7), which is the NIV translation. Here the NIV is doing an inclusive language deal, but it is not a good translation. The Greek word does not mean 'partner', but literally 'human frame'. Husbands and wives are in certain senses partners, but it is not saying that here. It is referring to the physique of women being weaker than that of men. Actually it has always been known that women, at least in the West, live longer than men, and female babies are less vulnerable than male ones. But in terms of muscle power, women are weaker.

One of the unhealthy trends of feminism and uni-sexism is the growing number of women who are getting involved in physical contact sports, which until recently were in the domain of men. I am referring to Rugby football, soccer, wrestling, and boxing. Having said that, no one is yet suggesting that a British women's team takes on the *male* All Blacks at Rugby football, or that women take on men in the boxing ring! Although the word 'weaker' here should be confined to physical frailty, it is worth remembering that the divine call to women to be in submission automatically casts them in a vulnerable position. This is where men have the specially important role of protecting, encouraging their gifts, listening to and affirming women whenever they can.

Truth not compromise

There is something else important to notice. In Titus 2:5 the submission of wives to their husbands has a reason attached to it: 'that no one will malign the word of God'. Paul believes that when wives do not accept their rightful place in submission to their husbands, the Word of God suffers. Why should that be? Surely because such an attitude is contrary to the Word, and so the will of God. As we have seen patriarchy, and the position of women in the family was then, and always has been, a universal fact. To trade it for some new concept of 'liberty' or 'equality' would be to malign the Word of God. And the apostle Peter says the same thing in 1 Peter 3:1. If any of the wives have unbelieving husbands, 'they may be won over without words by the behaviour [submission] of their wives'.

These verses are a healthy corrective to optimistic statements that are made about the inevitable fruit which will follow after women are ordained. The impression given is that once women are ordained the Church can look the world in the face again. As Dr George Carey said in the General Synod debate, 'we must draw on all available talents if we are to be a credible Church engaged in mission and ministry to an increasingly confused and lost world. *We are in danger of not being heard if women are exercising leadership in every area of our society's life save the ordained priesthood.*' Or as Mark Santer, the Bishop of Birmingham, put it in the same debate, 'I cannot see any way in which the liberating power of the gospel of Christ is commended to an unbelieving world by the assertion that only men can be priests. *That for me is the conclusive argument.*' Personally I don't see how the statement that 'dogs have five legs' can possibly commend the Gospel to anyone. I would have thought too that *truth* is more important than impressing people.

Sadly, the evidence in other churches that have taken this step is not encouraging. The churches may win a few, but ordaining women generally accelerates their decline. The majority of the population, who actually are not feminist, and would much prefer the old order to remain, are not impressed. It is the humble submission of women to the headship of men which is a winning formula in evangelism according to both Peter and Paul, and', it would seem, to the general public today.

In the decades leading up to the 1960s the churches began to remove the Ten Commandments from their chancels. In Chapter 18 we shall see how this symbolised the churches' growing confusion over moral issues. At the same time the

Church of England, which in the 1928 Prayer Book had first left out the word 'obey' from the marriage service, began to make this more the rule than an option. Brides were no longer required to promise to obey or submit to their husbands, as Paul and Peter required the Christians of the first century. In the new Church of England Prayer Book there are now alternative vows, one of which leaves out the wife's vow to 'obey' her husband. Also it is left to the wish of the couple, not the Church, as to which vows should be said. I understand that most couples leave the word out, and that this is encouraged by many ministers, who thus malign the Word of God.

As one would expect in one of the more liberal churches in the Anglican Communion, the New Zealand Prayer Book, or the He Karakia Mihinare o Aotearoa, to give it its Maori name, has eliminated the vow to obey entirely, and in two of the forms of service there is an exact reciprocity of vows, truly egalitarian, but hardly biblical. The Canadian Anglican Church, as liberal as they come, in a supremely liberal society, has likewise dropped the vow to obey entirely.

Now there are no doubt admirable arguments that we cannot expect modern young people to accept what the Bible says about submission. Certainly the modern condition of marriage in the Western world does not commend itself to would-be progressive thinkers. It is doing very badly. Yet today many women want an equal relationship in their marriages, and find the thought of submission demeaning. By the same token many men don't want the responsibilities of loving and caring for their wives and their children, as God's Word tells them they should.

Actually, the egalitarian marriage is a very poor substitute for the biblical one of submission and love. Elisabeth Elliot says 'equality is a human impossibility in marriage'.[3] The home 'is a place where we ought to be allowed to be unequal, where everyone knows everyone else's inequalities, and knows furthermore that it is the inequalities that make the home work'. C. S. Lewis discusses the practical importance of having a 'head' in each marriage in *Mere Christianity*. 'The need for some head,' he writes, 'follows from the idea that marriage is permanent . . . When there is a real disagreement . . . they cannot decide by a majority vote, for in a council of two there can be no majority.'[4] That's being practical, not theological. But the

theological principle of headship is there in the Bible as we have
seen, and correct theology will always be practical if accepted.

Larry Crabb comments on the egalitarian marriage:

> the emphasis on marriage as a partnership between equals
> left me strangely unwarmed. Certainly my wife is a person of
> equal value, but more importantly, she is enjoyably different.
> Learning to express our differences with the other's wellbeing
> in mind seems a far warmer ambition than asserting mutual
> equality. Something wonderfully possible seems to be missing
> from the egalitarian framework.[5]

Elisabeth Elliot again expresses it well in her book *Let me be a
woman*:

> if we have become so mature and open minded and adaptable
> and liberated that the commands of scripture directed to wives
> – 'adapt', 'submit', 'subject' – lose their meaning, if the word
> 'head' no longer carries any connotation of authority and
> hierarchy has come to mean tyranny, we have been drowned
> in the flood of liberation ideology.[6]

We shall be seeing later how the moral resolve of our society has
been undermined by the collapse of family life and indiscipline in
the home. When the Church also disregards God's order in the
family instead of upholding it, and seeks to turn the order of
nature upside down and teaches that dogs have five legs, it is
extremely serious. As the Psalmist wrote (Ps. 11:3), 'when the
foundations are being destroyed, what can the righteous do?'

Sheldon Vanauken gives a good example of how this can work
out in practice in his book *Under His Mercy*.[7] Four women, all
in their thirties, had been meeting for Bible study, when they
came to 1 Corinthians 11 about the headship of the husband.
There was silence apart from one woman who muttered, 'Jim
just could not do it.' They had all realised that *they* were the
head in the marriage, not their husbands. Someone said rather
weakly, 'Does Paul say anything else about it?' They turned to
Colossians 3:18; Ephesians 5:22f. and 1 Timothy 2:11f. There
was some discussion. Finally the leader said, 'Well girls, what do
we do?' Someone else said, 'We've *got* to do it.' Another said,

'They've got to – the men.' They got their men together and did a role reversal to *the right way round*.

In less than a year the four women with amazement and delight were telling each other, and every other woman they knew, what had happened. All four husbands had quietly taken over. Every one had grown taller in his wife's eyes: bigger, stronger, wiser, more humorous. All of the marriages came to a new depth of happiness – a *rightness*. They realised too that their husbands had never demanded the headship – *it could only be a free gift from wife to husband*.

In his prize-winning book *A Severe Mercy*, Sheldon Vanauken tells the moving story of the death of his wife Davy. Their marriage had been a model of feminist rectitude. It was based on complete equality. But as her life was slipping away, their marriage changed. Her husband describes it in these words:

> near the end of her life she began to change. Reading deeply in the Bible, especially her beloved St. Paul, she began to *want* to be wifely and obedient to her husband . . . She was finding it *liberation* to be a traditional [Christian] wife. Not a comrade, not a partner, but a *wife*.[8]

This is the divine way for marriage. Let us follow it, as the old Prayer Book says, 'reverently, discreetly, advisedly, soberly, and in the fear of God'.

Chapter 9

Symbols

Listen, O high priest Joshua and your associates . . .
who are men symbolic of things to come . . .

(Zc. 3:8)

We have just seen that there is no firm case for the ordination
of women in the teaching of the Old and New Testament. We
shall see in a moment, that the Church Fathers unanimously
condemned the practice, and classified it as heresy. To change
all that in the twentieth century you need to find formidable
arguments. The evidence produced by the advocates of such a
radical change is just not good enough.

I could say, 'I rest my case,' because you cannot improve on the
authority of the Word of God. We shall see in a moment that the
Church Fathers based their main arguments against what they
regarded as heresy, on the same scriptures that we have been
examining in the preceding chapters. But we should also look at
what today is the main Catholic argument against the ordination
of women. We can summarise this under the word 'symbol'. We
will look at the argument that only a man can 'represent' Christ
at the altar.

I have to admit I find this argument weaker than the scriptural
one. Indeed, if asserted independently of the Scriptures, it is hard
to sustain. If combined with the Scriptures it helps to strengthen
the main position established in the Word of God, and affirmed
by the Church Fathers. In a conversation I had on this subject
with an Orthodox bishop, he felt the argument was weak also.
The incarnation is about the *humanity* of Christ, not about his
masculinity. We are saved because God became human, not

because he became masculine. In other words, Christ's humanity is more significant than his gender. Having said that, Jesus Christ was not an androgynous creation. Otherwise he would not have been truly human. He was masculine, and the Scriptures make clear that the Messiah would be male, a King, not a queen, a Prophet, not a prophetess, and above all a Priest, not a priestess. So it is a waste of time to consider the academic question about a possible female saviour.

Before we go further, we need to look at the whole question of 'symbol', and its place in the life of the Church. The Western Protestant world usually looks with some suspicion on religious symbolism. I have been in some churches where there are no symbols at all, not even a cross or a painting. There are just bare walls. The opposite extreme is found in many Orthodox churches, where the walls are covered with symbols, particularly holy icons, which are not understood, and frequently misunderstood, by Protestants.

Because of my long association with Roman Catholics, and more recently with the Orthodox, I have had to face this issue from time to time. One memory springs to mind. In 1989 an ecumenical group, of which I was chairman, had to decide where in the world to hold an international conference on the theme of evangelism. It was obvious that the Roman Catholics present wanted somewhere which had symbolical meaning or status. Most of the rest of us wanted a place which met the practical criteria, otherwise it really did not matter.

When the town of Brighton, England, was mentioned, the facilities met all our criteria. But the Roman Catholics, particularly from Latin America, objected. In the first place most of them had never heard of Brighton, and those who had, felt it did not have the right symbolism. The situation was saved by Bishop Moses Tay, the Anglican Bishop of Singapore. He reminded us that it was on Brighton beach that Hudson Taylor received his vision for reaching China with the Gospel. Everyone breathed a sigh of relief, and we all agreed to go to Brighton for the conference.

Like many Protestants, I grew up without much awareness of the importance of symbolism, and suspicious of what I did know about it. If we turn to the Bible we will see on many occasions significance attached to symbols. The Old Testament abounds with examples. To select at random, there were the altars which

Abraham built to the Lord, the specifications for the tabernacle
and later the temple in Jerusalem, the ark of the covenant, itself
containing important symbols, and the twelve stones taken from
the middle of the Jordan and set up in Gilgal. Later generations
were encouraged to ask the question of the stones from Jordan,
'What do these stones mean?' (Jos. 4:21). They were symbols
designed to provoke questions, and redolent with meaning.

Even more important than these were the symbols of the
redemption of the Israelites from Egypt, which found expression
in the Passover meal, celebrated by Jesus Christ with the
apostles just before our own redemption through his death on
the Cross. The Passover symbols were designed to remind the
Jewish nation constantly about what God had done for them, and
how God made them a people for his praise.

When we turn to the New Testament, we find symbols and
signs everywhere. St John's Gospel is built around a series
of signs, and the institution of the Lord's Supper, as a com-
memoration of the death of Christ, became central in the life
and worship of the Early Church. Here the signs and symbols
of bread and wine, appointed by Christ, are almost everywhere
used by churches, even those which give symbols a low rating and
a small place in their life. In addition water baptism is commonly
practised, where immersion in water is a powerful symbol of
death and resurrection.

Interpreting symbols

How we interpret symbols is another matter, and churches do not
always agree on what the symbol means, nor of the relationship
between the symbol itself, and the truth the symbol represents.
Thus the Anglican Reformers taught that the sacraments are
'effectual signs'. That is, they actually *do* something when practised, provided there is true faith to accompany them. On the
other hand, the Zwinglians and Anabaptists and other more
radical Protestant groups would see them as merely signs.

This word 'symbol' is what the word literally means in its Greek
origin (*sumballein*), to 'throw together'. So a symbol is a throwing
together of two realities. Of course, if one begins to deny the
reality of truth, then symbol dies with it. If you deny, as many

do, the reality of human sin, there is no place for a Saviour, and little relevance to the symbols of bread and wine. It would have been the same if an historical revisionist in Israel had proved that the story of the Israelites leaving Egypt was fiction and not truth. The Passover would have been made irrelevant.

It is an interesting fact that those who dismiss symbol, often move in the feminist direction. The most striking example is Paul Tillich, who has been described as the most important figure behind the rise of feminist theology, and who rejected any emphasis on particular Christian symbols, in spite of the fact that many of them derive directly from the words and declared will of Christ. Tillich wrote of moving beyond the Trinity concept of God, to God as the 'ground of our being'. He taught that this pointed to the mother quality of giving birth and embracing. Karl Barth is another theologian who was very ready to dismiss symbols, but on this issue he affirms them. Referring to Ephesians 5:22–33 he sees the submission of women as a 'particular form of the obedience that the Christian community owes to Jesus Christ'.[1] He sees in the Old Testament a symbolism in man and woman as an 'emblem of the Covenant'.

Another interesting example of conflict is in the sphere of psychology, where symbols often play an important part. Sigmund Freud has been described as the psychologist of Protestantism. With his emphasis on the father, and his often sexist denigration of women, he has provided in this field some of the ammunition for the feminist movement. On the other hand C. G. Jung has done for the feminists what Freud did for the sexists. It was Jung who said that the mother symbolises God at least as much as the father.[2] We are not surprised then to see Jung described by Gilles Quispel as having developed 'the most important Gnosticism of our century'.[3] He was deeply influenced also by religions like Hinduism and Buddhism. One can see the androgynous aspect in his 'neither male nor female' proposition, when he sees all men and women as a mixture of the male and the female. This is what someone has called 'gender blending'.[4] 'Heaven defend us,' E. L. Mascall writes, 'from the notion that a man must be effeminate if he is gentle, or a woman masculine if she is brave. Religious art has suffered badly from the former of these assumptions.'[5]

Frank Schaeffer, the son of the late Francis Schaeffer, blames rationalistic Protestantism for the rise of the feminist movement.

In an article in the Orthodox magazine *Again* he finds fault with the Protestant desacralising of women and its marginalising of the Virgin Mary as *Theotokos* ('the bearer of God').[6] The place of Mary, as a symbol of the Church, will be discussed later.

Symbols and the ordination of women

How then does 'symbol' affect our thinking about the ordination of women? A great deal depends on what we mean by 'ordination'. What is ordination for? There are different emphases as to what we mean by 'priesthood'. Father Thomas Hopko, the Orthodox theologian, states that *clericalism* is inherent in the debate about women's ordination. 'If in fact *the Church* means *the clergy*, and if in fact the clergy is a power position . . . then one would say "let's get into the clergy", whether we fall outside of the biblical qualifications or not.'[7] If the sole focus of it is the celebration of the Eucharist, then questions may fairly be asked as to whether a woman can be the celebrant at the altar, and be a valid representative of Christ. If it is the Church that is 'represented', then a woman could even be a more suitable representative, since, as we have seen, the Church is 'female' in the symbolism of the New Testament. Father Hopko answers such a proposition, 'priesthood . . . is in fact the paternal function, the sacramental calling to be a *father* in the community. Do you not then have to be a man to be a father? Can a woman be a father? Can every man be a father?'[8]

The priest, or presbyter, is the 'father' of the Christian community. He is 'father' not only at the altar, but in every other aspect of his ministry to the people of God. It is as 'father' as well as 'priest' that he rightly presides at the Eucharist. He is one of the 'heads' of the Church on earth, and thus represents and symbolises the One who is the Head of the universal Church. We have seen that patriarchy is 'inevitable', and it is the norm for all families on earth. We have seen too the close link in the New Testament between the family in the home and the church family. It is thus impossible to conceive of a church family with a 'mother' as the head (apart from a female religious order, which is not strictly speaking a church).

But the symbolism of this is important too. It is not true that

God is male, and the Church female, in any literal sense. If women are offended by the thought that God is 'male', they might spare a thought for the men who are in the Church which is 'female'. But the symbolism is important. The relationship between Christ and the Church is like that between a husband and wife. The husband is the initiator, as God the Father always is. The husband leaves his father and mother to be married to his wife. The Son of God left heaven to be 'married' to the Church. In one's sexual life, the husband again is usually the initiator, the wife has a more passive and receiving role. God is always the initiator in his relationship with us. The husband is the one who protects, and even gives his own life for his wife. So it was with Christ.

So we should not be surprised when we notice that the analogies for God in the Bible are usually male, and the analogies for the Church are usually female. The patriarchal nature of the family, whether Jewish, Christian or any other religion or no religion at all, is derived from the revealed patriarchal nature of God himself. As we have already pointed out, Paul indicates this in Ephesians 3:14–15 when he refers to God the Father 'from whom his whole family [literally 'every fatherhood'] in heaven and on earth derives its name'. Thus it is impossible to conceive of a matriarchal alternative in the family or in the Christian family of the Church. The symbol of God should always be male.

Symbols and Mary

It is no coincidence that the two churches that have the highest regard for the Virgin Mary, also have the strongest opposition to the ordination of women. I refer of course to the Roman Catholic and Orthodox Churches. Father John Meyendorff has written 'there is no doubt in my mind that the Protestant rejection of the veneration of Mary . . . is one of the *psychological* reasons which explain the recent emergence of institutional feminism'.[9] Mary has for centuries been regarded as the model woman as well as the model mother. Stress has been made on her meekness and her submission to the will of God. She is certainly not a model for the feminist movement! Simone de Beauvoir puts this appallingly when she writes, 'for the first time in human history the mother [Mary] kneels before her son; she freely accepts her inferiority.

This is the supreme masculine victory, consummated in the cult of the Virgin, it is the rehabilitation of woman through the accomplishments of her defeat'.[10] Thus Mary is depicted by de Beauvoir as a woman who betrayed her sex; she is seen as poor and cringing, an inferior creature, to be despised not honoured.

But the Scriptures, our faith, and history are against the atheist de Beauvoir. C. S. Lewis in his famous essay *Priestesses in the Church?* shows the folly of such an assessment. 'The Middle Ages,' he writes, 'carried their reverence for one Woman to a point at which the charge could plausibly be made that the Blessed Virgin became in their eyes almost "a fourth Person of the Trinity".'[11] This is hardly 'inferiority' or 'defeat'.

The true honouring of the Virgin Mary, as Mary says of herself in Luke 1:48, calling her 'blessed' through all generations, is one of the greatest safeguards against those false assessments of the role of women, which include their ordination. Father Max Thurian, the Taizé theologian who has converted to Roman Catholicism, in an article on the ordination of women, says that ordaining women 'would contradict their true nature and the specific gifts they possess'. He accuses those who want to impose on women a masculine form of ministry of 'a lack of theological imagination'. He then goes on to write of two lines of ministry, the Petrine, which was the origin of priesthood and episcopacy, and the Marian, characterised by 'maternity, contemplation and intercession'.[12]

It is interesting to see Mary as the model of femininity, and in some senses of humanity as a whole as it relates to God. Her classic words, 'I am the Lord's servant, may it be to me as you have said' (Lk. 1:38), are archetypal for all Christians, as a statement of belief and commitment. But additionally some see her as a model of the whole Church. At the end of the Second Vatican Council she was called by Pope Paul VI 'Mother of the Church'.

It was Irenaeus who was the first of the Church Fathers to see the connection between Eve and Mary. Paul had established the Adam/Christ connection, that the Fall came through one man's disobedience, so salvation has come through the obedience of one man (Rom. 5:12f.). Contrastingly, Irenaeus writes of the sin of Eve 'knotting us up', and Mary untying the knot through her obedience.[13] He is not, of course, saying that

Mary is the Saviour; but showing the importance of Mary's act of obedience, as a shining example for all Christians in their relationship with God. Hauke here describes her as 'the first and exemplary Christian'. The Roman Catholic theologian H. U. von Balthasar has developed this still further. He writes, 'in Mary, the Church already has physical existence, before it is organised in Peter'.[14]

Balthasar rejected the idea of the ordination of women, because ordination and office in his view are essentially masculine functions. But women should not view this as discrimination, rejection, or subordination. If anything, the masculine is subordinate to the feminine, for everything in the Church is ordered to the feminine receptivity of faith. Thus a woman who would strive for a male role in the Church would strive for a less and would deny the more which she is. For him it was a matter of equality in diversity. 'Every theory,' he writes, 'which puts vocations in an order of higher or lower "perfection" is an insult to woman, and especially to the mother of the Lord.'[15] Mary, in other words, has something different and more.

There are, as we have already noticed, several allusions to the Church as feminine in the New Testament, the most common being the Church as the Bride of Christ (Jn. 3:29; Rev. 21:2, 9; 22:17). Paul uses the same language when he writes to the Corinthians, 'I am jealous for you with a godly jealousy. I promised you to one husband, to Christ, so that I may present you as a pure virgin to him' (2 Cor. 11:2). Another text links this with the Virgin Mary. In Revelation 12:1f. a woman (the Virgin Mary or 'Israel'?) gives birth to a child, who is the Lord Jesus Christ, because it is said 'he will rule all the nations with an iron sceptre' (v. 5). The woman's child is snatched up to 'God and his throne' (v. 5), and then the woman flees into the desert 'to a place prepared for her by God' (v. 6). So the woman (Mary) becomes symbolically the Church. We need to stress the word 'symbolically'. Obviously Mary is not the Church. The Church is the Body of Christ. But again we see the Church symbolically seen as female.

For some the concept of Mary as the Mother of the Church will be disturbing. To others it is helpful. The argument against the ordination of women is in no way dependent on our agreeing to the concept of symbolism outlined in this chapter. But it does, I believe, reinforce an argument that has already been established. To Anglo-Catholics and Roman Catholics it is a valid argument, namely that a priest, who is representing God at the altar, must be male for the symbolism to be authentic. A woman theologian and philosopher, Gertrud von le Fort, writes, 'the Church was not able to entrust the priesthood to women, since she would thereby have destroyed the proper significance of women in the Church, she would have destroyed a part of her own essence, that part whose symbolic representation was entrusted to women'.[16]

Chapter 10

Truth back-to-back
A summary of Part 1

One standing alone can be attacked and defeated,
but two can stand back-to-back and conquer.
(Ec. 4:12, Living Bible)

We began our study of the biblical passages with this verse
(Ec. 4:12), and it is fitting to end with it. I like the Living Bible
translation. It conjures up a picture of two warriors standing
back-to-back, each protecting the other from an attack from
the rear. God's revelation often comes to us in back-to-back
formation. Thus we have seen in the biblical passages from
Genesis to Jesus Christ, Peter and Paul, that men and women
are called both into sexual equality *and* order.

A revealing aspect of the debates about gender in the churches
is the attitude of people to the Scriptures. There are many
who will be thoroughly dogmatic when it comes to the *social*
arguments for women teaching and taking authority over men
in the Church, but who are as weak as water when it comes to
the biblical arguments.

As we shall see, throughout this century there has been
intense pressure to move the arguments away from the Scriptures. In Sweden the Lutheran Church concluded that there
was no case for the ordination of women in the Scriptures; it
was decided purely on social grounds. In 1970, some years
after the first women had been ordained, a committee was set
up in Sweden by the bishops to examine amongst other things
the relevant biblical texts. *It was stated that it was impossible
in the apostolic church to ordain women, but the developments in*

secular society required it.[1] A German Protestant theologian, Eva Senghaas-Knobloch, has stated, 'theological justifications play no role in the supporting arguments [for the ordination of women] . . . the general exegetic and dogmatic lines of thought lead only to restrictive, or totally negative results'.[2]

In the Roman Catholic Church there is the same problem. As we have observed, Hans Küng wanted the subject moved from the theological field to the sociological. He was involved in a progress report to the House of Bishops on the ordination of women in 1966 which stated, 'there are no dogmatic or biblical reasons against it . . . The solution to the problem depends on the sociological conditions of time and space. *It is entirely a matter of cultural circumstances*' (italics mine).[3] Karl Rahner advanced the same argument.[4] In 1973 a working party of American Catholic bishops published a paper in answer to the increasingly shrill demands in America for the ordination of women. The statements from Scripture, and especially the passages from the letters of St Paul, are described as 'full of provocative words' and are dismissed without much ceremony as 'socio-historically conditioned'. They warn 'these Pauline texts should not be cited as arguing against the ordination of women'. Manfred Hauke concludes, 'a theological case . . . was not even attempted, but instead, reference was made to the traditional structures of the Church . . .'[5]

The same approach has been taken by those who have argued for ordaining women in the Church of England. The committee which prepared for the Lambeth Conference of 1968 declared, 'We find no conclusive theological reasons for withholding ordination to the priesthood from women as such.' All through the long debate on this issue in the Church of England, the theological aspects have been circumvented wherever possible. Liberals have trivialised the Scriptures, and Evangelicals have found new ways, as we have seen, to explain away the passages which are to them difficult.

The Thirty-Nine Articles

The Thirty-Nine Articles of the Church of England affirm the importance of the Scriptures in determining matters of doctrine and morals. They declare, 'the Old Testament is not contrary to the New' (Article 7). It is especially important to notice that on the gender issue both Christ and the apostle Paul quote from the Old Testament, definitely implying that they accept its authority. The Old Testament is obviously patriarchal, and all of the New Testament writers affirm this. There is not a single case of this being challenged.

In Article 20 it is plainly stated that the Church may not ordain anything 'that is contrary to God's Word written, neither may it expound one place of scripture that it be repugnant to another'. In other words, the ordination of women must not be contrary to God's Word written. We have seen that it patently is. And we are obliged to make sure we do not teach anything from one part of the Bible which is 'repugnant to another'. For instance, we may not interpret 'neither male nor female' (Gal. 3:28) as allowing women to be ordained, while at the same time ignoring the Pauline passages which teach that it is wrong to do so. As I have tried to show, properly interpreted, there is no conflict between these passages.

There are some who argue that the Scriptures are silent on the ordination of women issue, that they neither affirm nor deny it. This is a further reason why some have felt it left the way open to argue for it sociologically rather than theologically. The culture of today, in other words, demands it. I hope we have been able to establish that Scripture is far from silent on the principles of gender that are of the essence of this issue, even if there are no explicit texts which settle the matter of the ordination of women. But we do need to listen to the silences of Scripture, what it does not say, as well as what it does. As Bishop Kallistos Ware has said, 'not everything is outwardly defined. Certain doctrines, never formally defined, are yet held by the Church with an unmistakable inner conviction, an unruffled unanimity, which is just as binding as an explicit proclamation.'[6] And we shall see in the next section that the ordination of women was often discussed in the early centuries, and was always declared invalid on the grounds of the example of Christ and the teaching of the Scriptures.

Conclusions

Let us see what I believe these scriptures teach us:

1. The first three chapters of Genesis are like three strands of a rope, each of which is important. The first chapter reveals the equality of male and female, both created in the image of God. The second chapter reveals that God gave the man authority not the woman, and created her to be his helper. The universality and naturalness of patriarchy is further evidence of this truth. The third chapter reveals how Adam and Eve spoilt the whole thing through their disobedience, a key part of which was the usurping by Eve of the headship of her husband.

2. All of this is demonstrated in the rest of the Old Testament, where the leadership of the nation, the responsibilities for the ordering of the temple worship, and the teaching office, are always held by men. This is the 'culture' which Jesus and the apostles inherited and affirmed.

3. Jesus Christ came amongst other things to restore the dignity and worth of women. He also affirmed the patriarchal character of human society, including the headship of men. He did this through his teaching and by appointing only men as apostles. In this he was a traditionalist.

4. Pentecost was a great day for women as well as men. Both were filled with the Holy Spirit. Women were affirmed in the Early Church, and given scope for their ministries, especially that of prophecy. They served alongside the men in many different ways, *but they were never appointed as elders or bishops*. In saying 'there is neither male nor female' Paul underlines the unity that they enjoy in Christ, and that gender is no barrier to membership of the family of God. Women have the same birth rights as men in the New Covenant.

5. Paul balances what he taught in Galatians 3:28 by making plain that there are areas of ministry which are 'out of bounds' to women. They may not hold any teaching office in the Church, or take authority over men, because the man, as specified in Genesis 2, is the head of the woman. This continues the teaching of the Old Testament, and is also a 'command of the Lord' and so has to be taken seriously. Karl Barth writes,

'the supremacy of man is not a question of value, dignity, or honour, but of *order*'.[7]

6. Peter and Paul's teaching on the marriage relationship is consistent with the rest of their teaching. The husband is the head of the wife, and is commanded to love and cherish her; the wife is to submit to her husband, as we all submit to Christ.

7. There is consistent symbolism in both the Old and New Testaments which show that God is Father and Christ is husband, while the Israel of God in the Old and the Church in the New are represented as female, in the case of the Church, the Bride of Christ.

In their book *Recovering Biblical Manhood and Womanhood* the editors, John Piper and Wayne Grudem, have tried to evaluate the arguments which evangelical feminists advance for women in leadership in the Church. They draw our attention to what they call 'the excluded middle'. They define this as 'strengthening one's position by exposing the short comings of an ugly alternative, while giving the impression that there are no other alternatives when in truth there are'.[8] This helps us to see the weakness of the arguments of those in favour of the ordination of women.

An example of the 'excluded middle' argument is the remarks made by Dr George Carey in the General Synod Debate of November 1992, which I referred to in a previous chapter. He said, 'we are in danger of not being heard if women are exercising leadership in every area of our society's life save the ordained priesthood.'[9] This implies that there are really no alternatives, if the Church of England is to be heard, but to ordain women, whereas between excluding them altogether, and ordaining them, there are many wholesome alternatives.

Steven Goldberg has another way of describing this defective way of arguing. He calls it 'the fallacy of the glancing blow'. This is how he describes it: 'Those who cannot face the implications of a basically sound theory, reasonable premise, or trustworthy observation, *totally* dismiss them by focusing only on their excesses and perverted uses, and would have us believe that such a glancing blow is lethal.'[10] This fallacy is commonly used to derail arguments for patriarchy ('bad fathers'), hierarchy ('the

Spanish Inquisition'), submission ('wife beating'), and authority ('slavery'). When the middle ground is excluded, and the glancing blow argument included, you raise the emotional temperature and can just about prove or disprove anything.

The quest of women for positions as ministers of churches and bishops of dioceses is greatly mistaken, and those who encourage such expectations are denying the teaching and example of Christ and the apostles. This cannot but damage Church life as well as family life. But saddest of all is the effect this will have on women themselves. John O'Donnell has written an article on the theology of the Roman Catholic theologian, Balthasar. He comments:

> I suspect that Balthasar is correct, when he sees a profound temptation for contemporary women to consist in seeking a male identity model . . . His answer is equality-in-differentiation . . . and testifies that our contemporary trend towards pansexuality may turn out in the end to be sexlessness and that unisex is a false version of liberty.[11]

Women stand to lose most in this quest for equality in the pulpit and at the altar. Their gifts are wasted there. They have a far more important role to fulfil as 'mothers in Israel', whether they are married or not. They should leave the other part to the men, as the Scriptures indicate, and the Church Fathers affirmed.

Sheldon Vanauken has a good way of describing it. He rejects the feminist argument that equality means identicalness 'like two ten-penny nails'. Rather it means 'equal in value, equal in importance . . . like a nut and a bolt that are of absolutely equal importance in holding something together but are different and complementary'.[12] This is what the Scriptures teach, and what the Church has practised until the sexual revolution of the latter half of the twentieth century.

In the end we must conclude that 'two are better than one'. By that I mean that the Scriptures compel us to accept both sexual equality *and* order in the relationship between men and women. These two truths complement rather than contradict each other. In the acceptance of both lies the only hope for the well-being of the Church and the human family.

Part 2

Such a great cloud of witnesses

Therefore, since we are surrounded by such a great cloud of witnesses, let us . . . run with perseverance the race marked out for us.

(Heb. 12:1)

Chapter 11

The democracy of the dead

History is more or less bunk. It's tradition. We don't
want tradition. We want to live in the present and
the only history that is worth a tinker's damn is the
history we make today.

(Henry Ford, 1863–1947)

Tradition may be defined as an extension of the
franchise. Tradition means giving votes to that
most obscure of all classes, our ancestors. It is the
democracy of the dead.

(G. K. Chesterton, 1874–1936)

Henry Ford was a great debunker. He not only debunked history,
but also 'exercise'. 'Exercise is bunk,' he once said. 'If you are
healthy you don't need it, if you are sick you shouldn't take
it.' It is probably true to say that most people today would
concur with Henry Ford's view of history rather than with
G. K. Chesterton's, though probably not with Ford's view of
exercise! If the General Synod of the Church of England had
extended its franchise to include its ancestors, they would have
voted by a large majority against the ordination of women. Is it
not questionable to dismiss those who have gone before us, and
assume we know better?

There might be some validity in such an argument if our culture
were better than theirs, or if our talents for discovering and
maintaining the truth were of a higher order. But who would
be so bold as to make such claims? Do we really think we are
superior in these ways to the Church Fathers, or the Reformers

or the Puritans, to quote three examples? In reality our grasp of theological and moral principles is much weaker, and the morals of the society in which we live are much lower. In so many ways we are pygmies whereas they were giants. The Roman writer Cicero criticised Cato the younger along these lines. 'He delivers his opinions,' he wrote, 'as though he were living in Plato's Republic rather than among the dregs of Romulus' (*Ad Atticum* II.i.8).

In this chapter we are not affirming that tradition is infallible. However, it is something else to *ignore* completely the past. As Harry Blamires says:

> it is both uncivilised and unchristian to brush tradition roughly aside in heady accommodation to the spirit of the age . . . When we think of the calibre of their thought and witness, we are surely, if we are humble, compelled to give them as ready a hearing as tonight's voice on TV or today's columnist in the newspaper.[1]

We do need a conscious and humble deference to those from whom we have inherited the faith, many of whom suffered persecution and martyrdom, and without whose faithfulness we would not now be Christians.

When this issue was discussed in the General Synod the Bishop of Guildford said that the ordination of women was 'required by tradition'. It is hard to see how anyone who has studied the traditions of the Church could make such a strange remark. When 60 generations of our ancestors have consistently said 'no', and a small minority of the present generation says 'yes', how can one say that tradition requires it? The only justification for such a remark would be if each generation made up its own tradition, and expected its successors to do the same. In that case it should not be called 'tradition'. Tradition according to the dictionary means 'passing down a culture from generation to generation', or 'any time-honoured set of practices or beliefs'. Ordaining women can hardly be called 'time-honoured'! Had the General Synod been able to make contact with our ancestors, the matter would have been settled there and then. They would have come to a different conclusion from the one arrived at by the bishop.

In the last few decades the Church has been surfing on a false wave of optimism. A good way of describing this euphoria is to quote the words of Bonhoeffer, when he said that the Church had 'come of age'. The suggestion is that the past has been only childhood and adolescence, and we are now in a golden age of adulthood. In 1963 John Robinson's book *Honest to God* encapsulated it all. It oozed confidence in the new liberal certainties. Liberal fundamentalism was being born, discarding the hesitancies of the past, and mocking traditional beliefs. In the end the 1960s marked the start of the largest exodus from the churches in the West that history has ever recorded. Come of age? You must be joking!

Another serious mistake has been made in the controversy over the ordination of women, by assuming that it is something the Church has never had to face before. Many have been taken in by some feminists who have asserted so imperiously that women all through the centuries have been oppressed, particularly by the Church. They talk about the dawn of a new day in which women will be free to be equal with men. Both suppositions are wrong. In the first place, as we shall soon see, controversy over the ordination of women began in the second century, and has continued on and off ever since. And secondly, women have had their golden ages in the Church, and on the whole they have been a great deal better off than their non-Christian counterparts. They have sometimes played a crucial part in the life of the Church as well as in society at large. *But at no time until now has the Church thought it right to ordain them.*

One of the features of the writings of the apostles is their fierce warnings about heresies that were coming. The second century was to prove the correctness of their prophecies. 'The Spirit clearly says,' Paul writes, 'that in later times some will abandon the faith and follow deceiving spirits and things taught by demons' (1 Tim. 4:1). In his last known writing Paul speaks of those who 'oppose the truth, men of depraved minds, who, as far as the faith is concerned, are rejected' (2 Tim. 3:8).

Peter warns the Church, 'there will be false teachers among you. They will secretly introduce destructive heresies, even denying the sovereign Lord who bought them . . .' (2 Pet. 2:1). John wrote of the 'many antichrists that have come' (1 Jn. 2:18). Paul cautioned the elders at Ephesus, 'after I leave, savage wolves will come in among you and will not spare the flock. Even from your own number men will arise and distort the truth in order to draw away disciples after them. So be on your guard!' (Acts 20:29–30). So one could go on. *One of the heresies which distorted the truth was the ordination of women. As we shall see, the Church Fathers consistently rejected it.*

It is not difficult to see why some in the Church at that time wanted to ordain women. Although pagan society was as patriarchal as Judaism and the Christian Church, there were strong pagan forces which meant that often women were at the heart of religious life and ritual, and also a feminist movement demanding equality with men. It has always been a temptation to water down the Gospel to make it more palatable to pagans, and to allow the spirit of the age to influence the teachings of the Church. That is even more true today than it was in the second century. Fortunately, the Fathers of the Church followed the advice of the apostles, and swam against the stream of pagan ideas, not with it; they rejected the spirit of the age they lived in.

Early heresies

In the second century there were three major heresies, all of which eventually ordained women to the priesthood. They were the followers of Marcion, the Gnostics and the Montanists. Let us look at them in turn.

Marcion was an effective person, who gathered a large number of followers. His main problem (as with the feminists) was the Old Testament. He reckoned there was an unbridgeable chasm between the Old and the New, so he got rid of the difficulty by simply teaching that Jesus Christ, the God of love, came to rescue us from the revengeful and misogynist God of the Old Testament. Marcion then did a scissors job on the Old and New Testaments by removing all those passages which offended his main thesis. Heretics have been doing the same ever since.

For Marcion all references to creation and the Law in the New Testament were suspect. Through Tertullian we know that Marcion was particularly offended by what Paul wrote about women. This comes out in Tertullian's *Adversus Marcionem*. He complained that the women were ignoring Paul's commands about their place in the Church. Marcion put the letter to the Galatians at the top of the Pauline letters, 'because everything else needs to be seen in the light of what is recounted there'.[2] Marcion also placed the Gospel of Luke ahead of all the others, partly because of its favourable references to women. He sees Galatians as a skeleton key to unlock the meaning of Paul to us, although he actually leaves out Galatians 3:27–4:1 probably because of their references to the Old Testament. No wonder Tertullian accused Marcion of 'murder upon holy scripture'!

Next we need to look at the Gnostics. Josef Lortz has shown that the volume of heretical Christian-Gnostic literature 'exceeded that of orthodox writing'.[3] The Gnostics attempted to do away with gender distinctions, which some are attempting to do today. In modern culture it can be seen in uni-sexism, and most obviously in men and women wearing the same clothes (like the ubiquitous jeans), adopting the same titles, having the same hair-styles and wearing the same jewellery. There is today a major revival of Gnosticism, not least in the New Age Movement. The Gnostics, like their twentieth-century clones, appealed to the new order of redemption, which liberated Christians from all inequalities with each other. The skeleton key (Gal. 3:28) was again used, and almost the same arguments were utilised as today in the cause of feminism. Heresy is seldom original. The apocryphal Gospel of Thomas states, 'for a woman who makes herself a man will enter the kingdom of heaven'.[4] This statement is almost word for word the strategy advocated by Simone de Beauvoir in her famous book *The Second Sex*.

The blurring of male/female differences was also extended to the distinction between those who are ordained and those who are not, and this can be seen in the feminist rejection of any concept of hierarchy. Mary Daly writes: 'it is quite possible, many would say inevitable, that the distinction between hierarchy and laity as we now know it will disappear. Since our age is characterized by the emergence of oppressed minorities, it is unlikely that the Church can hold out against this rising tide.'[5] In our day the wholesale questioning of any form of authority, and the devaluing of any sort of leadership, fits into the same category, and is a fruit of the prevailing undercurrent of egalitarianism. Some are now talking about the post-modern period, by which they mean the end of the Age of Enlightenment. Part of being 'post-modern' is to reject all forms of authority, and to give no place to the idea of someone being 'over' another person.

Tertullian, an African Church Father whom we mentioned earlier, makes fun of this confusion. 'So then,' he writes, 'one person is bishop today, and another tomorrow.'[6] He goes on to refer to the heretical women, 'how cheeky and presumptuous they are!' The Church Fathers don't mince words when confronting the feminists of their day. Tertullian is referring here not to the Gnostics, but to other groups, particularly the followers of Marcion, Apelles and Valentinus. Another Gnostic writer puts these words into the mouth of Mary Magdalene: 'Peter threatens me, and despises our sex.'[7] The Gnostics were often putting their own words into the mouth of Jesus, the apostles, and especially the women, to express their views about the ministry of women. Tertullian backs Paul when he writes, 'It is forbidden for a woman to speak in church; she is also not allowed to teach, to baptize, to sacrifice or to presume to the rank of male office, not to mention priestly service.'[8]

Tertullian is regarded as one of the greatest of the Church Fathers, although he did later join the Montanist movement, which was a kind of second-century Charismatic Renewal, which later ordained women. What, however, adds to the authority of Tertullian's quote above (from *De virginibus velandis*) is the fact that it was written after he had become a Montanist. In the same period, Irenaeus roundly condemned women who 'felt themselves driven to celebrating the Eucharist by the Holy Spirit'.[9] Presumably this means claiming the authority of the Holy Spirit overruling that of the Church. Today we have women claiming that the Holy Spirit is calling them to be priests, *as if this in itself justified the practice*.

The Montanist heresy began in Phrygia in Asia Minor, fertile soil for the experience of religious ecstasies. Later when the region became Moslem, the dervishes thrived there too. Priscilla, one of the early prophetesses of the movement, claimed to have an experience of Christ coming to her *in the form of a woman*. According to Jerome, Montanus himself, the founder of the movement, had been a priest of the goddess Cybele before becoming a Christian. It would, however, be unjust to write off the early Montanists. A theologian of the calibre of Tertullian would hardly have transferred his allegiance to them if they had not been an impressive community. The early Montanists did not allow women to become priests, but they allowed them to be prophetesses and to bring prophecy in the meetings, which, as we have seen, accords with apostolic practice and teaching. It was 200 years later that it was reported that they were ordaining women, and another Church Father (Epiphanius) reports that there were female bishops and presbyters. There are no prizes for guessing the text they used to justify this![10] The differences between the sexes was held to play no role, for in Christ Jesus 'there is neither male nor female' (Gal. 3:28).

The Church Fathers' teaching

We have here a complete re-run of the current arguments. Hauke writes that they used 'the same argument that serves today as a password (Gal. 3:28) in almost all writings favouring the ordination of women'.[11] Since they used Paul, Epiphanius countered with 1 Corinthians 11:8, 14:34 and 1 Timothy 2:12 – the same texts used today by traditionalists. He accuses them of 'ignoring the word of the apostles'.

One of the most famous Church Fathers was Origen. He also opposed the ordination of women. He used 1 Corinthians 14:34 as his main argument against the Montanists, and enforced the fact that it was a command which had to be obeyed. He also cites 1 Timothy 2:12. He went further than I believe Scripture does, in banning women from even prophesying in the congregation. He did not ban women from all teaching, but only public-official teaching when women would take authority over men.

It is most important for us to note, that the Church Fathers, in unanimously condemning the ordination of women, appealed to the example of Jesus, and the Scriptures, rather than arguments about the need to have a male to represent Christ at the altar.

Another factor to bear in mind is that throughout this long period of some 500 years, there is little mention of the ordination of women, which would indicate that in general the Church assumed that women would not become priests. The only people who thought differently were heretics. Some people, clutching at straws, have cited a few archaeological finds in Rome, which allegedly show a woman celebrating the Eucharist. It is not necessary to refute this, because there will always be people who will act against the teaching of the Church. The important thing, for which there were no exceptions, is that when the issue arose in the Church, the Fathers always condemned the ordination of women to the priesthood.

So the pattern continues with unerring consistency. The Didascalia, a third-century Syrian document, prohibits women from holding a teaching office or performing baptisms, and it appeals to the behaviour of Jesus as authority in this matter. This is even clearer in the Apostolic Constitutions, the first part of which was based on the Didascalia. This document from the fourth century says this about women, 'if we do not allow women to teach, how can anyone agree that they, in contempt of their nature, should assume the office of priest? *For it is ignorant heathen ungodliness that leads to the ordination of priestesses for female deities, but not the command of Christ.*'[12] This is interesting not least because it makes the point, relevant in the present argument, that women cannot possibly be priests if they are not allowed to teach, and also because it refers again to 'the command of Christ' (see 1 Cor. 14:37).

It is Epiphanius, whom we have already seen in action against the Montanists, who is most caustic in his attack on women priests. He refers to a situation where women had been ordained as, 'godless and sacrilegious, a perversion of the message of the Holy Spirit; in fact the whole thing is diabolical and a teaching of the impure spirit'.[13] As we shall see Dr Philip Potter, when Secretary General of the World Council of Churches, was to call the views of those *opposed* to women's ordination 'demonic'. How opinions have changed! Epiphanius looks at the Old Testament and concludes, 'nowhere did a woman serve as priestess'. He also argues that since the Old is fulfilled in the New, there can be no female priests. This he sees as based on the will of God. The exclusion of women does not suggest they are inferior, and he gives the Virgin Mary as evidence for this.

Feminists have targeted Epiphanius for his comments on women. 'Every heresy is a bad woman,' he writes. 'The female sex is . . . without much sense' and 'we must dispel this madness of women' are other remarks he made. Epiphanius was not referring to women in general, but to the bad ones! It is hardly likely that he would have made the same remarks about Mary, the mother of Jesus. More clearly than any other of the Fathers, this man sees women priests as a heresy. Their prohibition as priests was based on the teaching of Christ and the apostles. The plain teaching of Epiphanius was endorsed by both Augustine and John Damascene. Both placed this matter in the category of heresy.

When we turn to John Chrysostom, alive at the same time as Epiphanius, we have further confirmation. 'The entire female sex must step back from so great a task, but also the majority of males,' he writes.[14] He bases it on the example of Christ, who appointed no woman as an apostle, and decisively on the authority of Paul. He allowed women to give non-official teaching, and encouraged them to study theology. He had in his church in Constantinople several hundred women deaconesses, the head of whom was St Olympia, his best friend and co-worker. The Orthodox theologian Father Hopko writes:

> It never entered the head of St Chrysostom to ordain St Olympia to be a presbyter or bishop. And I don't think that she felt she was being particularly discriminated against by not being one. It has to be remembered that the Eastern Church had an order of deaconesses, but they were not allowed to be involved in the specific ministry reserved for men.[15]

This is not an exhaustive survey of the Church Fathers and their teaching about the ministry of women in the Church. For that I would recommend Manfred Hauke's book *Women in the Priesthood?*, upon which I have leant heavily for this chapter, for the fullest and best treatment of this aspect of our subject. But there is one further matter of importance we need to cover.

The Church Fathers have had a bad press from feminists, who quote them, I have to say, rather selectively. They like to show them as misogynists to a man, and so their judgement on the issue of the ordination of women cannot be trusted. Jerome and Ambrose come in for special attention. Now it has to be admitted that these men did say some strange things about women (as indeed about other matters). Some of it was directed against women who were subverting the Church. It needs to be remembered that Amos once spoke of certain women as 'cows of Bashan' (Am.4:1), and Isaiah tells the women of Zion that God is going to make bald their scalps (Is. 3:16–17). The apostles also pointed out the faults of women when that was necessary.

But the one thing we must not deduce from this is that the Fathers did not accept women for the priesthood *because they were inferior*. That reason was never given. In fact to be fair to the Fathers, their general teaching on sexuality was consistent with that of the New Testament, and was revolutionary for those days. Ambrose, for example, so often quoted as a disparager of women, once wrote that what God had made was called 'very good only *after* the creation of woman'. Together with Tertullian, Irenaeus and Justin he writes, 'just as sin began with women, so too the good had its beginning with a woman'.[16]

When we look at the lives of the Church Fathers we see in practice a remarkable respect for women. They were given many opportunities for ministry. The Empresses Irene and Theodora ruled for long periods and played a significant role in the iconoclastic controversy. Women in this period were encouraged to be educated. Origen's lectures were well attended by women, and Clement of Alexandria recommended women to study philosophy. Gregory of Nyssa was taught the faith by his sister, for whom he was always grateful. Chrysostom was closely associated with a large group of women. We have already mentioned one of them, a deaconess called Olympia, who had a vital influence in the Church. Jerome, another target of feminists, had a group of women around him in his work, and he dedicated his biblical commentaries to them. He had special Bible studies with women, and taught them Hebrew. A woman called Marcella took a public stand in Rome against heretics, when even the priests were wavering. It was said of her 'she had a mind to please God rather than men'.[17] She, together with some other educated women, won the day against these heretics.

The exclusion of women from the priesthood cannot in the light of this be attributed to their weakness, or lack of education. Such arguments were never used. The reasons given by the Fathers is the same as I am using in this book. First, that Jesus did not appoint any women to the office of apostle. Secondly, the various statements of Paul (in 1 Cor. 11; 14; 1 Tim. 2). These were the reasons why the Church throughout this period had a common mind on the subject. There was also the question of the symbolism of the sexes. Increasingly Mary was being seen as a type of the Church. But it was from the example of Jesus and the fountain of the Scriptures that the Church Fathers drew the strength of their arguments and the unanimity of their convictions.

Chapter 12

The age of chivalry

> I thought that ten thousand swords would have leapt
> from their scabbards to avenge even a look that
> threatened her (the Queen of France) with insult.
> But the age of chivalry is gone. That of sophisters,
> economists, and calculators has succeeded, and the
> glory of Europe is extinguished for ever.
>
> (Edmund Burke, 1790)

In May 1993 my wife and I had a holiday in Tuscany. It was a time of reading and reflection on the subjects covered by this book. We stayed in a house, lent to us by friends, not far from San Miniato and Siena.

Most will have heard of Catherine of Siena, but few of Countess Matilda, who was born in the small town of San Miniato in 1045. She was a remarkable woman, the last of the imperial vicars of the Holy Roman Empire, as they were called. She was an earlier version of Joan of Arc, and actually commanded the papal army of Gregory VII against the German Emperor. She was the friend of popes and saints, the terror of kings, admired and courted by everybody from the Byzantine Emperor to the sons of William the Conqueror. By the time of her death in 1115, she owned huge estates, and had left an indelible mark on the history of Europe.

Catherine of Siena, or Caterina Benincasa, to give her full name, had a short life. But in that time she played a decisive part in the history of that period. She was born into a large family. She had no less than 24 brothers and sisters! In 1363 she became a nun, giving herself to contemplation and ministry to the poor and sick. Very soon she was intervening in the politics of the day, and prevented a war between the cities of Tuscany and the Pope. But her major claim to fame was her visit to the Pope in Avignon in 1376. She persuaded him to return to Rome, thus preventing another war, and two years later was involved in supporting Pope Urban VI. She died that same year, but in her short life achieved international fame as a peacemaker. Many of her letters to kings and prelates had great influence on them, and have survived to this day.

The period covered by this chapter is called 'the Middle Ages', and stretched from the fall of Rome in 476 to the Renaissance in the fifteenth Century, thus covering a thousand years. This millennium was the link between the ancient and the modern worlds. But it has also been called 'the age of chivalry', a period in which women became held in high honour, not least the Virgin Mary. According to Edmund Burke, the treatment meted out to Marie Antoinette, the Queen of France, marked the end of the age of chivalry. As we shall see in Chapter 13, it certainly marked the beginning of the age of equality. The Guillotine and the Gulags have been great levellers.

Some have distorted history by claiming that only in the twentieth century have women played any significant part in the history of the world and the Church. Such claims are ungrounded. Matilda and Catherine are two examples of many women who played a crucial part in history during what has been called 'the age of chivalry'.

Few periods of history have been so universally maligned as these Middle Ages. Many have regarded them as an arid period. Some still speak of parts of it as 'the Dark Ages'. Such assessments need revision. In fact, this period was probably one of the most creative and fruitful epochs in the whole of world history. During these years Europe came nearest to a cultural unity between Church and State, and in this setting many women came into their own. It was also the age of the feudal system, one of the most brilliant and successful social and economic systems ever devised by man. More about that in Chapter 13.

It was not only on the continent that women played their part in Church and State, but also in Britain. The most outstanding example in this period was Hilda of Whitby. She was descended from the kings of Northumbria, and so had royal blood. She was largely responsible for organising in 664 the Synod of Whitby, where she was the Abbess of a community. This was arguably the most important Synod ever held in England, because it united the Celtic and Western Roman Churches in the British Isles. The historian Bede reports that five bishops were produced from her school at Whitby Abbey.

This is not intended to be an exhaustive survey of this whole period. This has been well done by Manfred Hauke, and I would recommend his chapter on this subject.[1] Instead I want to draw attention to the part women played in what today we call politics. We will see that the Church throughout this period welcomed and encouraged women to play a full and at times leading part in public life, while at the same time maintaining the consistent practice of the apostles and Church Fathers, of not ordaining women, or allowing them to hold a position in the teaching office of the Church. Although this is a period in which Church and State became intertwined through the cultural unity that was largely achieved, they were never regarded as the same. Because women could achieve positions of leadership in the State, it did not follow that they could do the same in the Church. And there was never any sense of inconsistency that a Hilda of Whitby or a Catherine of Siena could do so much and yet not become priests.

Thomas Aquinas

Again, as with the Church Fathers, it has to be admitted that in this period there were prominent teachers like Thomas Aquinas who made misogynistic remarks. But it is by no means general, and by the same token one can find other statements from these authors which praise and affirm women. One has to remember that throughout this period the Virgin Mary was highly regarded, as the art of this era shows. In 1210 Pope Innocent III wrote, 'no matter whether the most blessed Virgin Mary stands higher . . . than all the apostles together, it was still not to her, but to them, that the Lord entrusted the keys of the kingdom of heaven'.[2] To this all the canonists, or teachers, of this entire period add their support. The ordination of women was invalid. According to Hauke, only John the Teuton reports others, who are unnamed, who regarded baptism as the sole condition for the validity of the ordination of women.[3]

Thomas Aquinas follows the Church Fathers in basing his opposition to the ordination of women on 1 Timothy 2 and 1 Corinthians 14. He adds the need for men to be tonsured, a cultural condition which is inapplicable today. But Thomas Aquinas expressly states that the position of women in the world is different from their place in the Church; he saw no reason to prevent a woman from functioning as a ruler in the temporal sphere. Throughout this period women were never denied ordination on the grounds that they were inferior. In any case the priestly office was not given to men because they were *superior*, rather it was given for humble service.

Thomas Aquinas was deeply influenced by the Greek philosopher Aristotle, whose misogynist view of women is well established. He speculated on the biological aspects of conception, drawing conclusions about the inherent weakness of women which have been proved entirely erroneous by modern science. If anything it seems that the male is born weaker than the female, and if there is a natural biological disposition towards any sex, it is towards the female not the male. There is another side to Thomas Aquinas. He quotes, for example, the well-liked interpretation of creation, that woman was created, not from the head of man to dominate him, nor from his feet for him to disdain her, but from Adam's side, to be loved and cherished.

As we shall see, a high estimation of women, far from declining in the Middle Ages, actually increased. One feature of this was the rise of chivalry, something which today is laughed at, and regarded by some women as a form of condescension. But through it women were raised in dignity and appreciation, almost to the point of being idolised. Men were expected to behave nobly to women; to honour and protect them. During much of the Middle Ages marriage was held in high esteem and through it men and women found completion. Sexual experience within marriage was to be enjoyed by both partners.

The Middle Ages also saw prophetesses coming into their own. One of the most outstanding was Hildegard of Bingen, whose influence was enormous. She was born in 1098 and died in 1179. She wrote a book on the natural sciences, and another on biology. She invented a language (like Esperanto), wrote poems, hymns and other music, and gave advice to Bernard of Clairvaux. Someone has written that her influence has 'no parallel in the whole of world history'.[4] Ignaz Dollinger writes, 'never before had a prophet commanded so high a degree of respect as she'. She was consulted by popes and princes, some of whom begged her to support them. One of these was the Emperor Frederick Barbarossa himself. She also produced a medical handbook, which amongst other things dealt in great detail with sexual matters. Nearly 800 years before the arrival of sex therapists, she was a proponent of the *mutuality* of sexual pleasure within marriage, and told men and women how to secure it! Some of the best teaching on sex from any age is contained in this handbook, and she apparently raised no eyebrows. So much too for the non-sexuality myth which Ferdinand Mount says 'is vital for the full feminist case'.[5]

In passing it might be good to ponder the words of prophecy given to Catherine of Siena:

> just as I (the Lord) once sent to the Jews and to pagan peoples men who, although inept, were equipped with my wisdom, so today I will send women, who are ignorant and frail by nature, but whom I will provide with divine wisdom, so that they can teach the high and mighty a lesson that will shame them.[6]

Another prophetess, who was a powerful political and military figure, was Joan of Arc. We have already mentioned Matilda, who, like Joan of Arc, was a commanding figure in these same areas of national life. There is no evidence that anyone questioned what they did on the grounds of their sex, although some might not have agreed with them politically. There was, for instance, Queen Theodelinde, who as her husband's representative acted as administrator of Lombardy, and worked alongside the Pope in fighting the heresy of Arianism. Then there was Adelaide and Theophano who governed the Holy Roman Empire for eight years without male trustees. Even Thomas Aquinas, who taught the subordinate role of women in the Church, wrote a friendly letter to the influential Duchess of Brabant, in which he acknowledged her right to rule in the temporal sphere.

It is often assumed that we have to wait until this century before women receive any education. This is then given as a reason why women were not ordained during these centuries. It is next advanced as justification for ordaining women on the grounds that today they are as educated as men, and so they can share fully in ministry alongside men. However, when we examine the facts we find this suggestion erroneous in the period of the Middle Ages. Thus A. Rosler writes, 'almost no other epoch has given women of distinction so many opportunities for unhampered measurement of their powers of mind against those of men as did the Middle Ages'.[7]

A striking example of this is Lioba, the sister of St Boniface. She knew the Bible almost by heart, and studied the Church Fathers, the councils and the whole of canon law. Princes and bishops sought her advice and help. Hauke comments about her, 'she was by no means an eccentric blue stocking, but rather a real woman'.[8] Women excelled in this period as doctors, pharmacists and teachers. They were members of guilds and directors of hospitals. In fact, according to Wenzel, 'women of noble lineage received a better formal education than did the men, who were trained for military careers'. It might be added that many of the men were away fighting so much that they were unable to further their education, whereas the women did. Amazingly in twelfth-century Bologna there were female professors in the university, who were installed by Pope Benedict XIV and other Popes! So much for the 'Dark Ages'.

Two trends

Also during the Middle Ages seeds were sown which ultimately burgeoned into the Reformation, which itself marked the end of the Middle Ages, and the beginning of the Modern Age or the Age of Enlightenment. This period is marked by two trends in the ministry of women. First there are groups like the Waldensians and Catharists, who ordained women, although in the case of the Waldensians their understanding of the Eucharist was the same as the Roman Catholic Church. This approach has been taken by other groups ever since, and has found its fullest expression in this century in the Pentecostal Movement.

It was the Reformers who established the second trend. It was an absolute prohibition of women teaching or holding the office of presbyter or bishop in the Church. Frank Schaeffer sees the roots of the modern feminist movement in 'rationalistic Protestantism'.[9] The warm acceptance of women in the Church (apart from ordination) and in temporal work, the concept of chivalry, taught by the Church Fathers and nurtured in the Middle Ages, were progressively lost by the Reformed Churches. Martin Luther even taught that 'no marital intercourse occurs without sin', which he probably learned from Augustine.[10] These two trends led ultimately to the polarising of attitudes to men and women into two extremes, sexism and feminism. The first denies the equality of the sexes, and the second repudiates a true understanding of headship and submission. So we can see how Protestantism was corrupted by its fatal exposure to the Enlightenment. As a result we are having to face at the end of the twentieth century an issue which is divisive and destabilising.

One aspect of this has been the insidious poison of misogyny from Aristotle to Kant, Nietzsche, and Schopenhauer. Werner Neuer reports that as late as 1908 a German doctor was writing a misogynist book called *On the Physiological Weakness of Women*.[11] P. J. Mobius' book went into nine editions. Another book by a German philosopher, O. Weininger (*Sex and Character*), had 25 reprints in ten years, and was translated into almost every European language. *Both these misogynist books have recently been reprinted*. This shows there is still in our society a strong sexist undercurrent, which justifies a feminist agenda. As we shall see, aspects of the feminist cause are justified, but feminist teaching, which addresses it, is often false. Some of the right questions are being asked, but the wrong answers are being given.

In conclusion, it is important that we draw the right conclusions from this brief look at a lengthy period of history. We have mentioned women who have played a significant role in both Church and State. However, we need to realise that without exception the women mentioned were either members of religious orders, and so not married, or members of the nobility, and so more free than the majority of women whose maternal duties prevented them from taking an active part in the wider world. The point we are making is that throughout this period women did not take leadership or teaching positions in the Church, and this was for theological reasons *not* because of deficient education or lack of leadership skills. Having said all this it needs to be remembered that very few women then or now have risen to positions of leadership in the State, compared with men, although it is more common today than it was then.

Chapter 13

The eleventh commandment?

The statement that all people are created equal is a
legal fiction.

(C. S. Lewis)

All animals are equal, but some animals are more
equal than others.

(George Orwell, *Animal Farm*)

One of the ironies of our day is the presence of enormous guilt
in people, and at the same time the denial of it. Dostoevsky said
that a time was coming when people would say, 'There is no
sin, there is no guilt, there is only hunger.' Today people, even
church people, say, 'There is no sin.' The word 'sin' seems to
have dropped out of the human vocabulary. Original sin is laughed
at. As Bishop Sheen once wrote, 'it used to be said that Catholics
were the only ones who believed in the immaculate conception.
Now everyone believes they are immaculately conceived.' There
is, however, a commandment which some have added to the
other Ten, and remains inviolate, 'Thou shalt not be unequal.'
Or as an American Democrat (Mario Cuomo) once put it, 'You
shall not sin against equality.'

Equality was one of the themes of the Greek philosopher
Aristotle. He wrote that 'inferiors revolt that they may be
equal, and equals that they may be superior. Such is the state
of mind which creates revolution.' Equality was rediscovered
by the liberal intellectuals of the eighteenth century. The poor
have often suffered from the clever ideas of intellectuals, who
have championed their cause, yet not really had their interests

at heart. Thus David Green bemoans the fact that what Professor Halsey calls 'ethical socialism', has been hijacked by middle-class intellectuals, and turned into what he calls 'egoistic socialism'. But more about that later.

Equality was once a pure word. It meant that everyone, regardless of sex, class, race, or income should be treated equally by the law of the land. The blindfolded lady on top of the Old Bailey in London is a symbol of that. But times have changed. As William Gairdner has pointed out, 'equality now means that everyone should be made the same by the law'.

The first rumblings of what was to become the most dominant influence in the Western world, and still occupies a prime position in the minds of many intellectuals, were heard in the War of Independence in the United States. This country, more than any other, today symbolises 'liberty'. It was Thomas Jefferson who wrote the famous words in the Declaration of Independence, 'We hold these truths to be self-evident: that all men are created equal.' That was 1776.

But the seeds of the 'equality revolution' were really planted in France, and were to throw out their first green shoots on 14 July 1789, when a mob stormed the Bastille prison in Paris. The news spread quickly around Europe, and in England, the famous poet William Wordsworth expressed his great joy at this fateful event. He was soon to become rather less enthusiastic when the mob turned ugly, and a reign of terror started in Paris and spread throughout France. The Church was a particular target, and the Cathedral of Notre Dame was turned into a 'Temple of Reason'.

One of the fruits of this was the ethnic cleansing of the entire Vendée region of France. Over 250,000 people – men, women and children – were sacrificed on the altar of reason and equality. Why were they killed? Because they cherished their personal freedom more than the enforcement of the ideology of equality coming from the central powers in Paris.

It is well known that the theme of the French Revolution was 'liberty, equality and fraternity'. William Gairdner has pointed out that this can easily become an evil cocktail, an incitement to violence, which, of course, it has provoked in all social revolutions. The first two terms are mutually exclusive. To enforce 'equality' you have to deprive fellow citizens of their 'liberty'. When you do that you don't exactly produce brotherhood![1] As Lord Runcie said in his Lambeth 1988 address, 'the trouble with earthly Utopias is that by leaving out God they take short cuts'. In other words, all men are brothers except those who in the name of brotherhood need to be eliminated. Or as George Orwell put it in his book *Animal Farm*, 'All animals are equal, but some animals are more equal than others.'

The illusions of equality

At first glance the idea of equality impresses. In Britain it has appealed to our innate liking of 'fair play'. But in fact it has been for 200 years a recipe for greed, envy and violence on a scale unprecedented in human history. The plain truth of the matter is that God has not created all people equal. Jefferson was wrong. The *inequality of people* is the self-evident reality of creation. From the barricades of Paris to the squalid killing fields of Cambodia, the quest for the holy grail of equality has seen more people sacrificed on its bloody altars than any other comparable ideology in the violent history of this planet. I mean that, and it makes me angry to think that people are still deceived by its subtle allure, and still pursue its hopeless goals.

To put it at its starkest, the main argument is that humans do not have liberty because they are not equal. People are supposedly oppressed by the inequalities of life and the orderings of society. So governments have to liberate people by removing the inequalities. It sounds all right until you see what has been done to achieve this utopia of equality for 200 years. If people are richer, cleverer, more powerful than others, then they have to be levelled down so that the poor, simple and powerless can enjoy the same privileges. In evil regimes this is done by force. Thus the French Revolutionaries got rid of the monarchy and the aristocracy; Hitler sent the Jews to the gas chambers; Stalin dispatched the farmers and the generals; and the Khmer Rouge liquidated the intellectuals and the middle class.

But most Western countries believe that force is an immoral way of achieving this, so they have chosen political means. Wealth is redistributed by punitive taxation, education is given equally to everyone whether they want it or not, and little incentive is given for any to be achievers. The most advanced and far-reaching country to try the democratic way to equality was Sweden. The Swedish dream has now withered on the vine. Equality has not been achieved fully there, any more than it has in China, Cuba or Russia. The quest for it simply bankrupts those nations which attempt it, whether by force or the processes of democracy. Now Canada has taken up the torch. It won't succeed either.

The illusion of equality was brilliantly expounded by Jean-Jacques Rousseau, who combined two thoughts, which have been entwined together ever since. One, the cult of reason, we have already mentioned. The second was the cult of nature. Reason was directed against the Church, the Bible, and their claims to Christian revelation. The second was directed against the biblical doctrine of original sin. Rousseau argued that men and women are basically good by nature, in other words 'immaculately conceived'. All that is needed is a good egalitarian society in which people can be nurtured. Society's failures are due to the inequalities it encourages, like the class system, which Marx attacked. If you get rid of these and have a classless society in its place, you won't need police or prisons. In fact, of course, the exact opposite has happened. It always does when you turn your back on God's revelation, and think up your own. So you have to build Berlin Walls and Gulags to make people equal!

In France this was enshrined in the document 'the Rights of Man and Citizen'. In it there was plenty about human rights, nothing about human duties. Actually duties were discussed, but deliberately dropped. It was the first of many Human Rights declarations. Today we even have animal rights! The unrighteous ignore them, and instead pursue their own interests. The righteous are not interested primarily in rights. They seek to fulfil their responsibilities to God and their neighbours. What came out of all this was communism, democratic socialism, and feminism. All three ideologies have had equality as their goal. That is the incentive that has driven them relentlessly forward. They all claim to be dedicated to the righting of the injustices in society.

The link between feminism and the French Revolution, and later communism, is an interesting one. The rhetoric of this revolution was about 'rights'. This was strongly focused through the writings of Thomas Paine, who wrote a book, which was published in 1791, called *The Rights of Man*. Meanwhile a revolutionary woman in France called Olympe de Gouge produced her own *Declaration of the Rights of Women* in the same year. She was unceremoniously guillotined as a counter-revolutionary. We must remember the Revolution was about 'fraternity' not 'sisterhood'.

It was the onset of the industrial revolution which raised much more seriously the whole question of women's rights, which forms the basis of what we generally call today 'feminism'. One of the front runners was J. S. Mill who wrote an essay called *The Subjection of Women*. But the major influence was to come from the writings of Marx and Engels, the intellectual founders of communism. Karl Marx once said, 'anyone who knows anything of history knows that great social changes are impossible without the feminine upheaval. Social progress can be measured exactly by the social position of the fair sex, the ugly ones included.' Between them they wedded the aspirations of feminism to the Marxist revolution. As we have seen, both workers and women had grounds for complaint about the injustices they had to suffer, and there was a ready ear for the communist and feminist arguments. Both, however, have failed to deliver the goods. Workers have on the whole suffered more under communism than they ever did under any other economic system. Feminism has helped the *position* of women in Western society, but not their happiness. And in the area of the family their influence has mostly been disastrous. As usual it is the innocent who have suffered most, especially children. Some feminists, as we shall see in the next chapter, have actively campaigned against the family.

Both Engels and Marx saw the goals of communism and feminism as two strings of the same bow. The priority was to overthrow all unjust power structures (the 'bosses' and 'sexists'). Then the 'new man' (sic) would be created, and men and women would be equal and free. They believed that all inequalities and economic slavery were caused by unjust structures. Once you get the structures right, men and women will be free and equal. Utopia will arrive. The political kingdom will have come. Everyone will be free.

Engels also interpreted this in the area of sexual equality. 'The husband,' he wrote, 'is the *bourgeois* of the family, and the wife represents the proletariat.'[2] Women need to be liberated from housework and child-rearing, which lowers them to the level of animals. Private families must be broken up and children raised by the State.

I want to make two comments in response to this brief statement about the feminist gospel of Marxism, and its attack on the family. The first is that it has been tried, particularly in Russia, and found wanting. Secondly, the goal of the State having the primary role in child-rearing is by no means restricted to the communist world; it has also been a goal of democratic socialism. As we shall see, it has been tried unsuccessfully in Sweden. It in being tried in Australia. During the last Australian election campaign the Prime Minister (Paul Keating) said, 'We [the State] will look after your children.' Strange, I thought parents were meant to do that!

The dismantling of hierarchy

There are a number of words all egalitarians and feminists dislike. One of them is 'hierarchy'. We said something about this in Chapter 2, but that now needs to be expanded. We have referred to the 'hierarchy of heaven', particularly the 'chain of command' within the Godhead. We also see the concept of hierarchy in the Pauline texts. First, we see it in the family (Eph. 5:22–24; 6:1–4), husband, wife, and children, each in a relationship of love and obedience. Then there is Paul's statement in 1 Corinthians 11:3, in which he links the divine hierarchy of Father and Son, with the human between man and woman. Because hierarchy involves knowing your position, and being in a humble relationship of submission, it riles feminists even to consider it, and people like Mary Daly dismiss hierarchy out of hand.

The concept of hierarchy is another victim of the egalitarian revolution. Before the French Revolution, hierarchy was part of the very fabric of Western society. This was particularly in evidence in what became known as 'the feudal system'. As we have already seen, the emphasis of the French Revolution was on 'rights'. The emphasis, on the other hand, of the feudal system was on 'responsibilities', or duties. Today 'feudal' is a derided word, describing unprogressive ideas, which are out of step with modern society. All systems can be abused, and the power that some had in the feudal system, was undoubtedly at times misused. Yet as a system it was in fact a kind of welfare state, which worked somewhat better than ours does in Britain, *because it was based on responsibilities, not rights*. No one could enjoy privileges without first fulfilling their obligations to the king or to the nobles. The feudal system was essentially hierarchical. Everyone had their place, and knew who the boss was. How different from our day!

Hierarchy cannot exist in an egalitarian society, it is a contradiction in terms. Hierarchy suggests that some people are 'over' others in the sense of authority *and responsibility*, not superiority. This was one of the merits of the feudal system, which is the object of scorn these days from liberal-minded people. Today the prevailing spirit is to reduce everyone to the same level. Yet there must be hierarchy if societies are to function properly. Steven Goldberg has written, as previously quoted, 'there has never been any non-hierarchical society, and there is . . . strong theoretical reason to believe that there never could be one'.[3] The original spark of the French Revolution was to topple all those who were thought to be 'over' others. The result was chaos, and the substitution of one form of oppression for a far worse. So it was to be in every subsequent revolution, not least the Russian, which Alexander Solzhenitsyn described as exceeding in cruelty and oppression the worst of the tyranny of the Czars. This is always the fate of those who try to improve on what God has provided, who try to change the course of nature. Dogs will always have four legs.

Chapter 14

Feminism, a flawed ideology

Custom will never conquer nature, for it is always
she who remains unconquered.
                    (Cicero, *Tusculanae Disputationes*)

If the feminist believes that it is preferable to have
her sex associated with authority and leadership
rather than with the creation of life, then she is
doomed to perpetual disappointment.
                    (Steven Goldberg, *The Inevitability
                    of Patriarchy* [p. 22])

We have been looking at the birth of egalitarianism, the pursuit
of equality. The crusade for economic equality and the classless
society found its strongest advocacy in communism. The quest
for sexual equality eventually became known as feminism, which
we will now examine.

In all the many arguments in the churches about gender,
cultural considerations have in recent years predominated. But
Cicero was right, *custom will never conquer nature*. Whatever
custom says about how many legs a dog has; it won't make any
difference, nature has decreed they have four.

It will come as no surprise to readers that I am not a feminist!
But I am concerned enough with its basic premises to warn people
'this product can harm your health'.

Time magazine has called feminism 'the most vexing thorn for
Christianity'. The same magazine has called the feminist movement 'a second reformation sweeping Christianity'. I would have
serious doubts about the rightness of calling it a 'reformation',

but that will depend which side of the fence you are on; however, it is no exaggeration to say that Christian feminism is a major movement in all the churches at the present time. It is likely to be the hottest topic for years to come, and not a single church will be exempt from its pressures. It will continue to be of primary importance in the social and political life of many nations.

Feminism has had an enormous influence on the thinking of our Western society, although it is as unacceptable to many women as it is offensive to many men. It has fundamentally affected the political agenda also. It has sometimes been difficult to get books published or sold in shops which are critical of feminism. For instance, Steven Goldberg's book *The Inevitability of Patriarchy* holds the all-time record in the Guinness Book of Records (1988 edition) for the highest number of editors' rejections of any book ever published. When a number of articles was published in the United States under the title *Gender Sanity*, every contributor told of written and verbal abuse hurled at them by radical feminists.[1] As I shall recount later, the sociologist Norman Dennis was so abused after giving a lecture in London, in which he challenged many of these modern suppositions, he vowed he would never return to the capital.

When William Gairdner's book *The War Against the Family* was published in Canada it was amongst the five top best-sellers. In it the author says a few home truths about feminism in defence of the traditional family. A bookshop chain in Vancouver, Duthie Books Inc., refused to stock it. The reason? 'The staff didn't like its ideas.'[2] Celia Duthie was reported as saying, 'I don't see it as censorship . . . we're ignoring him.' Gairdner was then accused of being a 'redneck' and a 'buffoon'. Actually they are referring to a former Professor of English, who did doctoral research at Stanford University.

Sadly the Christian feminist world is not averse to censorship either. David Ayers in the book *Recovering Biblical Manhood and Womanhood* documents an example of censorship of an article.[3] He also reveals the feminist bias found in many articles published in the secular press. Feminism easily becomes doctrinaire and dogmatic in its assertions, and intolerant of opposition. An example of this is the remark of Simone de Beauvoir in 1975: 'no woman should be authorized to stay at home and raise her children . . . *Women should not have that choice*, precisely because if there is such a choice, too many women will make it.'[4] Such is the attitude of those who in the pursuit of an ideological goal, in this case equality, will force others to conform. Thus their freedom is offered without their permission on the altar of the 'cause'. Allan Bloom, author of *The Closing of the American Mind*, points out that the feminist vision ultimately favours equality over freedom. It ends, he writes, 'in forgetting nature and using force to refashion human beings to secure that justice'.[5] In other words, back to the Gulags.

The most serious thing about all this is the lack of communication between men and women. While feminist literature has poured off the presses, mostly, one presumes, to be devoured by women, men have made very little contribution to the debate. Neil Lyndon's anti-feminist book *No More Sex War*[6] was not exactly an olive branch to feminists. This was followed by Ben Greenstein's *The Fragile Man*,[7] which was described by David Sexton in the *Daily Telegraph* as 'another own goal for men'.

One of the most striking stage dramas about this lack of communication is seen in David Mamet's controversial play *Oleanna*, which came to London from Broadway in 1993. It is a story about a Professor, called John, and one of his students, called Carol. She accuses him of sexual harassment, which ruins his career. When he actually physically attacks her on the stage, the audience reaction is invariably to clap, presumably because their sympathies are with the Professor, and she only gets what she deserves. The American actress who played Carol was booed on the streets of New York. Lesley Garner, writing about the play in the *Daily Telegraph*, sees what perhaps many of those watching the play didn't, that the main point of the drama is about a man and a woman who destroy each other *by speaking two different languages*. She goes on 'both characters were calling blindly across a comprehension gap too wide to be crossed . . . You don't have to look very far to see the mayhem and unhappiness caused by basic "missed communication" between male and female.'[8] *I have to say with sadness that most men don't begin to understand feminism, and most feminists don't understand men; between the two there is a great gulf fixed. Neither side is listening to the other.*

The changing face of feminism

One thing I have noticed about feminism is that its front-runners don't stay still for very long. Mary Daly, for example, started out as a church person, introducing feminism to the Roman Catholic Church, whereas now she has dropped the Christian label entirely, and has moved away from any kind of commitment to the Church. Then there's Germaine Greer, the Australian feminist, who ruffled the feathers of the establishment with *The Female Eunuch* in 1970. This was as radical as you can get. In her later book *Sex and Destiny* she argued, to the loud protests of feminists everywhere, for women's traditional role as mothers. She was accused of the betrayal of feminism. Now she is advocating motherhood like the best, and recommending women to 'go out and be batty old hags'!

Another example is the intrepid Betty Friedan who more or less recanted from her views in *The Feminine Mystique*. In her book *The Second Stage* she warns women not to be trapped by a 'feminist mystique' that could prevent them from experiencing the joys of a family.[9] Clearly this lady 'is for turning'. One hears rumours that a third wave of feminism is on the way. William Gairdner is not impressed: 'by the time the third wave washes over the second stage we will all be eunuchs'.[10]

It is also worth mentioning Kathy Gyngell, who in the 1970s was a feminist student at Cambridge University, and who returned in 1993 to propose at the Cambridge Union debate the motion 'A woman's place is in the home?' In an article in the *Daily Mail* she said that she had once believed all the major tenets of feminism: 'We read Betty Friedan's *The Feminine Mystique* and learnt to look down on our own home based mothers, who in our view had achieved nothing. We conveniently forgot that without their nurture and interest, few of us would have made university in the first place.' Why did she change? She tells us in these moving words: 'no one had warned me of the pain and separation both my baby Adam and I would suffer each morning and the way his anxious face would haunt me during the day'.[11] More about this and Kathy Gyngell's new understanding in Chapter 19.

We have already traced the origins of feminism back to the Parisian barricades of 1789, and the arguments of Marx and Engels. Its major thrust is sexual equality for women and men.

It is satisfied with nothing less. It has produced a wide range of arguments, some extremely radical. Shulamith Firestone, for example, in *Dialectic of Sex* argues that child-bearing is the centre-point of women's oppressors, so she advocates artificial reproduction. Betty Friedan mocked the calling of mothers to stay at home with their children. She called it 'the happy housewife *heroin*'. In one extraordinary passage she compared American society with Nazism, and described the traditional home as 'a comfortable concentration camp' whose prisoners are housewives, brainwashed by 'femininity', and who are not fully human.[12] William Gairdner comments that this should have enraged Jewish readers, who know the difference between concentration camps and suburban boredom. 'Buyers of her book,' he writes, 'should ask for their money back.'[13]

Politics and feminism

While feminists were on the attack, there was one government in the world which came near to achieving the feminist utopia. Sweden under its radical Prime Minister Olaf Palme sought to eradicate all distinctions between men and women, and to use legislation and public money to achieve this goal. He set up an Equal Opportunity Commission with massive public funding to get rid of all instances of unequal treatment. The declared aim was to make the roles of men and women exactly the same in all areas of work and life. *All* women should be brought into the work-force, and, when necessary, husbands should receive child-support benefits and maternity leave rather than their wives.[14] But the plans failed in 1990, when the country virtually went bankrupt. Poor tax-payers, what a waste! The Canadian *Financial Post* declared this Swedish model dead. 'It passed away last Friday afternoon.'[15]

The greatest influence on the modern feminist movement was undoubtedly Simone de Beauvoir, who for many years was mistress to the famous existentialist Jean-Paul Sartre. Her book *The Second Sex* is still regarded as the 'Bible' of feminism. Her basic thesis was that women become women through the influence of society. 'One is not born a woman, one becomes one' is her most famous maxim. She advocated the total removal of sex differences. For women to be free they had to become men. She represents the adult woman as an 'abortive man'. De Beauvoir has influenced the whole feminist movement, and Mary Daly, one of the first feminist theologians, based her book, *The Church and the Second Sex*, almost entirely on de Beauvoir's ideas.

It has been in the United States where feminism has had its greatest influence, although men still predominate in leadership, not least in the Senate and Congress. Some have mistakenly seen the United States, the most powerful country in the world, as a matriarchy. But if one looks beneath the surface of the rhetoric, it is still firmly patriarchal. The movement burst out in the 1960s about the same time as it did in Britain. It was for a short time called 'women's liberation', and was accompanied by symbolical bra burning, at about the same time as the rather more influential draft card burning, which symbolised opposition to the Vietnam War.

It must be remembered that feminism prior to the 1960s was not anti-family. Since the 1960s it has been the traditional family and its values which have been in the feminists' sights. But Betty Friedan declared war on the 'housewife trap' for women, and demanded equality for women, so that they could pursue their careers as men did, with the men sharing equally with the women in child-rearing. Friedan herself founded the influential National Organisation of Women, with a 'Bill of Rights' providing for the abolition of all discrimination against women.

The movement went into overdrive in the 1970s, and the front runner was Kate Millett, a radical lesbian feminist, whose book *Sexual Politics* was sensational. Marxists have always blamed capitalism for all society's ills. She shifted the blame to the privileges of men and patriarchy. Men not women were to blame for the capitalist system. To liberate women she called for no less than the abolition of the family, accusing it of being 'the fundamental instrument and the foundation unity of patriarchal society'.[16] One of the fringe groups at the time called itself SCUM (Society for Cutting Up Men). One can laugh, but they were serious. Gross hatred of men was bred by radical feminism. In its most extreme form, some feminists came to regard the traditional sexual union of men and women as on the same level as 'rape'. One must hasten to add that only a small proportion of women, even in the United States, have bought the radical feminist ticket. But that does not alter the fact that this kind of radicalism, even if it was not taken on board by the majority of women, was highly influential from the 1960s onwards.

Beyond the fringe

Another unsavoury aspect of radical feminism is its link with occultism, including witchcraft, and New Age. A recent book, entitled *The Absent Mother*, has the subtitle, 'Restoring the Goddess to Judaism and Christianity'.[17] This approach says that goddesses were around before monotheism took over (and, of course, their arch-enemy patriarchy). They were 'feminine deities of great power and creativity'. They apparently originated in the Great Earth Mother. Contributors to the book include Stewart and Janet Farrar, who have been practising witches for twenty years. Another is Deike Rich, an astrologer, who writes about the feminine side of Saturn. More relevant to our subject is a chapter written by Roger Horrocks, on 'the divine woman in Christianity'. Apart from an attempt to deify the Virgin Mary, he follows the New Age line on the signs of the Zodiac. We are leaving the age of Pisces (Christianity with the fish sign), and moving into the new age of Aquarius. He asks if this change will mean that masculine values will be replaced by the feminine. He quotes approvingly the words of the radical feminist Mary Daly in *Beyond God the Father*, when she writes about 'the second coming of the female presence'. Mary Daly actually admits she sees the feminist cause as 'beyond Christolatry' and to 'constitute the primordial, always present, and future anti-Christ'.[18] The Catholic nun has come a long way. In a chilling book called *Ungodly Rage*, the author, Donna Steichen, documents the spread of witchcraft amongst Roman Catholic feminists in the United States.[19]

We will be looking into the family issues in Chapters 18 and 19. But it needs also to be mentioned that many of the leaders of the feminist movement, particularly in the United States, are professing lesbians. A great deal of attention is given to males adopting same sex relations; but women probably far outnumber men in same sex behaviour. Lesbianism has always had an important role in the development of feminism. A familiar slogan of the movement in America is, 'feminism in theory and lesbianism in practice'.

The link between the ordination of women and gay rights is often denied, but there are clear connections. The liberation of homosexuals and lesbians and the acceptance of their life-style is often seen as part of the same feminist programme. This was made clear when Jane Dixon was consecrated Suffragan Bishop of Washington. The Bishop of Washington (Ronald Haines), as reported in the *Church Times*, described her as the latest of 'a small but growing group' and said that the new inclusiveness towards women, *as well as gays and other marginalised groups* 'is the beginning and not the end'.[20] This was also made clear when an avowed lesbian, who had been ordained priest by the Bishop of Washington, was chosen to be one of the 'ministers of the table', and deliberately placed 'centre stage'. The first woman diocesan bishop in the Anglican Communion, Bishop Jamieson of Dunedin, New Zealand, as reported in the *Church of England Newspaper*, has said that 'gay clergy can make good clergy. I don't believe this damages their function as priests, but it unquestionably would be difficult.'[21]

Europe, as usual, lags a little behind the United States. But it may be interesting to record what happened in a conference in Munich in 1979. It was held at the Catholic Academy, and the topic was *The Emancipation of Women: between Biology and Ideology*. A biologist there made a suggestion that the female sex is naturally endowed with an emotional orientation toward 'caring for the brood' so far as raising of children is concerned. It met with such violent debate that the astonished biologist commented: 'the reaction could not have been worse if I had said that women all have the itch'.[22]

Christian feminism

There will be many Christians who will want to repudiate most if not all of the radical feminism I have been describing. But Christian feminism draws from the same poisonous well of egalitarianism. The Christian element which is added should not deceive us. It is the same thing we are dealing with. It is the pursuit of equality of men and women without the complementary truth of the roles determined for them by the Creator, which are non-negotiable. When George Carey, the Archbishop of Canterbury, said, 'there is no connection between the ordination of women to the priesthood and feminism', he was immediately corrected by the former Bishop of London (Dr Graham Leonard) in an article in *The Times*.[23] It has always been an ingredient in the debate on the ordination of women.

Christian feminism as we have said is different from the radical feminism that I have written about. All Christians are committed to the family; Christian feminists would not accept in any way the radical suggestions of Friedan and Firestone, for example. But, as we shall see Christian feminism is potentially against the family too. It may not condemn the family as such, but by making its goal equality it undermines the basic God-given hierarchical framework, and the defined roles of men and women as specified by the Scriptures.

It needs to be understood that so far as the Church is concerned, feminism has been around a good many years. It may use different vocabulary from the radicals, but its goals are the same. A spokesperson for Christian feminism is Elaine Storkey. In her book *What's Right with Feminism?*, she treats radical feminism with sympathy. Her conclusions are that such feminists 'want the fruits then, but deny the Source'.[24] She goes on 'many of their diagnoses are correct. Much of what they say about patriarchy needs to be listened to.' Where are they wrong? They have faith in themselves, she concludes, not in God.

A great many Christian feminists would agree with Elaine Storkey's comments. It is similar to the approach that some Christians used to have to communism. If you could somehow 'baptise' it or 'sanctify' it, all would be all right. After all, so we were told, communism is based on the Sermon on the Mount. All we need to do is to convert communists to Christ, and all will be well. Those of us who spoke about the inherent evils of Marxism were ridiculed and called bad names like 'fundamentalists'. The collapse of one communist country after another, and the revelations which have come out of them of the truth, hidden for years by communist lies, reveal how much deception there has been. Feminism is the gender equivalent of communism, and it has some of its strongest roots in that system.

It is in essence wrong because its goals are based on a false view of the Scriptures. It needs to be dismantled, not sanctified with a Christian veneer. There is still in our society sex discrimination – that is evident. Men against women, and women against men. But feminism only worsens the situation rather than cures it.

One of the surprising features of this is the hold that feminism now has over Evangelicals in Britain, the United States and other Western countries. Evangelicals are split on this issue, and this is particularly noticeable in the United States. There are now two new organisations representing the opposing sides. One is called the 'Council on Biblical Manhood and Womanhood', and the other 'Christians for Biblical Equality'. The battle lines are drawn up. The first one has goals that are contained in the *Danvers Statement*. The other group, which also started in 1987, consists of Evangelical feminists, and is linked with the London Institute for Contemporary Christianity in the UK, which was founded by John Stott, and which is now served by Elaine Storkey among others. The first group's understanding is contained in a book called *Recovering Biblical Manhood and Womanhood*. It is edited by John Piper and Wayne Grudem, and has as its sub-title 'a response to evangelical feminism'. It is one of the best and most comprehensive studies I know on the subject.

The divisions amongst Evangelicals are also evident in Britain, and they voted on both sides in the General Synod debate. Following the decision, they have split into rival camps. Those against the ordination of women have started a new organisation called Reform, and are distancing themselves from Evangelical groups like Eclectics, which was started in the 1950s by John Stott. Those who are in favour of the ordination of women are called 'open' Evangelicals. It needs to be added that the ordination of women is not the only issue that separates them.

David Ayers sums this up in his chapter in *Recovering Biblical Manhood and Womanhood*: 'the feminist viewpoint is destructive because it is grounded in a set of false pre-suppositions regarding the created order. It leads to coercion, failure, and censorship. It contributes, directly and indirectly, to the growing uncertainty and confusion of the post-Christian world.'[25]

In these last two chapters we have traced the origins of egalitarian thought, the quest for equality, which was the seedbed in which both communism and feminism were first planted.

Communism, if left to run its course, would have destroyed every society and family forced to accept it. Fortunately a sufficient number of people have now seen through its fantasies, so that much of it has been overthrown. Feminism, if we allow it to continue unchecked, will similarly destroy the family and a lot else. We must see to it that it does not succeed.

Converted from feminism

Earlier we have noted the important testimony of C. S. Lewis to his conversion from paganism, and his instinct that priestesses do not belong to Christianity. It would be appropriate to link this with the story of the conversion of Sheldon Vanauken, also from paganism, and indeed largely through the influence of C. S. Lewis himself. It has added importance because Vanauken was also converted from radical feminism to a view similar to the one I am taking in this book. Both Lewis and Vanauken were English specialists, both having held university professorships in this field. Let Vanauken tell his story again.[26]

He joined the feminist movement in the early 1960s. In his book *Under the Mercy* he tells how the first cracks appeared in his feminist apologia: he went for a walk with his dog Nelly up Cedar Mountain. He thought of the *realities of nature* 'where cows are not bulls nor mares stallions'. His dog nuzzled his hand and he thought 'how feminine – how ladylike – she was'. He saw what he calls 'the real world'. He goes on, 'I suddenly and treasonably felt, not that feminism was wrong but that it was – silly.'

He was completely committed to feminism. It was he who introduced to the English language the words 'sexist' and 'sexism'. But he was to change. As we have seen, he began to see flaws in the feminist ideology. The cracks became fissures. As an English scholar he disliked what he calls 'this tin-eared abuse of English' in inclusive language.

In the end it was the artificiality of feminism that convinced him it was wrong. He saw it was contrary to the natural order. The breaking-point came one night as he was reading something about the possible aftermath of a nuclear holocaust. He realised that feminism would not survive a minute in nature or in survival conditions. 'I had wanted feminism,' he writes, 'to be the true natural order between man and woman, the true relationship. I reluctantly saw that it wasn't.'

His mind went back to another time when feminism flourished in the Rome of the Antonines on the eve of what Gibbon called 'the decline and fall'. The modern Roman woman had abandoned her traditional duties and pleasures in order to compete with men in literature, law, hunting, and even the gladiatorial arena. They wore men's clothes. This is all documented in the sixth satire of Juvenal. Sexual liberation was the order of the day. Vanauken comments, 'but Rome fell – and feminism can *only* flourish in a sophisticated society with strong protective laws and weak moral standards. Roman feminism perished with the imperial civilisation that protected it.'[27] The parallels with our own day are only too clear.

Chapter 15

The walls come tumbling down

More and more I come to regard 'churchiness' as
a survival of the useless: it was necessary once;
without the dogmatism and ecclesiasticism of the
early medieval church the whole of Christianity
would have gone into smoke. But the walls built to
protect now only confine and cramp, and should be
pulled down.

(William Temple, 1906)

Then I [Nehemiah] said to them, 'You see the
trouble we are in: Jerusalem lies in ruins, and its
gates have been burned with fire. Come, let us
rebuild the wall of Jerusalem, and we will no longer
be in disgrace.'

(Ne. 2:17)

In 1906 people were stunned to learn that the Bishop of Oxford
had refused to ordain William Temple. This young man of 24 was
the most brilliant Anglican of his generation. His father had been
Archbishop of Canterbury, so he had an exemplary background.
Everyone knew that a dazzling career lay ahead of him and he
was a Fellow of Balliol College, Oxford. The reason why the
bishop would not do it was because William Temple could only
very tentatively accept the doctrine of the Virgin Birth, and 'with
rather more confidence', to quote his own words to the bishop,
that of the bodily Resurrection of our Lord. The bishop in his
letter to Temple said that he believed these two doctrines to be
'essential'.[1]

William Temple wrote to his brother in Berlin about this, referring to 'churchiness as a survival of the useless'. He went on, 'it was necessary once . . . *but the walls built to protect now only confine and cramp, and should be pulled down*'.

Eventually after two years' deliberation between William Temple, the Bishop of Oxford, and Randall Davidson, who was then the Archbishop of Canterbury, Temple was ordained, later to become Archbishop himself. But throughout the years since then the walls have been tumbling down. And how things have changed since 1906! Now bishops as well as young budding ordinands can express not merely doubts, but full-blooded denials of the Virgin Birth and the bodily Resurrection, and even make fun of those with whom they disagree! It has to be added that William Temple soon moved in the other direction, towards an orthodox position on the Creeds, and their statements about the Trinity, Virgin Birth and bodily Resurrection. His biographer, F. A. Iremonger, says that Temple received 'absolute certainty at a second of time during a symphony concert at the Queen's Hall'.[2] It is interesting also to note that as early as 1916 William Temple wrote to a friend, 'personally I want to see women ordained to the priesthood'. But he regarded Christian unity a more important objective, and he was wise enough to say in the same letter, that the two were not compatible. A situation which still pertains today.[3]

From 12 November 1992, the day after the General Synod of the Church of England approved the ordination of women, the lessons for the following days came from the prophet Hosea. One verse stood out, 'Judah's leaders are like those who move boundary stones' (Ho. 5:10). The Church of England and all the other major Protestant churches have been moving the boundary stones, slowly but surely, all through this century. The walls today are in ruins. We are no longer sure where the boundaries of theology or morality are. Almost anything goes. You can place them where you like. But they have been moved so slowly, many have not noticed it. A minister once had a disagreement with his people about where the piano should stand in the church. In order to get his way he moved it six inches every Sunday, and no one noticed or complained. That is how it has been happening in the churches throughout this century. Prophets like C. S. Lewis, E. L. Mascall and Malcolm Muggeridge have warned the Church, but they have been ignored. Canon Eric Mascall once wrote, 'the real dividing-line today is between those who believe in the fundamentally revealed and given character of the Christian religion; and those who find their norms in the outlook and assumptions of contemporary secularised culture, and are concerned to assimilate the beliefs and institutions of Christianity to it'.[4] The Protestant ship continues to move further and further on to the rocks.

In 1912 William Temple was involved in a book called *Foundations*, which reinterpreted Christian truth 'in terms of modern thought'. Ronald Knox, a Roman Catholic convert from Anglicanism, wrote, 'they are not concerned how they can represent truth most adequately, *but how they can represent it most palatably*'. The desire to please has always been an ingredient of heresy. The heretic is more concerned that truth is relevant to the world than to God and his revealed Gospel. What Malcolm Muggeridge once called 'a humanistic, materialistic orthodoxy called the consensus'.[5]

Changes in society

When we look at the twentieth century, soon to run its course, it has been dominated by the two World Wars, the increase of national wealth in the Western world, the extension of education to both men and women, and by staggering advances in science and technology. All these have stimulated the cause of women's rights and encouraged the growth of feminism. Not all of this has been loss, some has been gain which we all can accept and for which we can be thankful. The two World Wars were the first in which conscription was used. Most men were compelled to leave home, and many of them country as well, sometimes for years on end. Women were left to do a lot of the things which men had previously done. Women came into their own in many fields new to them. The creation of wealth, and its more even spread in society, enabled the State to provide free education for all its citizens. When feminists complain about the lack of education for women, it has to be remembered that few *men* received much education until the twentieth century. However, there was sex discrimination, and men were given priority over women. The development of technology has increasingly taken the sweat out of work. Much manual work, which at one time only men were perceived as capable of doing, is now done by machines, which women can operate as well as men. The rapid expansion of education has opened up many more careers for women.

Feminist activism in the twentieth century can be divided into two periods. The first strove to redress the political, economic and moral discrimination against women in Western society. In Britain it became known as the suffragette movement. They were successful in alerting society to injustices, which were increasing in the light of the changes in twentieth-century society already outlined. Although the focus was on 'votes for women', the agenda was wider, but not as wide as the feminist movement of the 1960s.

Feminism sometimes distorts the truth and muddles the facts. It is worth remembering that the major opposition to votes for women came from women themselves rather than men. A recent study by Susan Marshall finds that women constituted 'the overwhelming majority of the counter-movement's leaders and members'.[6] They were so devoted to their families they feared that the commercial market would lure young single women first into commercial life, then into political life, thus undermining the family as the basis of society.

The second period of feminism came from the 1960s onwards and was initially inspired by the famous book *The Second Sex* by Simone de Beauvoir. This was more radical and far reaching than the first period. William Gairdner has summarised the two stages, 'this former feminism insisted that society be structured to protect children *inside* the family. The feminism we have today is, in contrast, attempting to structure society to protect women *outside* the family.'[7]

Some have said that there is no link between the issue of the ordination of women and feminism. But, as already pointed out, the correlation is close. Many supporters of the ordination of women are feminists, and feminism has influenced the thinking of all of us in varying degrees. It is now part of the culture of the twentieth century. It has contributed positively to the enhanced standing of women in our society.

Sweden takes the lead

The first ordination of women as priests, within the Protestant mainline churches, took place in the 1950s in the Danish State Church. Then in 1960 the Swedish Lutheran Church took the plunge, and as this Church is in full communion with the Church of England, and has close historical and cultural connections, it is worth looking more closely at what actually happened. I have already mentioned that the two World Wars were a contributing factor in advancing the cause of feminism. We need to remember that during war itself, the male macho image is dominant, as stories of male heroism overshadow everything else. After the war is over the same macho influence continues for some years, as the survivors return, write their books and the movies endlessly recall the great stories of gallantry. It takes a new generation born after the conflict to change this strongly masculine image.

But Sweden took no part in either of the two World Wars. While Norway and Denmark, occupied by Nazi Germany, were blacked out, just across the Skagerrak and Kattegat the lights of Sweden blazed. Sweden had embarked in the 1930s on a policy of democratic socialism. The architects for this were Gunnar and Alva Myrdal. He was an economist, his wife a radical feminist sociologist. The aim was to produce an egalitarian society, and the feminist component was to make men and women equal. In the 1970s the policy had gone further than one of equal opportunity, it now pursued one of equal results or outcomes. No longer was the family unit to be favoured in any way. The Swedish Prime Minister, Olaf Palme, in 1973 put it bluntly: 'no one should be forced into any preconceived role because of his or her sex; rather all should be afforded better opportunities to develop their personal capabilities'.[8]

It should, therefore, not surprise us that Sweden led the way in sexual emancipation, and sadly the Swedish State Church was too liberal and timid to oppose the permissive trends. But on the issue of the ordination of women the Church was bound to clash with the expectations of the State, which partly controlled the Church anyway. Also the rest of Europe would of course lag behind Sweden. This was especially true of Britain, which was involved in World War 2 longer than any other country. Thus feminism had to wait until the macho atmosphere had passed, and was not to rise to prominence in Britain until the 1970s, well after the Swedes.

The Swedish State Church thus became the trend-setter for the rest of the Protestant world. The clash between Church and State in Sweden was inevitable. As the clergy were actually employed by the State, they were accused of discrimination in not ordaining women. Sweden regarded itself at the time as the flag-bearer for the crusade for equality in every area of their society, and an example to the rest of the world. The Church was out of step, and so intense pressure by the State was brought to bear on the Church to conform.

The State started a well-orchestrated campaign to canvass the public so as to end the impasse. This reached a crescendo in the 1950s, and by 1958 the General Synod was forced to make a decision on the matter. Some of the laity were highly politically motivated and so voted in favour, as did later a majority of the bishops, whereas the ministers mostly rejected it. The first women were ordained on Palm Sunday in 1960. What has happened since? Swedish friends of mine, the Rev. Carl Gustaf Stenback, and Bishop Bertil Gartner, inform me that the situation is still a running sore over 30 years later. The Swedish State Church like the Church of England has a high proportion of Catholic-minded priests in it. Bishop Gartner has also reported to me that most appointments, since the decision to ordain women, have been made from amongst those who were willing to conform. Those who hope for peace in the Church of England now that the decision to ordain women has been taken, are going to be disappointed. Tension and division will continue for many years to come. It is estimated that still 35–40% of the Swedish clergy are opposed. A Swede in favour of women's ordination wrote in 1972 of the traditionalists, 'their morale is unbroken; they have the confidence of the faithful. In spite of constant pressure, they appear to be the victors!'[9] The problems in England and elsewhere in the Anglican Communion will be a 'thorn in the flesh' for a long time to come.

How did the feminists in Sweden succeed against strong opposition? The arguments are interesting in the light of our present situation in the Church of England. A Bible Commission of the Swedish Lutheran Church examined the biblical foundations of their Church relevant to this subject. They agreed that the scriptures in 1 Corinthians 14 are clear, and that the teaching is a command of the Lord (v. 37). However, *it was thought permissible to disregard that command since Paul and Jesus had derived the directive from the rabbinical conception of women, which is no longer relevant today.* Because of the change in the social culture of today, to continue to follow this scripture would even contradict the central biblical intentions of Galatians 3:28.[10] There you have it in a nutshell. Scripture bows to culture, not culture to Scripture. And the skeleton key (Gal. 3:28) is used yet again, interpreted out of its context. Michael Novak puts it well when he writes, 'the heart of the matter then is that the "advanced" culture of our age thinks of itself as normative'.[11]

This is always being overlooked by feminists. They forget that they themselves are totally surrendered to late-twentieth-century culture. Sheldon Vanauken writes about this, *'every* age has its characteristic illusions . . . the feminist vision of woman, of equality as sameness, may be the great illusion of our age'.[12]

There is another slant on this which is also revealing. Mary Daly in her book *The Church and the Second Sex* quotes with approval the Swedish biblical scholar Krister Stendahl.[13] He wrote that both sides in the dispute agreed on the historical meaning of the relevant biblical texts, that when a reason is given in those texts, it is always by reference to the subordinate position of women in creation. The real problem and disagreement concerned the application of these texts to modern times. One side regarded the texts as normative for all time. Professor Stendahl argues that *it is almost impossible to assent to the political emancipation of women while arguing on biblical grounds against the ordination of women.* So when Scripture conflicted with the political agenda, Scripture lost. Many of the speeches in the General Synod debate of November 1992 read like a re-run of the Swedish debate, almost word for word. The issues are the same, the arguments are the same, and the result was the same.

Others follow Sweden

When we turn from Sweden to Germany we find another interesting slant on the debate. Karl Barth believed strongly that the role of women in marriage and in the Church should be one of submission. But his student Charlotte von Kirschbaum, whom Barth himself naively affirmed was continuing his own thought, believed that women should be ministers, claiming they are needed *under present-day conditions if the Church is to reverse its decline in membership*. Germans had got used to women ministers during World War 2 because of the absence of so many men at the Front. In the discussions there were a few brave dissidents, the most notable the Bishop of Bavaria (Hermann Dietzfelbinger). Again we see that the same arguments from experience ('women do such a fine job in the Church') and the need to make the Church relevant ('women will reverse church decline') were vigorously put forward by the Church of England. The important theological arguments were barely taken into account. Cultural pressures won the day.

The influence of the World Council of Churches in this matter has been considerable in the twentieth century. The question was addressed at the first meeting of the newly formed body in Amsterdam in 1948. 'The Church consists of both men and women,' the preamble went, 'and both have the same degree of personal worth, even if this fact is often disregarded in practice.' The goal of women's liberation, including their ordination, has been vigorously and persistently pursued by both the Commission of Faith and Order and the Department on Co-operation of Men and Women in the Church, Family and Society.

The WCC, with the sole opposition of the Orthodox, have more and more demanded the ordination of women, and have particularly influenced Third-World leaders, by attaching female liberation to the wagon of racial liberation. Pauline Webb, an English Methodist, called the idea of female submission 'heresy',[14] and Philip Potter, when Secretary General of the WCC went further and called it 'demonic'. Any such submission was regarded as comparable to treatment of blacks (racism) or workers (capitalism). As Manfred Hauke points out, 'the struggle against sexism is seen as an integral part of liberation theology', which has dominated the WCC agenda since Uppsala 1968.[15] There Paul Hanson called for the elimination of the Old Testament masculine image of God, which he accused of being a mechanism of oppression.[16] Almost exactly word for word the revival of Marcion's heresy of the second century! The ordination of women has always been part of the political agenda of the WCC.

It is interesting that Jacqueline Field-Bibb in her history of the movement towards women's ordination should sub-title her book 'ministerial politics and feminist praxis'.[17] It has been constantly apparent that political arguments have increasingly been preferred to the theological, and that the praxis (accepted practice, custom) of the twentieth century is favoured to that of the first century. She also politicises the issue as 'the struggle between the forces of liberation and the forces of oppression'.[18] The feminist theologian Schussler Fiorenza in her book *In memory of Her* goes so far as to assert that revelation is not found in the canon of Scripture, but in the ministry of Jesus and the life of the community called forth by him.[19] This is, of course, another way of by-passing the 'problem' texts of St Paul.

Anglicans follow

The story of the Church of England in the twentieth century, as we have already seen, is one of slow but relentless erosion of orthodox Christianity. What happened in Sweden and Germany was now to take place in England, although it took longer. In the 1960s, when feminism was making all the running, the Church of England did not look as if it would follow suit. There was, however, one freak happening which was to influence the events which followed. In 1944, the Anglican Bishop of Hong Kong ordained a woman to serve in Macao when no man was available. This move was condemned by the Lambeth Conference of 1948, and the woman had resigned two years earlier because of the controversy. The Lambeth bishops mentioned only tradition and ecumenical relations as the reason for their disapproval. The Lambeth Conference of 1968 could find no conclusive theological reasons against the ordination of women (or for it, as it happened), and further study was encouraged. But significantly the word 'theological' was quietly dropped from then onwards, something which did not escape the notice of E. L. Mascall.[20]

It was Hong Kong that again made a pre-emptive strike in 1971, by ordaining two women, a step sanctioned by the international body (the Anglican Consultative Council). At the

1978 Lambeth Conference the green light was given for the ordination of women, each Province being free to make its own decision. The Church of England's approach to the subject of the ordination of women has been either wise or crafty, depending on which way you look at it. I would call its methods 'Fabian', and let me explain what I mean. The Fabian Society was formed in 1884 by radical socialists in Britain. Members included Sidney and Beatrice Webb and George Bernard Shaw. Their goal was to introduce socialism in Britain by stealth – that is, by easy stages rather than the kind of radical confrontation or revolution advocated by Marxists. That is why they called themselves Fabians. The name comes from a Roman general called Quintus Fabius Maximus. He did not believe in what Saddam Hussein would call 'a mother of battles'. His policy was to harass his enemies mercilessly, but never to join them in all-out battle. It was wise, and it worked.

The Church of England realised that the ordination of women was a large pill for many to swallow all at once, so they cut it up into easily digestible parts. The Fabian method to a 't'. One has also to note that the constant and deliberate pressure from groups like the Movement for the Ordination of Women harassed and canvassed church leaders for many years. Also there were the endless discussions in the General Synod. By 1992 many Anglicans were battle weary, and some voted in favour, not because they agreed, but because they could not face any further pressure. Quintus Fabius Maximus' method won in the end.

The 'fabians' won the first skirmish in 1975 when the General Synod agreed that 'there are no fundamental objections to the ordination of women to the priesthood'. This effectively defused the issue of any theological time bombs which might have been ticking away. It seemed to indicate that the only objections were practical and superficial ones, which were bound to be overcome in time.

The next fabian encounter with the opposition was in the 1980s when it was proposed and agreed by the General Synod to ordain women to the diaconate, a form of ministry previously being a year's apprenticeship for men before they became presbyters or priests. In the first place this was a form of sex discrimination, because it did not provide men with the possibilities of a permanent diaconate (as granted by the Roman

Catholic Church through the Second Vatican Council). Secondly it was a master-stroke because it got the Church used to women presbyters or priests. They were able to wear men's clothes (e.g. dog collars), and do everything else that a man does in the priesthood except celebrate Holy Communion or serve as the vicar of a parish or the bishop of a diocese. Moreover an increasing sense of injustice built up because women, who were just as able and committed as the men, could not go on to the presbyterate or priesthood as the men did after only one year.

The next fabian clash was the matter of female bishops. It was thought wiser not to introduce the consecration of bishops in the same measure as the ordination of women to the priesthood. No doubt it was thought best to do it in two stages, so that the Church could get used to women priests before women bishops. This in spite of the fact that the Bible does not draw that kind of distinction between priests or presbyters and bishops. The two words in the Greek are interchangeable, and it has always been Anglican doctrine that the presbyter or priest's ministry is an extension of the bishop's. But here as elsewhere expediency came before Scripture or theology.

It is even more important to notice the subtle innuendos of the debate which were included in the whole process. For example, in November 1962 the Church Assembly of the Church of England passed a resolution asking the Archbishops to appoint a committee to examine the various reasons 'for withholding of the ordained and representative priesthood from women'. It has been a consistent feature of the debate on the ordination of women that traditionalists have been called upon to prove that women should not be presbyters or priests, rather than feminists being asked to prove that they should. It has been a debate, in other words, about a negative, rather than a positive. Thus traditionalists have been put on the defensive. Both the Scriptures and Church Tradition require formidable arguments to prove that women can be ordained, because for 2,000 years they have not been eligible.

Traditionalists do not need to prove anything. It is the feminists, not the traditionalists, who should have been in the witness box. In other words, the arguments have been about the wrong issue. A friend of mine in a letter put it well: 'the principal error the bishops have made was to take the Church of England into the debate on a negative. At the marriage feast at Cana, Mary said, "whatever he tells you to do, do it". She did not say "do what he doesn't tell you not to do".'[21]

Lord Runcie, when Archbishop of Canterbury, recognised this. In a letter to the Vatican in December 1985, he said, 'it is insufficient simply to state that there are no fundamental reasons *against* the admission of women to the priesthood . . . It is also necessary to demonstrate compelling doctrinal reasons *for* such a development.'[22]

Let me give an illustration. For many years there were proposals about building a Channel Tunnel. The discussion did not start out with the assumption that there should be a tunnel, and then its detractors asked to supply arguments to show that it should not be built. There had never been a tunnel, so the arguments hinged on whether it should be constructed or not. The British and French governments had to be convinced that a good case could be found for building it. The arguments were about building a tunnel, not about refraining from doing so. So the debate in the Church of England should have been about whether a good case can be found in the Scriptures and Church Tradition for ordaining women, not whether it can be proved that they are ineligible. No doubt the feminists knew, like the theologians of the Swedish Lutheran Church, that no such case can be found in the Scriptures and Church Tradition, so they sat on their haunches and asked the other side to prove their case rather than proving their own.

The 'walls of Jerusalem' need to be rebuilt, and we should not be put off by those who accuse us of 'fundamentalism'. Nehemiah and his co-workers were also ridiculed. The churches in the West are suffering from a spiritual disease like AIDS. People die because the virus attacks the body's immunity system, and so the body is no longer able to defend itself from outside attacks. So our churches have lost their spiritual immunity system. For Anglicans this consists of the Scriptures, Church Tradition and reason. During this century the churches of the West have discarded the authority of the Bible; they have not listened to our ancestors, and now they are denying what is natural, namely that dogs have four legs.

We need to look next at some of the side-effects of this liberal trend within many churches. Before we do so, we need to summarise what we have learnt from history.

Chapter 16

The cloud of witnesses
A summary of Part 2

Every time history repeats itself, the price goes up.
(Anonymous)

Someone once wrote, 'The only thing that history teaches us is that it teaches us nothing.' He was clever, but he was wrong. Sadly we live at a time when there are far more debunkers of history than those who respect it. In July 1993 Mrs Barbara Mills, the British Director of Public Prosecutions, in the course of a conference address on the right to trial by jury, referred to Magna Carta as 'overwhelmingly important in its day. But we aren't still in 1215.' The editor of the *Sunday Telegraph* commented, 'the chief problem that besets Mrs Mills and her kind is . . . that they are anti-historical'.[1] He goes on to comment on the phrase 'a record as long as your arm', and then says, 'that is what the human race has. *We should all study it, not pretend it isn't there.*'

We have only been able to look sketchily at the history of the way the Church has handled gender, and particularly the ordination of women, over the centuries. When I was a student I was warned about accepting theological novelties. I was told that these were nearly always heresies, and that anyone who came up with a doctrine which up-staged the apostles was almost certainly wrong. The doctrine that accepts women for ordination not only up-stages the apostles, it claims to be an improvement on the view of the 60 or so generations which followed them.

It is worth remembering the famous Canon of St Vincent of Lerins: 'we within the Catholic Church are to take great care that we hold that which has been believed everywhere, always and by all men . . . and that we shall do if we follow universality, antiquity and consent' (Commonitorium, 2.). This Canon has always been understood in a relative rather than absolute sense. But E. L. Mascall has written, 'if there is anything to which the Vincentian Canon does apply absolutely, it is surely the restriction of priesthood to the male clergy'.[2]

I think it would be useful briefly to summarise these last few chapters, to help us to see more clearly how things have got to where they are today. When we understand this, we shall be in a better position to work out what to do about it.

The Church Fathers

The Church had to face grave threats in its early history from heretics. The major areas of conflict concerned the Trinity, and the Person of Christ. We today benefit from the careful way they protected the apostolic faith and teaching from heresies, which would otherwise have undermined and destroyed it. The question of the ordination of women was one of these threats. The Church Fathers were unanimous that the testimony of Jesus Christ, his appointing male apostles, and the teaching of Paul in 1 Corinthians and 1 Timothy made such ordinations invalid. It was heresy to suggest otherwise.

The age of chivalry

In this chapter I have given examples of the important role that women often played in both church and secular life during this period. Yet throughout these years the view of the Scriptures and Church Tradition was upheld, that women were ineligible for ordination. The period itself is interesting because in Europe, Church and State enjoyed a reasonably harmonious relationship, not excepting Thomas à Becket, murdered in Canterbury Cathedral by Henry II's henchmen. Yet throughout this period women were not regarded as eligible to become priests and bishops in the Church. The reasons given were theological, not educational or social.

Even today, following the emancipation of women and the wholly changed social environment, very few women reach the top in society. We can see this by looking at those countries which have gone farthest in seeking undifferentiated equality for men and women. In the 1970s all 13 members of the Swedish cabinet were men. In Cuba, 20 out of the 21 ministers and all 15 members of the Political Bureau were men. In communist China 13 of the 14 leaders of the Standing Committee of the National People's Congress, all 17 members of the State Council, and all 67 heads of the General Ministries were men. All but one of the Politburo were men, the one exception being the widow of Mao Tse-tung. In the old Soviet Union, 96% of the members of the Central Committee were men.[3] Some may respond to these figures and say, 'It's obviously due to sex discrimination.' There may be some truth in that, but one has to remember the examples quoted are from countries dedicated to sexual equality. If they can't achieve it, who can? The plain truth is that women, with a few exceptions, are not constituted physically, mentally or emotionally to compete with men in places of leadership. Their gifts lie in other *equally vital* realms.

The ideology of equality

In the French Revolution there surfaced streams of thought that had been fomenting in the *Ancien Regime* for many years. These were anti-hierarchical, and confronted the sections of society which most buttressed 'hierarchy', the Church and the Monarchy. The desires for equality soon developed into socialism and ultimately communism. Sexual equality moved higher and higher on the political agenda, and ultimately found its focus in what we now call feminism.

Feminism

The word covers a large area of thought, some of it confused. The 1960s and 1970s saw the birth of a new radicalism, which took feminism to the ultimate. Feminism has also invaded the

churches, and has influenced its policies towards women, especially in the promotion of their ordination. It is now possible to talk
about feminist theology, as something distinct both in method and
content from 'masculine' theology.

The liberal flood

Finally, we have seen the way theological liberalism has come like
a flood within the churches to pull down the walls which previously
distinguished truth from error, right from wrong. We see how the
ordination of women is a vital part of the liberal agenda.

We have seen the slow but steady erosion of basic Christian
doctrines. This was epitomised in the Church of England by the
appointment of Dr Jenkins as the Bishop of Durham in 1984,
thus institutionalising heresy in a way that has never been done
before. All this has prepared the churches to make important
decisions based on ephemeral factors rather than the timeless
truths of the Scriptures and the wisdom of many generations of
Christian Tradition. Bishop Kallistos Ware writes cogently, 'if
women can and should be priests, then their exclusion for two
millennia is a grave injustice, a tragic error. Are we to attribute
a mistake of this magnitude to the Fathers and Ecumenical
Councils, to the apostles and the Son of God?'[4]

History is not easy to interpret, and the reader may question
some of the ways I have done it. I would not want such
questioning to lessen the impact of the first part of the book.
Ultimately truth is discerned from the Scriptures, not from
Church history. That is where I rest my case, and the best of
our ancestors have always done the same.

Part 3

Side-effects

Jesus said, 'every good tree bears good fruit, but a
bad tree bears bad fruit. A good tree cannot bear
bad fruit, and a bad tree cannot bear good fruit . . .
Thus, by their fruit you will recognise them.'

(Mt. 7:17–20)

Chapter 17

Equality and order in the Godhead

It is only in the light of the dogma of the Trinity
that human beings can understand who they are and
what God intends them to be. Our private lives, our
personal relations . . . depend upon a right theology
of the Trinity.

(Bishop Kallistos Ware)

We have seen the prominence given to God as our Father in the
Old and New Testaments. It is this vision of the divine Father
which is reflected in family life universally, both in the home and in
the Church. So it is natural that the head of the family and the head
of the Church is the father of the community. The association is
made many times in the Bible. For instance, in Psalm 103:13
we read, 'As a father has compassion on his children, so the
Lord has compassion on those who fear him.' Another text is
Hebrews 12:7–9: 'God is treating you as sons. For what son
is not disciplined by his father? . . . Moreover we have all had
human fathers who disciplined us and we respected them for it.
How much more should we submit to the Father of our spirits
and live!'

Radical feminists dislike the word father, and regard patriarchy
as a form of male oppression, although they do not demand
a matriarchal alternative. They want to remove hierarchical
relationships altogether. Christian feminists would keep the
revelation of God as 'Father', reduce its significance for the sake
of 'equality', and a growing number would argue for 'Mother' as an
alternative title for God. This will bring us later into the subject of
inclusive language.

A bizarre example of the above was when the Episcopal Church of America instructed its members to cease calling priests 'father'. Let me hasten to add that Christ's admonition 'call no man father' had nothing to do with it. Many Christians never have called their ministers 'father' anyway. The reason given by the Committee on the Status of Women is the impropriety of parental terms for ordained people. They have also ruled out 'mother' for women priests. So priests are now to be called 'pastor' or 'reverend', which are uni-sex titles. Those who object and say the word 'reverend' is an adjective, not a noun, are accused of 'upper class bias', which means they are better educated than others, which you should not allow to influence your judgement. Amazing!

There are some who challenge the Fatherhood of God as divine revelation. Instead it is said that humans started the idea of 'father', and it is they who have projected their ideas of father on to God. In other words, God becomes 'Father' because we have earthly fathers, and not the other way round. Mary Daly sees this as a source of sex discrimination: 'Since God is male, the male is God' is the way she puts it.[1] For feminists fatherhood is often seen as tyrannical. They see the need to liberate people from this patriarchal emphasis. The radical feminist view denies the Christian revelation of the Fatherhood of God, and instead regards it as a human invention, and often as a conspiracy with which to tyrannise women.

We see here two ways of assessing the truth; the one in which God reveals himself, and we reflect him as an image or a mirror – we are like God. The other in which we reflect our culture, and so become like it. When we do that, without realising it, we begin to create God in our image. So we see him/her as 'Mother' as well as 'Father', and in between we replace the distinctive roles of men and women, fathers and mothers, with the holy grail of equality, itself a secular concept. To make God in our image, and to reflect back our mortal concepts onto him is palpably wrong. Yet that is constantly being done. God is described and understood in a falsely egalitarian way. We bring our egalitarian concepts into the very courts of heaven.

To understand all this we need to do some theology. The Trinity is not the easiest teaching to understand, yet its importance cannot be stressed enough. Bishop Kallistos Ware writes:

men and women, so the Bible teaches, are made in the image of God, and to Christians, God means the Trinity; it is only in the light of the dogma of the Trinity that humans can understand who they are and what God intends them to be. Our private lives, our personal relations, and all our plans of forming a Christian society *depend upon a right theology of the Trinity.*[2]

V. Lossky has said, 'between the Trinity and Hell there lies no other choice'.[3] And here the Orthodox Church has some important insights to share with us.

Some of the differences between the Western and Eastern Churches can be measured in terms of contrasting emphases. The Western stresses the unity of the Trinity, while the Eastern emphasises the 'threeness' of the Persons. The West sees more the equalness of the Persons, the Father, the Son and the Spirit being co-equal, or 'of the same substance'; whereas the East stresses the diversity of the Persons.

The importance of this for the subject of this book cannot be stressed enough. Within the Trinity we see both unity and diversity, or we might say, equality, yet diversity of roles or order, and submissiveness of functions. That is exactly what we are saying about men and women. They are created equally in the image of God, yet they are designated different roles by God, the man the role of head, woman the role of helper. This should not surprise us, when we realise that men and women are made in the image of God.

Now I want to go a little deeper into this, because I believe the Orthodox Church has a real contribution here to help us see the truth. The Holy Trinity is a mystery of unity in diversity; so is the relationship between men and women. We are one, yet we are different, and there is a mysterious ingredient about the link between the two. The Eastern insight, which is largely missing in the Western Church, was the work of the Cappadocian Fathers. They said that there is one God because there is one Father. Bishop Kallistos Ware comments, 'The Father is the "cause" or "source" of Godhead, he is the principle (*arche*) of unity among the three; and it is in this sense that Orthodoxy talks of the "monarchy" of the Father.'[4] The Son and the Spirit trace their origin to the Father, and are described in expressions of their relationship to him. 'The Father,' writes Ware, 'is the source of Godhead, born of none and proceeding from none; the Son is born of the Father from all eternity; the Spirit proceeds from the Father from all eternity.'[5]

We can learn a great deal from this special insight of the Orthodox Church concerning the inner life of the Trinity, and it is helpful to our subject. If men and women are made in the image of God, then we can learn about that relationship from the way the Persons of the Godhead relate to each other. We are told in Genesis 1:26–27: 'God said, "Let us make man in our image, in our likeness" . . . So God created man in his own image, in the image of God he created him; *male and female he created them.*' So here we see the man as an individual, and the woman as an individual, created in the image of God. But this verse says something more than that. It is saying that there is a real resemblance with God in the gender distinctions. In other words, men and women are both equally created in the image of God, and, therefore, share the same destiny. *But also the distinctive roles of men and women, what differentiates them, is created in the image of God.* If that is true, then there is much we can learn from the nature of the Trinity, and we can see the roles of men and women in relationship to each other reflecting those of the Trinity of Persons.

We see, firstly, that the Father has a leading role. He is the Head of the Trinity if you like. It is he who sends the Son, and later the Holy Spirit (Jn. 6:57; 14:26). That does not deny the equality of the natures (*homoousios*) within the Trinity. It is only saying they have different functions. The obedience of the Son does not in any sense imply his inferiority. Jesus himself was well aware of this in his life with the Father, and expressed both truths on a number of occasions. He was accused, for instance, of 'making himself equal with God' (Jn. 5:18), and also made the statement, 'the Father is greater than I' (Jn. 14:28). In the first we see his equality with the Father, in other words that the Father and the Son are 'of the same substance'. In the second he verbalises the different roles within the Godhead, so that *in that sense* they are not equal. The Father is 'greater', not in the sense that he is a better, more divine, or a more important person. He is greater in the sense in which his role is different. He is the 'head' if you like, and the Son submits to him. Bishop Kallistos

Ware writes: 'within the Trinity, God the Father is the source and "head" (1 Cor. 11:3) of Christ, and yet the three Persons are essentially equal. *And the same is true of the relationship of man and woman.*'[6]

Because this is true, we are not surprised to see this reality reflected in the lives of men and women. Thus we shall expect to see the father as the head of the community. We shall also see women, although equally human and gloriously godlike, being in submission to their husbands, and honouring that position given to them by God. We shall not equate submission with inferiority. We shall remember that Christ, although having the very nature of God, 'did not consider equality with God something to be grasped, and . . . humbled himself and became obedient . . .' (Phil. 2:6–8). Such is the very substance of God, and such is the substance of the human relationship between men and women. In the words of Graham Kendrick's song, 'meekness and majesty' is the astonishing blend of deity. *We gasp in amazement, but we can hardly then be haughty and reject as unsuitable and undesirable for ourselves something which is part of the very nature of God.*

Christ, therefore, is revealed to us as the supreme example of humility and unselfishness. He was not grasping for honours. He would rather people discern his deity through his works, than through boastful words. When we look at the life of Jesus, we see no grounds for women grasping for equality of roles with men, not least because Jesus Christ himself refrained from aspiring to equality with God. Jesus did not cease to be God when he became man. He was equal with God, and when challenged about this, never denied it. But he was also submissive to the Father. 'The Son can do nothing by himself,' Jesus said, 'he can do only what he sees the Father doing, because whatever the Father does the Son also does' (Jn. 5:19).

The Western Church, as we have seen, tends to present a more monochrome, and perhaps 'dull' concept of the Trinity. It stresses the unity and equality of the Persons, rather than their dynamic interaction. The Western Church wants us to grasp what is the same about the Persons, whereas the Orthodox what is different. There is no conflict or disagreement between the two. Both are right and both are important. It is not difficult to see the relevance of this to our subject. Feminism stresses the unity and equality of the sexes, full-stop, or 'period', as the

Americans would say. But it is only half the truth, and half truths are dangerous. They are the seeds of heresy. The whole truth can only be grasped when we see the corresponding truth, that men and women are placed by God into the roles of head and helper, and these roles are no more interchangeable than the roles of the Father and the Son are. The greatest mistake, and, therefore, the greatest danger, in ordaining women is that it reverses the roles of men and women in defiance of God the Creator. It weakens our understanding of the Trinity, by rejecting the dynamic of the interpersonal relationship between the Persons. It reflects a rejection of the principle of submission which is part of the Trinity's relationship within itself. It lifts the false banner of egalitarianism, and waves it in the face of God. Manfred Hauke has put it well: 'feminist theology is the perfect example of a false understanding of democracy, extending its demand for equality even to the image of God'.[7]

When men and women claim to have found an equality of relationship *without* hierarchy, and without the biblically defined roles of headship and submission they are claiming something which is not true of God. By doing so they miss a vital part of the understanding of God's very nature, and as a result are fundamentally impoverished, and distorted within themselves.

It is common these days to try to equalise the relationship between God and men and women. One of the worst examples I ever saw was the American car sticker *God is my co-pilot*. It is becoming more and more clear how pervasive this attitude to God is. It is part of the anti-hierarchy, anti-authority spirit of our day. At times it is almost as if people are saying of God, 'Who does he think he is?' Or to quote the words of Jesus in his parable of the talents, 'his subjects hated him and sent a delegation after him to say, "We don't want this man to be our king"' (Lk. 19:14). There is scant reverence for God, and little honouring of his name. The commandment 'you shall not take the Lord's name in vain' is of wider application than swear words, or blasphemous utterances. It includes occasions when we treat God and his name as if he is on a level with us. Charismatics are particularly prone to this, and the overemphasis on healing and deliverance from evil spirits, easily puts us in the centre of the situation, with God on the outside, whose business it is to do our bidding. The reality is that God is in the centre. We are there to serve him, not he us.

Inclusive language

The language of gender is another area of change in our world. It was brought home to us in a practical way the first time my wife was referred to as 'Ms'. We were waiting to catch a flight from Maui to Honolulu when an airport announcer asked if Mr and Ms Harper could go to the ticket counter. In order to avoid the distinction between Miss and Mrs, especially when women are unmarried and cohabiting, the two states of life are united in the one title 'Ms'. Sheldon Vanauken has called it 'that ugly unpronounceable growl'. It is felt unfair that men get away with the one title 'Mr', whether they are married or single. So for equality's sake, it's Ms only, from now on. The change to Ms is only one example of the gender language battle. The British government has taken steps to see that no official letter or leaflet will now refer to husbands, wives or spouses. They are all to be referred to as 'partners'. Equality marches on.

But the much more critical issue is inclusive language as it relates to God himself, the demand from feminists that the excessively patriarchal vocabulary of the Bible be balanced by references to God as 'Mother'. The whole inclusive language debate has now spilled over into much more serious areas, such as the text of the Bible and the nature of God. You can't get more serious than that.

God and inclusive language

In 1992 the British Methodist Conference discussed the issue of inclusive language. A working group of their Faith and Order Committee wrote the Report, and it is worth noticing that five out of the seven members were women. The use of inclusive language, and female imagery for God was strongly encouraged. When one looks at the Report one sees how closely the issue of inclusive language is linked to that of the ordination of women. For instance, Genesis 1:27 is quoted several times, but Genesis 2 and 3 are ignored. We are not surprised to find Galatians 3:28 quoted, as usual out of its context, and with approval, and the other Pauline texts ignored or rejected. The basic assumption which is made in this report is that 'subordination' or 'submission' is out of the question for sexual relations, because it implies inferiority. So the Report dismisses totally the Pauline and Petrine texts, ignores the example of Christ and his appointing male apostles, and reads back the rejection of submission and hierarchy into the Trinity itself, exactly as we have already reported others doing. A plea is made for 'fairness' in divine imagery, and so in order to include feminine imagery for God as well as the masculine, they affirm that God is 'Father'. But since God is not male they say we should talk rather of the 'parenthood of God'. So in a subtle way, the route is open for God then to be referred to as either Father *or Mother*.

A feminist theologian, Alwyn Marriage, is quoted with approval when she suggests that since God the Father and God the Son are predominantly male, God the Spirit may appropriately be spoken of in female terms. She also insists that the Third Person is co-equal with the second and the first, *otherwise Trinitarian theology simply reinforces the subordination of women to men*.[8] We see in this argument the twin errors of wanting to get the feminine into the Trinity to balance the masculine, and also the assumption, mistaken as we have seen, that there should be no place for female submission on earth because the Persons of the Trinity are 'co-equal'.

The theologian, Jürgen Moltmann, has taken this route himself in his book *The Trinity and the Kingdom of God*.[9] In it he rejects hierarchical and hence patriarchal ordering of human society, since if human society is to be modelled on the life of the Trinity it should be egalitarian and co-operative rather than authoritarian and hierarchical, thus reflecting the inner life of the Trinity, which is a loving sharing of co-equal persons.[10]

We have seen that one of the major routes to feminising God is via the Person of the Holy Spirit. Catherine Halkes has written, 'a feminist theology must be primarily pneumatological theology'.[11] Some have drawn attention to the fact that the Hebrew word for 'spirit' (*ruach*), is feminine in gender. But the adjective in 'Holy Spirit' (*ruach qadosh*) is always masculine. As Donald Bloesch points out, 'if the feminine form of "holy" were used with *ruach* it would probably indicate a cult prostitute. When Spirit is personified to mean "Spirit of the Lord", the accompanying pronouns and possessive adjectives are consistently masculine.'[12] He accuses those who try to feminise the Spirit in this way of 'a lack of both solid biblical scholarship and linguistic understanding'. We need to remember there is no necessary link between sex and gender in Hebrew, because it has no neuter gender.

So we see how egalitarian assumptions, with their feminist overtones, finish up interpreting the doctrine of the Trinity, rather than the Trinity being the true model for our human relationships. As we have shown earlier in this chapter, the Persons of the Trinity are not in an egalitarian relationship, for both the Son and the Spirit are in a relationship of submission to the Father.

The Pronoun War

In 1992 a row developed in the United States over a new lectionary for the Roman Catholic Church there. It had been under pressure from feminists for a long time, and one of the areas of conflict had been over the lectionary. Apparently the more traditional liturgists had dropped out. A Roman Catholic priest called Peter Stravinskas in an interview in *The Catholic World Report* said they left because they were 'battle weary'.[13]

The feminists had been pressing for years for more inclusive language, and they got their way. Instead of keeping to the text of the new translation, produced by biblical scholars in 1987, they rewrote the text themselves. The new text of the lectionary does not correspond to any published translation of the Bible. The new lectionary was put to the American bishops at their conference in November 1992, and passed *without debate*. Perhaps they too were 'battle weary'. It then had to go to the Vatican for approval, which at the time of writing has not been given.

The point at issue is the sacred text of the Bible, faithfully transmitted to us by our ancestors. Should that text be changed for ideological/political reasons? In practice what does this involve? Let me give one example. The Bible says, 'blessed is the man who does not walk in the counsel of the wicked, or stand in the way of sinners' (Psalm 1:1). Feminists object to that because of the exclusive use of the masculine gender. So they want to change the singular to the plural, 'blessed are they who . . . etc.' Peter Stravinskas comments:

it is important to keep the singular, first of all, because the Bible has a singular. Secondly, to change everything into the third person plural, in effect, destroys the notion of an individual relationship between a believer and Almighty God with everything subsumed into a collectivity. Therefore, this move would involve great arrogance as well as a faulty understanding of theology.[14]

Even worse than this is the attempt to avoid wherever possible the masculine 'he' or 'him', when referring to God, and to 'neuter' it by changing it to 'God'. To call God 'he' is a form of sexism to many feminists. Writing in *L'Osservatore Romano* Mgr. Robert Sokolowski stated that to change the text of the Bible like this, 'conflicts with the duty of the Church to hand on what it has received'.[15] So we see gradually the new items of the feminist programme coming to the top of the agenda. The 'Pronoun War' has only just begun.

It is in the United States that Catholic feminism is strongest. A Roman Catholic journalist and mother, Donna Steichen, has surveyed this area and published her finding in a book called *Ungodly Rage, the hidden face of Catholic Feminism*. She writes about this,

their [the Catholic feminists'] ultimate rebellion against God . . . has been disguised for public consumption as a campaign for 'inclusive' liturgical language . . . But in private, and in their own publications, feminist theologians reveal, behind that mask, naked denial of the objective existent, transcendent Father God. They hope to replace him with a gnostic deity, androgynous, immanent and worshipped in themselves.[16]

A similar controversy broke out in 1993 over the English version of the new Roman Catholic catechism, which delayed its publication. Again inclusive language was the difficulty. The Vatican was unhappy with variations from the original French text using 'non-sexist language'. Part of the problem is that English grammar is not naturally inclusive, and this affected almost every paragraph of the text. 'People' and 'persons' are words which were substituted for male pronouns. So we note another skirmish of the Pronoun War.

Most serious is the attempt to apply inclusive language to God himself. This came to a head in New Zealand, where the Anglican Bishop of Dunedin (Penelope Jamieson) is referred to liturgically as 'Mother in God'. She is the first ever female diocesan bishop, and is committed to a feminist agenda. She also agrees, as reported in the *Church of England Newspaper*, with the Portuguese feminist Maria de Lourdes Pintasilgo that 'in the 21st century feminist theology would be seen at the centre of the way the church should move'.[17] The Anglican Prayer Book in New Zealand has adopted inclusive language for God. It refers to 'God as Father' rather than 'God the Father', a mode rather than a person. The link between the ordination of women and inclusive language is made clear in the introduction to the new Anglican Prayer Book in New Zealand. After mentioning women priests (first ordained in 1977 in that country), it says '*Thus* there has been an increasing need to choose language which is inclusive in nature and which affirms the place of each gender under God.' Bishop Jamieson has described inclusive language as 'contemporary poetry, every bit as poetical as Cranmer'.[18]

It has been in North America that feminism has most obviously affected the churches regarding inclusive language, not least the Episcopal (Anglican) Church. Both the 1979 American and the 1985 Canadian Prayer Books have adopted lectionaries in which all references to female submission in the congregation and other unfashionable ideas have been cut out, including readings from the New Testament.

Many of us believe that the ordination of women does inevitably lead to a distortion of one's understanding of the doctrine of the Trinity. It is also evident that inclusive language, as descriptive of God, is part of the same package, whatever disclaimers some put forward. The one unavoidably leads to the other. What is equally serious is the effects undifferentiated sexual equality can have on family life, and to that matter we now turn.

Chapter 18

Equality and order in the family: fathers

This triangle of truisms, of father, mother and child,
cannot be destroyed; it can only destroy those
civilisations which disregard it.

(G. K. Chesterton)

All anthropology indicates that society must be
based on the family, and the family cannot exist
without marriage.

(Steven Goldberg)

Human history began with a family crisis or two. Adam and Eve's
discord in Eden was soon followed by the sibling rivalry of Cain
and Abel, which ended in murder. So it has continued ever since.
Today the family is again in serious crisis. If we fail to find a
solution we will be plunged into a new dark age of lawlessness
and chaos, which could destroy our civilisation.

Perhaps the most serious aspect of the decision to ordain
women is that it ignores the gender distinctives created by
God. It is the replacement of his natural laws with egalitarianism.
Male and female roles become interchangeable, and this deals
a body blow to the basic structure of the human family. It is a
sign that the churches who do this have lost their way and are
not hearing what the Holy Spirit is saying. At just the moment
the family is disintegrating before our eyes, the Church begins
to dismantle its biblical framework. As more and more families
become fatherless, the Church begins to replace fathers with
mothers at the altars and pulpits of some of its churches. Just
when it becomes clearer by the day that mothers need to give

their children priority over their own careers, the Church opens a new career up to women, some of whom are mothers, which will take them away from their children when they most need them. Just when people need clear guidelines on taking moral decisions on family matters, such as cohabitation, abortion, birth control, divorce, most of the churches fudge the issues and offer people little or confusing guidance.

The Church sometimes is even ambivalent about the family itself. In an article in *The Times* entitled 'We can do it far better together' the Anglican and Roman Catholic Bishops of Liverpool (David Sheppard and Derek Worlock) wrote that the family as we know it is of modern origin, and that from biblical times until the nineteenth century it was *extended*.[1] They criticised Mrs Thatcher, who was then Prime Minister, for not encouraging the State to be that extended family. Amongst other things they urged a greater redistribution of wealth so that the State could achieve these goals. But the bishops were wrong. The so-called extended family has never been anything else but the traditional family, parents and children, with others added on, servants, cousins, in-laws etc. The basic framework has always been the same. What the bishops may not have realised is that their arguments are the same as those of the radical feminists who have been attacking the traditional family for years. Thus Shulamith Firestone writes in *The Dialectic of Sex*, 'the modern nuclear family is only a recent development'.[2] Again, Germaine Greer in *The Female Eunuch* says, 'the single marriage family . . . is possibly the shortest lived familial system ever developed'.[3] Avant garde sociologists and church leaders seem often to concur with the statement once made by Sir Edmund Leach that the traditional family 'is a most unusual kind of organisation and I would predict that it is only a transient phase in our society'.[4]

In Britain one of the bastions of the family has been the Mothers' Union. There was a time when divorcees could not be full members. Now one of their former Vice-Presidents, herself a divorcee, writes in their magazine *Home and Family* of the 'inflated importance given to the family'. Mrs McMullen goes on to say that the nuclear family of mother, father and children is not a blueprint with divine endorsement. With respect, she is seriously wrong. The nuclear family was created by God, it does not need God's endorsement, but it does need ours.

Ferdinand Mount, in his well-documented book *The Subversive Family*, counters all these myths when he writes, 'the family is not an historical freak . . . it is neither a novelty nor the product of unique historical forces. The way most people live today is the way most people have always preferred to live when they had the chance.'[5] In this book he documents how both Church and State have tried from Plato onwards to diminish or even to destroy the family. There will always be those who would want forcibly to divert the resources and goodwill of the family to 'better' causes, 'God, nation, community or class', as Mount categorises them. The Church herself is not free from blame because it often puts an inordinate work-load on its ministers and lay people, and the family suffers greatly as a result. But let us be of good cheer, the family usually triumphs. As anthropologist Margaret Mead once said, 'no matter how many communes anybody invents, the family always creeps back'.

The fearful legacy of the 1960s

In the 1950s a rock and roll star called Jerry Lee Lewis was due to come to Britain for some shows. However, when it was revealed that he had a scandalous sex life his hotel bookings and all his shows were cancelled. The 1960s were to change all that. From the 1960s onwards a scandalous sex life was almost a condition for doing a show! The decade of the 1960s was a moral watershed in our society. The seeds sown in that decade have produced a lamentable harvest, and the family has suffered most.

There were three major contributing factors to this in the 1960s. The first was the introduction of the oral contraceptive pill. It was first released in 1953, but did not become widely used until the 1960s. It provided women with a much safer and easier way of preventing a pregnancy. The second was the discovery of new and more successful drugs to treat venereal disease. And the third was David Steel's Abortion Bill of 1967, which meant there was now back-up if contraception failed. The fears of either an 'unwanted' pregnancy, VD, or a back-street abortion, had for many years acted as a check on unrestrained sexual adventures. Although AIDS was probably around in the 1960s, it had not yet become the scourge it was later to be. For women there was also a new sense of equality with men. They had always before had the worst of sexual encounters when a pregnancy occurred. Now they too could 'have fun' without fear of getting pregnant.

Neil Lyndon refers to the 'Class of Sixties women'. They were born around the time of World War 2, and grew up with common and conventional expectations of adult and especially married life. He writes, 'they had been taught to expect that boys should do all the paying and all the driving and that if you didn't keep your hand on your halfpenny and make sure that they kept their hands on the wheel and their eyes on the road ahead, all the hell of a teenage pregnancy would be the outcome'.[6] All that was to change, as Lyndon points out: 'they now found themselves the vessels of a technology which afforded them absolute and infallible protection against pregnancy, and if they slipped up, they could take advantage of a safe and speedy technique for abortion'.[7]

The figures of what happened speak for themselves. In 1961 in Britain there were 27,000 divorces (at that time regarded as scandalously high), in 1989 there were 164,000. More than one third of marriages now end in divorce, *nearly double the European average*. In 1961 only 5,000 marriages took place between people who were divorced. In 1989 it had risen to 50,000. In 1961 less than 5% of people cohabited before marriage. By 1988 it had risen to over 50%. It has also been shown that couples who cohabit are three times more likely to break up than those who don't. If one thinks that remarriage is the answer, the divorce rate for second and third marriages is higher still – two out of every three, according to a recent survey.

Some people question whether the period I am writing about is markedly worse in terms of morality than other times. The statistics are revealing, but they have been challenged. What is certain is the absence of shame which marks the period from the 1960s onwards. Immanuel Jakobovits was the Chief Rabbi in Britain throughout this period (1967–91). In an article in *The Times* he wrote about this, 'there is a most important distinction between moral lapses then and now. Pain protects health . . . whereas without shame we would disport ourselves like the brutes . . . today shame is being systematically displaced by brazen vulgarity . . .'[8] The prophet Jeremiah wrote of his generation, 'are they ashamed of their loathsome conduct? No, they have no shame at all; they do not even know how to blush' (Je. 6:15; 8:2). Today unmarried couples cohabit without shame, fathers abandon their families without shame, and illegitimate children are conceived without shame. Societies also accept widespread abortion without any qualms of conscience. Jakobovits goes on, 'the removal of shame has changed our moral vocabulary'.

Another serious side-effect of the decline of the traditional family has been the growth of the cults and sects. The sensational affair of David Koresh and his followers in Waco, Texas, raised the seriousness of the issue. Stephen Robinson, writing in the *Daily Telegraph*,[9] spoke of the mushrooming of such groups 'in part because of the collapse in family structures and a general sense of alienation'. He goes on to say that Americans are encouraged to explore their dysfunctional family background. He adds, 'such a national obsession makes a good hunting ground for any ambitious cult leaders'. The 1960s was also the seed-bed years of the modern radical feminist movement, which as we have often said was anti-family, in favour of liberated sex, abortion, gay rights, and above all, anti-patriarchy.

What were the churches doing and saying during the permissive 1960s? To be fair to them, I doubt whether people would have taken much notice whatever they did or said. But what they did say and do was in the main unhelpful. As we have already noted this was about the time when the Ten Commandments, which used to be displayed in thousands of sanctuaries, were removed. C. S. Lewis once wisely said that the very things that people of any period would most like to change are probably the very things they most need to hear. It was the decade of the 'New Morality', which in essence was no morality at all. It was popularised by John Robinson in *Honest to God*. He described the sanctity of marriage as 'an occult view of life'. He went on, 'it is far from obvious that it has any basis in the teaching of Jesus or the New Testament'.[10] Instead Dr Robinson introduced his readers to the new and trendy 'situation ethics' of Joseph Fletcher, which was based on 'love', although no clear idea was given what such 'love' was, it was assumed everyone knew. In fact by the 1960s it had become one of the most debased words in the English language.

The churches also have been somewhat selective in their

moral judgements. Issues like *apartheid* have been treated as clear-cut and judged accordingly. Whereas in sexual matters, the churches' conclusions have been very hazy. A leader in *The Times* says, 'one of the fastest growing ideas of the past 30 years has been the belief that no chosen lifestyle is inherently superior or inferior to any other. It has been the axiom that there should be the fewest possible limitations on the individual's happiness and rights, including rights both to have children and to get divorced'. It is well said. One might add to this hedonistic scenario, that *responsibilities* are secondary to rights, if they are considered at all. A few decades of socialism has also indoctrinated many people into believing that everyone has the right to be supported by the State in whatever circumstances. The churches have talked a lot about 'lifestyle', but have stubbornly refused to have any value judgement on anything, least of all traditional family values, or aberrations like homosexual and lesbian practices.

Sheila Lawlor of the Centre for Policy Studies sums this up in an article in the *Sunday Telegraph*, 'there are many obvious causes for the decline of traditional marriage and family life. For instance, the 1960s culture of sexual liberation; the feminist ideology that wants women to free themselves from men; the spread of secular morality in place of Christian; and the dogma of the Left which sneers at tradition.'[11] She goes on, '*but none of these has been as potent as the hidden hand of government*'. She might have gone on to point out that our system of taxation and social security is systematically biassed against the family, especially since the 1960s, when the effects of feminism were beginning to be felt.

The whole taxation and social security system in Britain, as well as other Western countries, is seriously flawed, because support for the so-called nuclear family has been in long-term decline. Over the last half-century the tax burden has been deliberately shifted from single people to families. During the period 1950–92 the income tax threshold for a married man with two children fell from 101% of average male earnings to 36%. Both Labour and Conservative administrations have been responsible for this steady erosion of support for the natural family. What makes it worse was the strident claim of Mrs Thatcher that her party was the party of the family. It has not been true of either party since 1945.

In an article in the *Sunday Telegraph*, Patricia Morgan and

Paul Goodman wrote about 'the great Tory betrayal'. They went on, 'the mother who stays at home to look after her children has gained nothing from Tory reforms of family taxation. Proposals to introduce transferable tax allowances (which would have allowed such mothers to transfer their tax allowances to working husbands) were withdrawn.'[12] How has this come about? Morgan and Goodman have come to the same conclusions I have arrived at: 'obeisance to the powerful and vociferous feminist lobby . . .'

This opens up a can of worms. It is worth mentioning that when Neil Kinnock, then the leader of the parliamentary Labour Party, was defeated twice at the polls in a General Election, the family issue may have played a bigger part than has usually been considered. The political Left, including Kinnock, poured scorn on what they called the Conservatives' obsession with the traditional family. They said that the family was not collapsing but *changing*, and that the rising rate of divorce and of births outside marriage should be seen as opening up new opportunities for women.

We will now look in turn at the three fundamentals of the family, the father, the mother, and the children. We shall see how the position of all three are menaced today by the State, by modern egalitarian dogmas, particularly feminism, and by the fact that the churches are following the spirit of this age, rather than the Spirit of God. Only when there is a reaffirmation that 'dogs have four legs', can the family be saved. The Church should be leading the way; instead it is often confused and indecisive. When the Church of England insists on the ordination of women it is part of this overturning of nature and the disobedience of the Scriptures; in other words it is saying, 'dogs have five legs'.

Absent fathers

Single-parent families constitute the greatest problem facing Western society today. In Britain they have more than doubled in the last twenty years. If trends continue more than 50% of all families in Britain will be single parent by the end of the century. In the USA the trend is the same, but much worse amongst black families. In 1950 in that country there were only 17% which were single parent, today it is 56%. The results are the same there as here: increased sickness, illiteracy, and crime. In America one young black in three is either in prison, on bail or on probation. In Britain 90% of single parents are women. That means the major problem here is *absent fathers*.

A Greek Orthodox layman, Frank Schaeffer, has written: 'The fate of tens of thousands of single women raising tens of thousands of fatherless children, in poverty and squalor, in our "liberated" culture graphically and tragically illustrates the price our society has paid *for the loss of Christian familial order and male responsibility*.'[13] A leader in *The Times* drew attention to the large body of American and British data demonstrating 'the disastrous effects of rearing children without fathers'.[14] In the United States more than 70% of all juveniles in state reform institutions are from fatherless homes. Also 60% of fatherless young people drop out of school or college.

If you look at the graph of crime (see p. 172), you will notice that notified crimes were negligible until the middle 1950s, but then took off, accelerating through the 1960s, and are still increasing in the 1990s. Here we see that the causes of crime have little or nothing to do with 'social deprivation'. In fact the big growth has taken place during the period when Harold Macmillan, the then Prime Minister, told the public, 'You have never had it so good.' Our country had far worse unemployment and social hardship in the 1920s and 1930s, a period in which the rise in crime was negligible. In addition to the personal cost, it needs to be remembered that the overall cost of sending a child to prison is greater than the cost of providing them with higher education.

Various reasons have been given for the rise in crime by modern sociologists and church leaders – paranoia, poor IQ, and low levels of ceratonin in the brain. When young people rioted in Newcastle Dr George Carey was widely reported as including 'social deprivation' amongst the causes. This has frequently been said over the years. Judging by the immediate response from people who actually lived in this part of Britain, it was inappropriate to apply the epithet 'social deprivation' to this example of mindless violence in Newcastle. But it has been common for church leaders and left-wing politicians to say this for many years. 'Society' has been held responsible when things have gone wrong, not individuals. This as we have seen is how

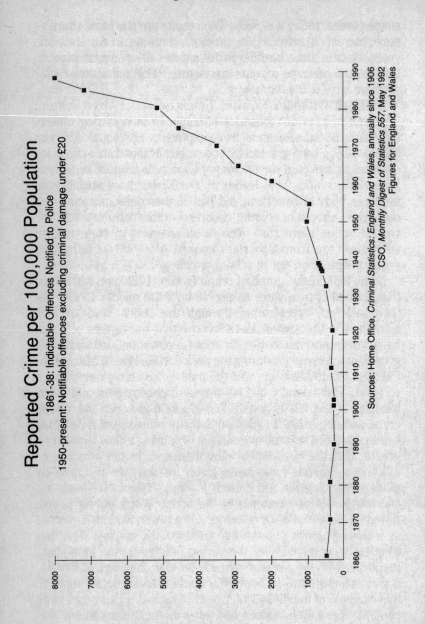

Reported Crime per 100,000 Population

1861-38: Indictable Offences Notified to Police

1950-present: Notifiable offences excluding criminal damage under £20

Sources: Home Office, *Criminal Statistics: England and Wales*, annually since 1906
CSO, *Monthly Digest of Statistics* 557, May 1992
Figures for England and Wales

Marx and Engels diagnosed the ills of their day, and Lenin, Stalin and other communist leaders tried to demonstrate the truth of it with the ideal classless society which the others had dreamed about. If you improve society, so the argument went, crime will decrease. If we read the true story of Russia since 1917 we find a different account of the matter.

The violence that George Carey responded to in Newcastle has now been well documented by Norman Dennis and George Erdos in their book *Families without Fatherhood*.[15] Dennis is a local, who has lived all his life in the North-East. They have closely examined the reasons for the riots. They took place in the autumn of 1991 and received world-wide publicity. Two youths stole a car for a ram-raiding burglary. They were pursued by police, and were killed when their car crashed. The younger of the two lived on an estate called Meadow Well, and their peers set fire to their neighbours' houses and shops. The careful research done by Dennis and Erdos reveals that poverty was not the cause. They were considerably better off than previous generations. Neither was homelessness the cause. They lived in pleasant post-war semi-detached houses with gardens.

They were in no sense of the word 'socially deprived'. Their area had been developed carefully and thoughtfully by the Tyne and Wear Development Corporation. It was said 'they had nothing to do and were bored'. In fact the area has every kind of sports' clubs, libraries, and self-improvement facilities. Neither could unemployment be given as a reason, since the estate had access to the considerable labour market of Tyneside, with a station on the new Metro system right in the middle of the estate.

Norman Dennis, a sociologist, who calls himself an ethical socialist, believes that the collapse of the family, and particularly the absence of fathers, is the prime reason for the meteoric rise in the crime rate. Some time ago this intrepid trend buster presented his views to an audience in London. Rather than following the vogues fashionable to the psychologists, he put the rise down to lack of moral fibre. 'I was subjected,' he reported, 'to such abuse from the great and the good . . . that I refused to travel down south again.'[16]

Dennis and Erdos summarise their findings by saying 'yes', it is true that 'unemployment' was the key to the riots, but not in the sense of absence of job opportunities. Rather it was in the sense of the 'weakening or complete disappearance of the expectation that a young man should prepare himself for the larger employment . . . for a lifetime . . . of mutual support of a mature man and a mature woman'.[17] The fathers of the rioters called their wives 'lass' and their house 'home'. Their children call their female partner, to whom they will probably not be married, 'the bitch' and their home 'the kennel'.

In an exposé of the shallow stuff served up sometimes by the media, the amoral Left, and then reprocessed by church leaders, Dennis and Erdos accuse them of 'self-centred celebration of the family's dismantlement and their unremitting attack since the 60s on all the taboos that protected family life' and 'wanton ignorance of, or open hostility to the known facts'.[18] There is something almost sinister about the new cast of mind where fathers view the State as responsible for the upbringing and support of the children they have sired. As Dennis and Erdos point out, they are really saying, 'My baby is the hostage through whom I, who will not do my duty, will hold you up to yours.' The Chief Rabbi, Dr Jonathan Sacks, writing in *The Times*, says, 'There is no greater faithlessness than having a child and then walking away. What we are in danger of losing is not the conventional family, but fatherhood.'[19]

We have stressed throughout this book the importance of fatherhood. The Old Testament was unashamedly patriarchal, and the ultimate responsibility for the welfare of the family rested with the father. The Chief Rabbi in the same article draws attention to the fact that the biblical word for faith (*emunah*) means loyalty. It comes from the same Hebrew word as the verb for bringing up a child. 'There is a connection between the two,' he writes; 'God's faith is portrayed in the Bible in the language of fatherhood.'[20] This law of nature, which is true for all human families whether they are religious or not, was confirmed by the Lord Jesus Christ, who chose twelve 'patriarchs' to match the twelve in the Old Testament, and the teaching of the apostle Paul that the man is the head of the woman.

Papa's missing

There is a story told about the famous American actress,

Lucille Ball. She was asked on an American TV show the question, 'What's happened to our country? What's wrong with our children? What's missing?' She replied, 'Papa's missing.'

The absence of 'Papa' or 'Daddy' should sound all the alarm bells, because it is, to quote the words of Leanne Payne's book, *a crisis in masculinity*.[21] I have been saying, especially in the early chapters where we have traced the biblical teaching, that this is essentially a theological matter, not sociological or psychological. Having said that, I would now want to add at once that a true theological understanding will lead to a correct sociological and psychological perception, *not the other way round*. We all have social and psychological aspects to our being. If we get the theology wrong it will affect the other aspects harmfully, *and this is what we are seeing all over the Western world*.

Leanne Payne wrote her book after several years of careful study and pastoral counselling, especially of men. She shows how in our gender-confused society it is men, not women, who face the greater problem. Because their masculinity is not affirmed, they evade their duties, turn to violence, and the resulting vacuum is filled by women. This, I might add, is what the churches are doing mistakenly in the name of sexual equality. Leanne Payne goes on to show that since all of us are 'born of woman', the path to maturity must involve us in emancipation from our mothers; this is where the father should come in to affirm the sexuality of his son or daughter. A mother figure cannot substitute for the father, although in exceptional circumstances God will provide. This should always be the exception rather than the rule. As Leanne Payne puts it, 'They need to hear in the male voice, "my son/my daughter, you are very special".' When this is lacking there can be serious identity problems, *of which homosexuality is one*.

Further support for this comes from a secular feminist, Alix Pirani. She writes, 'patriarchy is seemingly making relentless progress towards global annihilation . . . If the supportive father abandons the family . . . who will survive? The crisis is not new, only the apocalyptic scale is new.'[22] Later she writes, 'the challenge at the present is to get the absent father to return'.[23]

It needs to be stressed that when we are talking about absent fathers, we are not only referring to those who have left home more or less permanently, although, sadly, there are plenty of them. I am also thinking of the many fathers who remain in the home, but effectively leave all or most of the nurturing to mother. They make little or no effort to relate to their children, and this is psychologically destructive, as Leanne Payne points out in her book.

What so many men need today is to be affirmed in their role as leaders in the home, Church and community. This is now beginning to be validated by people working in the social sciences. For instance, Margaret Mead, the famous anthropologist, writes, 'To deprive a man of his authority is to make him irresponsible and cause him to act irresponsibly.'[24] Another American writer, George Gilder, writes about this, 'it is difficult to relax and be a man, for manhood is only expressed in action . . . Men are dependent on constant initiative or *the reserving of certain roles as distinctively male*.'[25] This further bears out the theological affirmations that men are called to be the heads of the Church family and the human family, and they will be greatly frustrated if prevented from doing so by women. Women, on the contrary, have been called to help men fulfil this God-given role.

This may be a factor in the alarming rise in male suicides in Britain and the United States. In Britain they have gone up by 80% in the last ten years (1982–92). Dr Chad Varah, the founder of the Samaritans, who specialise in helping such people, blames this rise in part on the concept of the 'new man', the voguish media model of the perfect partner. He said that many men do not know who they are or what is expected of them, particularly in significant relationships. He calls it 'an identity crisis'.[26]

It is the recovery of fatherhood that is the greatest need in our society, not least because the father more than the mother has the responsibility of instilling discipline and respect for authority into the children. The writer of the Letter to the Hebrews *assumes* that fathers do this. 'For what son is not disciplined by his father? . . . Everyone undergoes discipline.' And 'we have all had human fathers who disciplined us, and we respected them for it' (Heb. 12:7–9). In fact the writer goes so far as to say that if children are not disciplined, 'then you are illegitimate children and not true sons'. The absence of fathers is probably the main contributing factor in the rise in crime, violence, delinquency, illiteracy, and vandalism. When the Church replaces some 'fathers' with 'mothers', it is adding to the problem, not helping to solve it.

Chapter 19

Equality and order in the family: mothers and children

> Children, obey your parents in the Lord, for this
> is right. 'Honour your father and mother' – which
> is the first commandment with a promise – 'that it
> may go well with you and that you may enjoy long
> life on the earth.'
>
> (Eph. 6:1–2)

There is an old Jewish proverb: 'God could not be everywhere, therefore he made mothers.' Of course, God can be everywhere, but there is a grain of truth in the proverb concerning the ubiquitousness of mothers. However, today there is a deeply tragic element to it. The anthropologist Margaret Mead has written, 'men suffer from too few roles at the moment, women from a multiplicity of roles. Women are exhausted.'[1] This is particularly true in the home, where women have often these days to be the main bread-winners, and care for the children also, not only in single parent families, but also in many other families where the father simply opts out of home and family responsibilities. So let's look at what has been happening to mothers.

Deflected mothers

If fathers have walked out of the home, and away from their duties in them, mothers have been deflected from theirs, the care and nurture of children. In my stress on the patriarchal

I would not want anyone to conclude that I am minimising the eminent role of mothers in the home. Their relationship to their children begins at conception, and they normally have a greater influence on them than the father at least until the children are five. It would be wrong also to attempt to evaluate who is the guilty party in the single parent scenario. There is usually blame on both sides. But the ultimate responsibility for the well-being of the wife and the home is the husband's. So it is the men who must shoulder much of the blame.

One of the main culprits in the break-down of family life is the message of radical feminism. One of its chief tenets was to take mothers out of the home and away from their children. They compared the drudgery and pettiness of the domestic scene, with the exciting life of a career alongside men. Day care centres became surrogate mothers. We have already mentioned Kathy Gyngell earlier in the book, who was once a militant feminist. She gave up her career because she could not be separated from her son Adam. 'Nobody warned me,' she wrote in the *Daily Mail*, 'of the near panic I'd suffer driving home through rush-hour traffic to feed him.'[2] When she decided to give up her career for motherhood, the idea was met with disbelief by female colleagues. They told her she would be 'bored'. One 'expert' told her not to feel guilty. 'Such is the power of feminist thinking,' she concludes. She lists a terrible indictment of feminists and the damage they have done:

1. They have undermined and denigrated the option of mother-hood as a career.
2. They have viewed children as commodities without unique individualised emotional needs.
3. They have perpetuated the myth that 'other' care is as good as 'mother' care.
4. They have not challenged the Establishment view that mothers are economically inactive.

She concludes by saying, 'feminists may complain that it is unfair that mothers are primarily responsible for the upbringing of their children. But it is an unavoidable fact of life.'

Here the question of higher education comes up. Usually in their interviews our daughters are asked what they are going to do when they leave college. What happens if they say, 'I am going to get married and have lots of children'? If they did say this, they might be refused entry. So from the outset there is pressure on women to choose careers rather than be mothers, unless they are prepared to have small families.

The churches have done very little to help in this family/career tension. However, there is always Mothering Sunday. But even this occasion now depresses some people. Minette Marrin, writing in the *Sunday Telegraph*, says she finds little to celebrate about it.[3] Motherhood is undermined from every side. How has this happened? Quite rightly she blames the 'experts'. First the smart counsellors, who show us how mothers have harmed their children. In the United States children now sue their parents for rearing malpractice. She writes:

> It is because of these beliefs that contemporary women cannot stand up to their children; terrified of traumatising them, hating their own mothers and fearful of the wrath to come, they appease them in every way, in the hope of being liked for just a little longer . . . They have made our own mothers obsolete; we are encouraged to sneer at their outdated ideas. But even in sneering we see the first intimations of our own obsolescence . . . they were wrong and our mothers were right.

There has been much controversy over the development of the European Community, and the sovereignty issue. Or in other words, who rules Britain, Westminster or Brussels? What has escaped the attention of most people is the influence of the United Nations, and its legally binding Conventions, which are never agreed in Parliament, and yet are signed by the government. One of these was the Convention on the Elimination of All Forms of Discrimination Against Women. This was passed by the United Nations on 3 September 1980, and ratified by the United Kingdom in 1986 by Mrs Thatcher's government. A great deal of this Convention covers non-controversial ground, which would carry general acceptance, matters like equality for men and women in law, education, and the franchise.

But when we look a little closer at it, we find the feminist influence has got in there too. It speaks of the need for a 'change in the traditional role of men as well as the role of women in society and in the family . . . to achieve full equality between men and women'. That is pure feminism for you. It condemns any 'distinction, exclusion or restriction' in the political '*or any other field*'. It calls on over 200 nations 'to eliminate practices based on stereotyped roles of men and women'. It then states that there should be no discrimination against women on grounds of marriage or maternity, and the need to ensure *their effective right to work*. It goes on to demand that nations 'provide child-care facilities to enable parents to combine family obligations with work responsibilities and participation in public life'. So we see that the world has been committed for many years now to the feminist doctrine of undifferentiated equality which makes no distinctions regarding the roles of men and women. It has pledged the entire world to giving the careers of mothers priority over their place in the home bringing up children.

I made some enquiries about the legal status in this country of United Nations Conventions, ratified by the United Kingdom. In a letter from the Foreign and Commonwealth Office I was told, 'these conventions *are legally binding* on those states that have ratified them. Although international treaties are not directly part of our domestic law unless incorporated by legislation, our law (statute and common law) *does protect the rights in the conventions, which we have undertaken to respect and ensure*.'[4] That's a little scary, but wait until we look at the Convention on the Rights of Children! Before we pass on, it is worth asking why the United Nations has never produced a Convention on the family? Has it ceased to believe in it too?

Neglected children

The pain of men and women going through the trauma of divorce, and the strain of many women caring for their families without fathers is immense. But they at least have chosen this path. They could have done otherwise. Children have no such choices in the matter. They cannot pick their parents like their parents picked each other. They are the innocent sufferers in situations of spiralling distress. 'The family will outlive its critics,' the Chief Rabbi (Dr Sacks) writes in *The Times*, 'but its temporary eclipse will cause pain to those who deserve it least, our children.'

No pictorial images have brought this home to me more powerfully than the photo of the American soldier Hollie Vallance holding her seven-week-old baby before leaving for Operation Desert Shield. Or another of a young father holding a child in his arms while waving goodbye to his wife, a soldier in the United States Army bound for the Gulf. Can we honestly say that is 'natural'? The feminist soldier Lori Moore sadly comments, 'children are the unsung victims of Operation Desert Shield'.[5]

The figures for child abuse itself are disgraceful for a society which calls itself 'civilised'. But what happens to the minds and personalities of these innocent victims? There is also the increasing risk that youngsters who go through an unstable childhood are much more likely to repeat the same pattern of mistrust and instability in their own family life. Most single parents do not stay single. They cohabit or marry again, before once again experiencing separation or divorce. Cohabitation is a recipe for disaster, because of the knock-on effect it has in instability. Today more than 30% of babies born in Britain are born out of wedlock. One in five children experience family breakdown by the age of sixteen. Every year in this country over 8,000 under-age girls become pregnant, *which is six times higher than in the rest of Europe*. Is it any wonder that we are seeing such a rise in suicides amongst young people? Statistics show that 86% of teenage suicides are in fatherless families. Having grown up in such misery they see no way of breaking out of the cycle of despair.

Larry Christenson, who with his sister has contributed the foreword to this book, told me how he recently bumped into a Professor from the Lutheran Seminary where he had trained many years before. Both were catching a flight at an American airport. Larry had not seen him since leaving college. So he asked the Professor, 'What change have you noticed most in these years?' The Professor replied that the thing that troubled him most was that in the United States, 'children are no longer cherished'.

A British economist, Sylvia Ann Hewlett, remarked to UNICEF some years ago that all United Nations agencies seemed to concentrate on the Third World when dealing with child-related problems. She was promptly asked to do a research job for UNICEF which has now been published. It is a damning indictment of two countries in particular, the United States and Britain. *They are the only two countries in the world in which the well-being of children is actually getting worse.*[6]

Birth control

Actually, at least in the West, it is becoming more and more unlikely you will even be conceived. This is because an increasing number of married couples are deciding not to have children because they interfere with their careers. An even larger number of parents are deciding to have fewer children, and the birth rate is plummeting dangerously in the whole of the Western world. For a stable population there must be a total period fertility rate of 2.1 children per woman; Britain has 1.8, Germany 1.6, and Spain 1.4. We are literally destroying ourselves, and, of course depriving millions of potential people of the right to live. The lowest birthrate in Europe is now Italy, where it is 1.25, the lowest recorded birthrate in the history of humankind. It has been estimated that if rates continue at this level the population of Italy will be nil in 150 years.

In 1968 Pope Paul VI issued the Encyclical *Humanae Vitae*, which plunged the Catholic Church into turmoil. A commission had sat and advised the Pope to liberalise the Church's laws relating to birth control. The Pope did the opposite. Paul Johnson, then Editor of the *New Statesman* caught the mood with his statement, 'most Catholic parents feel they know more about the practical problems of married life than an elderly bachelor in Rome'. But times have changed. In the Encyclical the Pope wrote that the mass use of contraceptives would 'result in marital infidelity and a general lowering of moral standards'. The elderly bachelor has been proved right in this statement. The problem in Europe at all events is not too many children, but too few. It is no longer the doomsday scenario of a population explosion, or 'popullution' as the Green Party now calls it. Instead we are facing population *implosion*. Easy contraception and abortion have deeply influenced the social mores of Western society. We are having to pay a terrible price for not heeding this particular warning of Pope Paul VI.

Neil Lyndon writes about this, 'the introduction of infallible contraception vitiated the offence of adultery at its root. If sexual intercourse outside marriage need not involve the risk of children being born, the act of adultery need not be seen automatically as offering a threat to the essential substance of the marriage contract.'[7] So the Divorce Reform Bill of 1969, passed two years after *Humanae Vitae*, was to be called 'the adulterers' charter'.

Another side to this in Britain is the ethnic mix. One in five of the white population is under sixteen, compared with one in three among coloured people. The birth rate among coloured people is higher (2.5%), but amongst Pakistanis and Bangladeshis it is more than twice the white rate (4.6%). Two out of three of such households are the traditional family unit, compared with one in four in the white community. In Britain the disintegration of the family is largely a white problem, whereas in the United States it is much more a black problem.

Abortion

Having overcome the first hurdle when conception takes place, the womb is no longer a place of security for some babies. In Britain at least 200,000 babies a year some time between conception and birth, are legally dismembered limb by limb, sometimes for no other reason than the birth is inconvenient. Abortion has been described as 'the invisible holocaust'.[8] Martha Crean, writing in the *Toronto Life* has said, 'the Victorians used to hide the pregnant woman. Now we hide the child. Permanently.'[9]

We have seen how 'rights' now dominate the thinking of modern people. One of the latest is the right of a woman 'to control her own body', which means to have an abortion whenever she likes, and whether the potential father is in agreement or not. It should be argued that women should control their bodies better *before* they get pregnant; and that what we should teach our children is less about birth control and more about self-control. This applies also to the men.

One of the new sugar-coated palliatives to the horrors of abortion is 'every child a wanted child'. The argument is simple. Only have a child if you want a child. If an accident takes place, get rid of it if you don't want it. We have seen throughout this book that society, when it is out of touch with God, will become more and more unnatural.

Uncared-for children

Then, if birth eventually is allowed to take place, the chances are increasingly slim of that child having a father, or a home instead of a day care centre. It has now been proved that such children are far more prone to illness, drug abuse, and a life of crime. They will also die earlier than children growing up in a healthy home. Someone has said about day care centres, 'working parents want day care. What children want . . . is their parents'.[10] It is increasingly unlikely they will get them.

We have already seen how feminism has wheedled its way into a Convention of the United Nations. We should not, therefore, be surprised when we find the same imprint on the Convention on the Rights of the Child. This extraordinary document was passed by the United Nations on 20 November 1989, and ratified by the British Conservative government on 19 April 1990. The Foreign Office assures me it is regarded in British law in the same way as other UN Conventions. It is Articles 13, 14, 16 and 18 which I want to refer to.

A person ceases to be a child according to this Convention when they attain the age of eighteen. So it includes most of the teenage years as well as childhood. Remember these are rights which are *legally enforceable*. So let us see what these rights include. Article 13 gives children and teenagers the right to 'freedom of expression'. This means that minors can choose what kind of sex education they receive, what TV programmes and videos they watch, and what books and magazines they read. The rights of parents can be overruled by the children.

Article 14 gives children and teenagers 'freedom of thought, conscience and religion'. There is here a rider that mentions the need to respect the rights and duties of parents. But the gist of the Article would suggest that children could overrule their parents, and they would have the right, for example, to join a witches' coven if they so wished, or engage in child sex, even if the parents disapproved.

Article 15 gives children and teenagers 'freedom of association and of peaceful assembly'. Here parents don't get a look in at all. So minors have the freedom to choose whether to join the church youth fellowship or the Hell's Angels. A twelve-year-old has legal rights to associate with whom he or she pleases.

Many in Britain now join the criminal class at a very tender age. Parents and the police can do little about it. In a speech in the House of Commons, Lady Olga Maitland horrified her fellow members with information about a gang that operates in her own constituency of Sutton and Cheam, which is by no stretch of the imagination an area of social deprivation.[11] The gang calls itself the 'Sutton Burglary Posse' and operates with business cards to leave behind after a visit. They are all aged fourteen or younger, and so cannot be touched by the law. One of the leaders has been arrested more than 40 times and has 200 charges against him. On one occasion he was in court to face 21 charges ranging from causing bodily harm to burglary, receiving stolen property, stealing cars etc. He walked out of court virtually free. The United Nations could have had no idea what legal minors are today capable of doing.

United Nation Conventions are little known, but there was an interesting article in *The Times* by Janet Daley reflecting on this one.[12] In referring to the changed relationship between parents and children in Britain she writes, 'the young do not consider their parent's authority to be either sacrosanct or fearsome. They are very aware (as their parents) that they may call in the law to protect themselves against over enthusiastic discipline.' Towards the end of 1993 a Gallup survey was published on the theme, 'youth crime in 90s Britain'. It reveals that the problems of discipline are almost too far gone for the police to handle, and that they are really *rooted in the home*. Janet Daley concludes that children today are suffering from deprivation, but of what are they deprived? 'Perhaps,' she writes, 'more than anything it is the privilege of growing up with an unequivocal sense of right and wrong.'

But the Convention goes from bad to worse. Article 16 grants them 'the right to privacy' and they are not to be 'subject to arbitrary or unlawful interference' in the pursuit of such rights. Thus parents have no rights to look into what a teenager does in his room, or even whom he might invite into that room. It also includes 'correspondence'. Any child can, therefore, receive hard porn literature through the post, and parents cannot stop it.

Article 18, clause 3, is an astonishing one. Let me quote: 'children of working parents have the *right* to benefit from child-care services'. In case you should think that I am exaggerating the artlessness of this extraordinary document, which gives children rights over parents, please note the Vatican's reservations expressed when they signed it. They insisted on the right to interpret them 'in a way which safeguards the primary and inalienable rights of parents, particularly in the field of education (articles 13, 28), religion (article 14), association with others (article 15) and privacy (article 16)'. The Islamic countries (Kuwait, Saudi Arabia etc.) rejected anything 'incompatible with Islamic law' (which would rule out all the articles I have mentioned). But Britain and all the rest of the Western world blithely signed without a single question mark about the way this Convention undermines almost completely parental rights and authority over their children. Again egalitarianism has triumphed over traditional family values.

Most will, I am sure, agree that the facts and comments I have made are gravely disturbing for the future of family life in our world. I do not blame the Church of England and the rest of the Protestant world for creating the problem. But they are surely responsible for adding to and confusing it, and for seriously undermining the basic biblical structure of the family. In other words the churches who have done this will increasingly themselves be part of the problem not the answer. The true solution is in recovery of biblical and traditional family values. These include the headship of the husband, the helper role of the wife in simple submission, the commitment of the mother to the home in preference to her career, and the care and authority of the parents, inculcating rule and discipline in the home as well as loving attention from the cradle onwards.

It is much more difficult for these family values to be expressed in our homes, if they are not also in the Church. The Church should be the model for home life. The substitution of mothers in place of fathers in the Church is not only disobedience to God's Word, but confusing the natural order of patriarchy. Ultimately it will do untold harm and the knock-on effect on the family will cause great damage to an institution which is already fragile.

I make no apologies for the time I have spent on the UN Conventions, because they show the *international influence of feminism* and its egalitarian principles. It is these precepts which have been embraced knowingly or unknowingly by those who are pressing ahead with the ordination of women. Thus men and women are deemed to be 'equal' not only in their natures, but in their roles. The logical outcome of this is that parents and children are also 'on the level'. You can hardly argue *against* the husband/wife hierarchy, and *for* the parent/child. Thus you raise the rights of children to the same level as the parents.

Our Western churches have become so utopian in their ideology, they are prone to a naivety which is positively dangerous. Thus biblical principles are laid on one side, in the pursuit of idealism, which has no chance of triumphing in a world prone to wickedness. We dream of perfect systems. Then no one is required to be virtuous. The natural law that God has set in place, and which we tamper with at our peril, is to restrain evil as well as to promote goodness. For authority to 'work', there must be an hierarchical structure in the home as well as in the Church and the world.

We live in a world obsessed with the pursuit of 'rights' and with the hunt for equality. Nothing else seems to matter. The United Nations continues to produce endless Conventions on Rights. These are eagerly signed by nations some of whom are indicted by Amnesty International for using torture to extract confessions from political prisoners. So much for Human Rights! Countries rush to sign agreements giving voting rights to women, when they don't even give them to *men* in their own countries. They are happy to grant rights of privacy to children, when their prisons are overcrowded with dissidents and others who have no hope of a fair trial. Rights without responsibilities are a dangerous delusion.

The debate about the ordination of women is in a large measure about women's rights. It is the claim for equal rights without the complementary truth of differing roles. It leads to the undermining of authority, because it denies the God-created and hierarchical structure of the family. The Church should be setting a good example through its structures of what family life is all about. By reversing male and female roles it is disobeying the Creator, and making a confused situation even more chaotic. It is a blow against the family not for it, when it is facing challenges which could bring about its complete collapse.

One of the most ancient symbols of the Cross and the sacrament of the Eucharist is the pelican, seen in ancient drawings using its own beak to draw blood from its own veins to feed its young. It would be a good symbol of father and mother love for their own children, their willingness to make personal sacrifices for their well-being. A recovery of what has in the past been normal and natural love for children is essential if the West is not going to slide into anarchy and ruin. We need no one to tell us that the future health of our society depends on our children.

Sylvia Ann Hewlett writes in her UNICEF report, 'the day will come when the progress of a nation is judged not by its military and economic strength . . . but by the health and civilised behaviour of its children. *Nothing is more important.*'[13]

Chapter 20

Ecumenical suicide

The real ecumenical crisis today is not between
Catholics and Protestants but between traditional
and experimental forms of church life.

(Harvey Cox)

In the last chapter we looked at the serious crisis affecting the
family in British society. We saw the urgent need for a return
to the traditional values of the family, and how the ordaining
of women is taking the churches in the opposite direction, in
defiance of God's order in nature, and his declared will in the
Scriptures. When we turn to the subject of unity, it is even
more obvious that the doctrine of the 'five-legged dog' is not
going to help our relationships with those churches which still
say they have four. And when these comprise the largest, oldest
and most international churches in the world, there is trouble
ahead. In fact for the time being we will have to forget the
possibility of unity with these churches.

Before we turn to the other churches, we need to look at the
obstacles which stand in the way of the unity of the Church of
England, and the larger Anglican Communion. On the broader
front about half of the Communion world-wide is still against the
ordination of women. In the Church of England the proportions
are about one third to two thirds.

A bridge down at both ends

It has often been said that the Anglican Church was 'a bridge church'. Its roots go back to Celtic Christianity, which was more Eastern than Western, more charismatic than institutional, and to do with the heart as well as the mind. The coming of Augustine to Canterbury (in 597) and the Synod of Whitby (in 664) meant that the Celtic and the Western Church were merged. At the Reformation the Church in England became 'Reformed', though retaining much of its Catholic heritage, and certainly its Catholic episcopate.

The Reformation Settlement tried, without success as it turned out, to retain within the one Church many strands of teaching and tradition (except the Roman Catholic). The ethos of the Church of England has often been described as 'tolerant'. Its history shows the opposite. In 1662, for instance, the Church of England insisted on the Act of Uniformity being passed, which unchurched 2,000 clergy without compensation. Some ended up literally as prisoners of conscience, others were transported from Britain. In the end it was Parliament that insisted that the Church should allow religious freedom to all British subjects. A Church which could not comfortably contain a Richard Baxter, a John Wesley or a John Henry Newman, can hardly be called 'tolerant'. Baxter, who has been described as 'the champion of moderation', was given the classic Anglican treatment for prophets – he was offered the Bishopric of Hereford! When he turned it down, he was made redundant, not being allowed even to return to Kidderminster, the scene of his greatest work.

John Wesley, arguably one of the greatest Englishmen of his generation, was never honoured by the Church of England. Instead he was ostracised to the day of his death, although he remained loyally an Anglican to the end. John Henry Newman was another man with a brilliant mind, who probably influenced the Roman Catholic Church more than any other person of that generation. One could add many other names to this list. In comparison the Roman Catholic Church has been more successful in retaining the services of its prophets and saints. The Church of England's toleration has tended to extend only to those who are themselves 'tolerant'. Moderates always find fellow moderates easier to get on with than enthusiasts! People with convictions are embarrassing to our national church.

A bridge has been defined as 'a structure providing a way across something' or 'something that joins or connects or supports other parts'. The British Parliament, which has sought to keep a weather eye on its spiritual partner, has insisted on toleration from the eighteenth century onwards. Without showing much enthusiasm for its 'movers and shakers', the Church has been forced to accept the Evangelical Revivals of the eighteenth and nineteenth centuries, the Oxford Movement of the nineteenth century, and the Charismatic Renewal of the twentieth. All three movements still have a place in the Church of England, although the continuing presence of the Anglo-Catholics, descendants of Pusey and Newman, is at grave risk because of the ordination of women. They make up, together with the Liberals, the arches of the 'bridge', which stretches between the Roman Catholic and Orthodox river-bank on the one hand, to the Evangelical and Free Church bank on the other. Thus the Church of England, while maintaining her Catholic roots going right back to the Celtic past, has embraced, albeit without much enthusiasm, Evangelicalism, the rebirth of Catholicism, and her ancient Charismatic heritage.

To return to the 'bridge' analogy. The Church of England has been a bridge also across the ecumenical divide. It has been a meeting place for different spiritual movements and emphases, a chance to see how they relate to each other, and function in unity. It has been one of the few examples in the history of Christianity of the successful combining of so many strands of the world-wide Church in one organisational structure.

Most of this now lies shattered. It is a dream which has become a nightmare. The Church of England has knocked down two arches of the bridge. The Catholic arch has gone. That means that the 'special relationship' which Anglicans have long had with the Vatican has vanished. The dialogue will continue, but now the Roman Catholics will be relating to a Free Church, not a church which has long claimed to be part of the Catholic Church and to have valid orders. Also the Evangelical arch has gone. It is true that some Evangelicals see no problems with the ordination of women. But there are many who do, and see this as a betrayal of scriptural principles. They will now turn in on themselves, and increasingly follow an independent line.

When we turn to the wider Anglican Communion the picture becomes distressing. Here we see a clash between our Western culture of equality and feminism, with the quite different and more traditional and 'natural' culture of Africa, Asia and Latin America. The pressure to conform to Western culture can so easily become a kind of 'neo-colonialism'. Michael Ovey and Peter Walker write about this in a booklet on the subject of gender.[1] They refer to what they call 'geographical arrogance'. They go on, 'We are in danger of baptising as eternal truth [i.e. the ordination of women] what is simply the opinion of some in the West in the late twentieth century.'

One hopes that the Third World will not buy into this. African, Asian and Latin American culture is strongly patriarchal, and family life is still largely intact. They are in no doubt that dogs have four legs. They have always believed it, and always will if left to themselves. However, there is mounting evidence that the diseases of the West are being spread, sometimes by Church leaders, and it will have disastrous consequences. The people who are hurt most are the poor. The West is able to cope to some extent with the problems of large-scale family breakdowns because of the Welfare State. But in most Third-World countries, *the family is the Welfare State*. If that goes, there is nothing left. We need to think twice before we export our feminist agenda to the Third World.

Examples of the distressing changes taking place in Third-World countries at this time are given in a book by William Hamilton-Dalrymple called *City of Djinns: a Year in Delhi*.[2] He visited Delhi after the passage of several years, and writes of the changes he saw. He refers to the damburst of Western goods and ideas now pouring into India which brought with them an undertow of Western morality. 'Adulterous couples now filled the public gardens,' he writes, 'condom advertisements dominate the Delhi skyline. The Indian capital, once the last bastion of the chaperoned bride, the double-locked bedroom and the arranged marriage, was slowly filling with lovers, whispering, blushing, occasionally holding hands . . . Delhi was starting to unbutton. After the long Victorian twilight, the sari was beginning to slip.'

This is not to say that the lot of women in these countries is all that it should be. Double standards are still common. Women's lives are often rigidly circumscribed. But to attempt to change this by turning nature upside down is not the answer. Sadly Western coercion, backed sometimes with hard cash, is affecting the Third World. Africans, tempted to want to be more Western, and to please their benefactors, are prepared to conform and ordain women. They are usually a small token number of women, counter-cultural, and so unacceptable within their own culture.

Closing doors

The determination to ordain women has caused a deep rift in the Church of England and the wider Anglican Communion. When we turn to relations with the Roman Catholic and Orthodox Churches, the decision has been disastrous, and the Church of England was warned well in advance. In our relationship with the Roman Catholic Church it has put back the ecumenical clock 70 years. It was in 1921 that the informal Malines Conversations started, the first ecumenical contact between the two churches. It is clear that the *chief* hope of reunion has always been a satisfactory agreement to recognise each other's orders. There is now no hope whatsoever that such an agreement will ever be reached while women are ordained. No doubt polite conversations will continue. There will be talk of 'co-operation', but the goal of reunion is now firmly on the back burner. The Roman Catholic position on the ordination of women was made clear by the statement *Inter Insigniores*, issued by the Pontifical Congregation for the Doctrine of the Faith in 1976. It described the unbroken tradition of the male priesthood as having a 'normative character'.

There have been frequent warnings circulated by the Vatican that they would regard the ordination of women as a serious hindrance to unity. Pope John Paul II has issued many cautions, as has the Council for Promoting Christian Unity. Cardinal Cassidy, the head of this body said, just after the decision had been taken, 'the Holy Spirit does not contradict himself. He has spoken to the Church for almost 2,000 years in one way on this issue. It would be very strange if he spoke in a different way now'. Or in other words, dogs have had four legs for 2,000 years, how is it you now say they have five?

When we turn to the second largest church in the world, the Orthodox, we find even greater concern expressed. A friend of mine, who is an African bishop, was attending a meeting with the Head of the Egyptian Coptic Church, Pope Shenouda III. Someone asked what he thought of the new female Episcopal bishop (Barbara Harris), who had just been consecrated in the United States. 'A woman cannot be the head of the Church,' he replied, 'and if she is she will be the headache of the Church.'

When the Episcopal Church of the United States (ECUSA) agreed to ordain women the Orthodox response was immediate and definite. Father Alexander Schmemann said, 'it is tantamount for us to a radical and irreparable mutilation of the entire faith, the rejection of the whole of scripture . . .'[3] Father Thomas Hopko called it 'disastrous'.[4] In Britain Bishop Kallistos Ware termed it 'a chasm of horrifying dimensions'.[5]

Archbishop Athenagoras has written that the demand for women priests is 'a contemporary fashion which overthrows the evangelical order and the experience of the Church'.[6] During the Anglican-Orthodox Consultations, the Orthodox Church has always stated their position clearly and firmly. At one of the meetings in Athens in 1978, the Orthodox went so far as to say that the 'foundation of Christian faith is at stake'. To ordain women 'is a violation of the apostolic faith and of the apostolical order in the Church'.[7] When the Convention of the Antiochian Orthodox Church in America met in 1973, *the women* instigated and passed a resolution that the matter not even be considered by the convention delegates.[8] The long-standing friendship between the Anglican and Orthodox churches has been deeply affected by what has happened.

At the Lambeth Conference of 1988 the Roman Catholic speaker (Bishop Pierre Duprey of the Council for Promoting Christian Unity) was tactful and did not mention the subject of the ordination of women directly. By contrast the Orthodox representative (Professor John Zizioulas, Metropolitan of Pergamos) tackled it head-on. In fact the major part of his address was on this subject. He described it as 'extremely undesirable'.[9] He then went on to urge that 'no decision should be reached without an exhaustive *theological* debate of the issue'. He then said that the churches had not yet begun to treat this matter seriously at the ecumenical level. The Bishop then went on to castigate both sides – 'traditionalists', for only producing arguments concerning traditional practice, and the 'feminists', arguments based on 'sociological concerns'. He counselled the Anglican Church to join with other churches in a theological debate 'at the ecumenical level'. This plea sadly fell on deaf ears. Nothing was ever done about it. It has often been claimed that a 'thorough' debate has taken place on the issue of the ordination of women. This may be true at a superficial level. But the *theological* debate never took place at the ecumenical level.

Sadly, the olive branch put out at Lambeth in 1988 by the Orthodox Church was never accepted. Rightly Professor Zizioulas accused the churches of making theology a secondary, or even an irrelevant matter in the quest for Christian unity. He warned that 'the cost can be too great for the Church of Christ to pay'. The cost to the Church of England is going to be heavy in the days to come. The cost to Christian unity is incalculable.

The Church of England has ceased to be a 'bridge' church, by its own decision which effectively demolished both ends of the bridge. It is not all loss, because it will now be closer to the Free Churches, Methodists, United Reformed Church and others. Some accused the Church of voting to become a 'sect'. A 'Free Church' is a better description. The Church of England has effectively lost its special relationship with the Catholic and Orthodox Churches, and with it any hope of future reunion. But all churches have suffered loss because of this, and the credibility of the Ecumenical Movement has been badly damaged.

Chapter 21

Spotting the elephants

There are theologians who claim to see fernseed
and can't see an elephant ten yards away in broad
daylight.

(C. S. Lewis)

C. S. Lewis was a master of the art of exposing error and
revealing truth through the use of simple analogies. The seed of
the fern plant is so small you can barely see it with the human eye.
The elephant only the blind can miss! So he saw some theologians
as experts at focusing on small and comparatively unimportant
things, while at the same time missing the big ones.[1] Jesus used
a similar analogy when he talked about those who 'strain out
the gnat, but swallow a camel' (Mt. 23:24). One thing about an
elephant is that it can't be hidden. It is too big for that. *You will
only miss it if you are looking in the wrong direction.*

There is something strange happening in our world. In the
last few years unprecedented concern has been expressed for
'Green' issues. Our polluted planet has been the subject of
endless debate. Depletion of the ozone layers, destruction of
rain forests, global warming and similar matters, have been
discussed at the highest levels. Christians have joined in, and
invoked God the Creator, and his concerns for what he has made.
But very few people seem aware that God created gender as well
as the material world and the animal kingdom. The Creator has
just as great concern for gender, and I don't only mean sexual
behaviour, as he has for ecology and conservation. How is it
that people have missed this huge elephant, or failed to see the
connection with the creation?

In my reading up of this subject I turned to James Houston's book *I believe in the Creator*.[2] This is a good thought provoking book on the creation, but when I turned up the subject of the creation of sex, I found *nothing*. It is hard to believe that someone writing about God the Creator, and who has brought up a family of five, should have nothing to say about gender. It may be a commentary on our times. Perhaps we have become so saturated with sex, and so sickened with its banality, we would rather keep off the subject. Perhaps feminist equality has so got through to us that the androgynous syndrome (male and female combined in one organism) is beginning to take over. Or maybe we are getting so used to gender confusion, the distinctions don't matter any more.

A devastating prophecy for today

In Isaiah 3 the prophet delivers a terrible indictment of the society of his day. As we read it we shall see that it speaks about our day too:

1. The people are about to become leaderless. The Lord is taking away the leaders of the army, the judges, the prophets, the elders etc. (v. 2).
2. In their place 'mere children will govern' (v. 4).
3. There will be a rebellion of the young against the old and the base against the honourable (v. 5).
4. There will be a retreat from leadership and taking responsibility; 'do not make me the leader of the people' is the cry (vv. 5–7).
5. Sin will be openly and unashamedly paraded as it was in Sodom, where homosexuality was practised as a legitimate lifestyle (v. 9).
6. Young people will tyrannise the people (v. 12).
7. *Women will rule over the people* (v. 12). They are described as 'haughty . . . flirting with their eyes . . .' (v. 16), so 'the Lord will make their scalps bald' (v. 17).
8. Judgement is predicted for the people of God. This will include the situation in which 'seven women will take hold of one man and will say, "take away our disgrace"' (Is. 4:1).

There are few passages in the Old Testament more applicable
to our day and situation than this one. Here we see a retreat from
the duties of leadership, which today is part of the egalitarian
message, the removal of hierarchy from Church and society, and
the determining of key matters by democratic voting. Here we
see society withdrawing from moral judgement, while flaunting
its immorality shamelessly as Sodom did. We too live in a society
with few moral opinions about homosexuality, divorce, abortion
or cohabitation, to mention a few. What is worse we have
Church leaders who are also ambivalent about many aspects of
morality, and sanction evils such as homosexual practices. Again
and again it is only the voices of the Roman Catholic and Orthodox
Churches, and Jewish leaders who are heard in protest.

We see in all this the inversion of the natural, and so often
its perversion. We see the young taking authority over their
elders, and women over men. So the divine laws of nature are
transposed, the young no longer submitting to their elders, or
women to men. 'Haughtiness' is a good word sometimes to
describe the radical feminists who have wrought such havoc in
our Western society. We see the judgement of God today exactly
as in those days, although the circumstances are different. Then
it was war which decimated the male population, so that many
women could not be married and have children. Now it is the
collapse of traditional family life which means that by the end of
this century over 50% of British homes will be fatherless.

When society forsakes God, life becomes unnatural. It is not
just the moral laws which are broken, God's natural laws are
also. Today the churches are as guilty of breaking these laws
as the society within which it is meant to act as salt, leaven
and light. One example of this is the constant attempt by church
leaders to affirm homosexuality. When in 1993 scientists claimed
they had found that homosexual inclinations may be genetically
transmitted, the media greeted the news as a moral bombshell.
Lord Jakobovits, the former Chief Rabbi in Britain, in a letter to
The Times urged ethically sensitive people to defeat this further
attempt to 'erode our transcendent moral values'.[3] He wrote as
a Jew what one longs to hear more Christian leaders declaring:

Homosexuality is a grave departure from the natural norm
which we are charged to overcome like any other affliction,

genetic or not. If natural or hereditary tendencies would entitle us to lay aside the sixth, seventh and eighth of the Ten Commandments we might as well abolish them altogether – and allow civilisation to relapse into moral chaos.

We are living in a period when there has been what Michael Novak calls 'the intellectual shift in our thinking from "natural law" to "natural rights"'.[4] The ordaining of women is another example of this attempt to reverse the laws of nature, and to ignore the principles laid down in both the Old and New Testament. It is the attitude expressed humorously once by Mark Twain, 'lump the whole thing – say that the Creator made Italy from designs by Michelangelo, or something else'. If society is manifestly under the judgement of God, so is the Church. In fact as Peter says, 'it is time for judgement to *begin* with the family of God' (1 Pet. 4:17).

Life in the West is becoming increasingly unnatural. We can no longer take for granted what was the norm a few years ago. An example of this was the photograph published in our newspapers during 1993 of the summit of Mount Everest. In the first place there was about twenty tons of litter there. But in addition there were human bodies, left unburied by successive groups of climbers. It is natural to show reverence for the human body, and all cultures regard the disposal of the human body as something sacred, for which the greatest respect needs to be shown. Different cultures and religions have different ways of showing that respect. In this case the bodies obviously could not be buried on top of the mountain, but they could have been brought down. Lord Hunt, who led the first expedition to climb Everest, commented, 'to leave them there would be unthinkable. It shows an astonishing cynicism about human life.' And Chris Bonington, another Everest climber, wrote 'it was ugly, in many ways a microcosm of all that we have done to our planet'.

But there are far more serious aspects of this turning of the natural laws of the Creator upside-down. Isaiah asks the question, 'can a mother forget the baby at her breast, and have no compassion on the child she has borne?' (Is. 49:15). The implication of the question is that it is a law of nature that mothers love their children and provide for them. It is natural to do so. But it isn't any longer. We talk now about the mother's right to abort a baby (in preference to the rights of the unborn child). Is that not unnatural? We know now of widespread child-battering. Is that natural? Many women now put their careers before their children's welfare. Some married women plan not to have children at all. How unnatural it all is!

When we turn to men, we find them neglecting or ignoring altogether their duties as husbands and fathers. The natural instinct is for men to be protective of their wives and children. To care for them, to spend time with them, teaching and disciplining the children and taking trouble to know them. As we know, in many cases today, the fathers have just walked away from the home. But even those who stay often take little interest in their children and do not share as they should with the nurturing. I say this is unnatural. The normal patriarchal instinct is missing.

Natural laws condemn paganism

One of the most searing passages in the whole Bible exposes the abandoning of the laws of nature. It is Romans 1. Here the apostle turns his searchlight on pagan society of that day, of which our own society has so many corresponding features. He writes of pagan society possessing a 'depraved mind' (v. 28) and 'doing what ought not to be done'. This includes reference to a feature of our own paganism, disobedience towards parents (v. 30). These people not only do awful and unnatural acts, but they 'approve of those who practise them' (v. 32). Here he identifies both lesbianism and homosexuality as the abandoning of the natural for the unnatural.

But the main point of Paul's letter to the Romans, and its terrible indictment of Roman paganism, is that he does not invoke the Word of God, although he could have done. He accuses them of 'suppressing the truth', *not* of the Word of God, of which they had no knowledge, *but of the created order*. They were guilty because the law of nature was 'plain to them' (v. 19), even if the Word of God was not. Paul argues that from the moment of creation God's nature had been 'clearly seen being understood from what has been made, so that men are without excuse' (v. 20). In other words, Paul does not condemn pagans because they had broken the Ten Commandments, of which they were ignorant anyway. The wrath of God is against them because they break the laws of creation, for which there is no excuse.

It is this which is the most serious indictment against the modern Church which ordains women in direct contradiction of both the creation laws of Genesis and the words of the apostle Paul, and condones the unnatural behaviour of homosexuals and lesbians. When Paul turns (Rom. 2) to the Jews, who do have the Law, he says that they too are under the judgement of God, and they have no excuse, because they cannot plead ignorance as the pagans can. The law of God is even plainer than the law of creation. They should know better. For those who reject the truth and follow evil, Paul writes, 'there will be wrath and anger . . . trouble and distress' (Rom. 2:8–9).

To return to the main theme of this book, the pagans of Paul's day were saying that dogs have five legs. Paul is saying they have four, and nature confirms this. Even if you were able through genetic engineering to produce a dog with five legs, it would be created in direct disobedience of the Creator, who decided that dogs should have four legs. That was his decision, and it is not for us to question it, or try to change it. God has created a world, in which men and women have different but complementary roles. Men cannot be mothers, and women cannot be fathers. Men are created to be the heads of communities. Women are called to be alongside the men to help them to do what they were created to do; they are not called to take over from them the role of headship. That is an act of disobedience towards the One who made us.

What makes this controversy so acutely painful and bewildering – the *imbroglio* I referred to earlier – is that equally intelligent and devout people are caught up in it and are coming to opposite opinions. George Carey, in his famous *Readers' Digest* interview said, 'the idea that only a male can represent Christ at the altar is a most serious heresy'. He went on to describe this view, held by many of his fellow Anglicans, as 'devastating and destructive'. That is strong language! Later he retracted the word 'heresy' and substituted 'serious theological error', which I suppose is a more polite way of saying it. I have pointed out that the Church Fathers usually put the ordination of women in the category of 'heresy', and they were less polite about it in those days than we are. How is it we have reached such an impasse?

The warning of old heresies

As we have seen in Chapter 11, the Church was soon embroiled in heated disputes with heretics. There were quite a few, but three stand out. The first, largest and most influential, and, therefore, dangerous was Gnosticism. The other two were associated with the names of Marcion and Montanus. If we look closely at them we shall see some common features, and, more significantly, similarities with our current problem over the ordination of women. The link is an obvious one, because all three heresies ordained women, although Montanism did it at a much later stage.

Let us look at them in turn. Gnosticism is a term applied not only to Christian heresies, but to a wide band of religious beliefs, many of which were common in the East before the coming of Christ. It is generally thought that Paul's letter to the Colossians was written with the rebuttal of Gnosticism mainly in view. Gnosticism also is a prime example of an early form of religious syncretism, the desire to combine many different strands of religious beliefs into one system. Christians for the first time were beguiled into introducing Gnostic ideas alongside the Christian truth. In addition to syncretism, Gnosticism thrived on compromise. Gnostics were prepared to accommodate their beliefs, not only to other religions, but also to the spirit of the age. What is now called 'New Age' is a modern form of this same heresy.

Looking at these three heresies we find a common feature in the way they separated what they believed to be irreconcilable elements. In the case of Gnosticism it was their belief in the evil nature of matter, which meant that God is entirely separated from it. This would rule out the Incarnation, and the Sacraments. There are strong links with the thinking of Eastern religions like Hinduism, as one also finds today in New Age. The denial of the essential goodness of what God has made led them not only to deny the Incarnation, but also God's work in creation, which to them was an accident or a mistake.

The other two heresies did the same thing. Marcion split the Old from the New Testament, and virtually edited out all references to the Old in the New. Jesus' coming was a rescue operation from the bad god of the Old Covenant. Gnosticism was

Christianity *plus*, Marcionism was Christianity *minus*. Both were attempts to over-simplify Christian truth for the more efficient and acceptable marketing of the Gospel.

As we have already noted in Chapter 11, it is unfair to judge the third, Montanism, as a heresy in its early stages. It began as a charismatic renewal movement in the churches, at a time when the churches had become formal and dull. It later became sectarian, and ultimately heretical. One of the major features of Montanism was the gift of prophecy. This was given to women as well as men, and was a frequent occurrence in their worship. Thus from the earliest moment women were ministering as well as men in the churches. It is not surprising that many years later, the Montanists began to ordain women to the priesthood, and this was roundly condemned by the Catholic Church at the time.

We have seen that both Marcion and the Gnostics blundered because they could not reconcile, in the case of Marcion the Old Testament with the New, and in the instance of the Gnostics, God with his creation. In the case of the Montanists, the grounds of their heresy was the splitting of the *ministry* of the Holy Spirit from the *offices* of the Holy Spirit. It was dividing the charismatic from the institutional aspect of the life of the Church.

There are obvious comparisons between Montanism and the twentieth-century Pentecostal and Charismatic Movements. In these we see the same tendency to minimise the place of office and authority in the Church and to maximise that of the charismatic ministries. Added to that is a downgrading of history and tradition, and the making of a fresh start with little or no reference to what has gone before. Since Pentecost, God has always poured out his Spirit on women as well as men, and women excel in many of the charismatic ministries, to which both Scripture and Church Tradition entitle them. But Montanism failed to distinguish between ministry and office.

As the years passed the Church was to be engaged in great disputes. Some of this revolved around the Trinity, but most were about Jesus Christ. Was he God, or just an inspired man? Was he fully human, or some kind of demi-god? Did he have one or two natures? Was he one or two persons? Was he born of a virgin or later 'adopted' by the Father? Various Councils were called by the Church to enable the bishops to discern the truth, and to condemn heresy. Two of these were held at Nicaea

(AD 325) and Chalcedon (AD 451). At the first the heresy of Arius was condemned. He taught that Christ was not fully God. At the second the heresies of Nestorius (Christ was two persons not one) and Eutyches (Christ had one nature not two) were condemned.

The main element in all these heresies was the attempt to reconcile what is irreconcilable, to simplify what is complex, and to make understandable what is mysterious. The Fathers of the Church were right, and the centuries have vindicated them, that finite human beings cannot define the infinite, and often you are bound to accept two apparently irreconcilable truths, rather than try to rationalise them or synthesise them. Thus we believe in three Persons, and one God. We believe in the one Person of Christ, and two natures. Later Protestants were to dispute predestination and freewill. In the end many were to see the truth in *both*, not in one or the other.

We need to apply this to the present dispute over the ordination of women. I believe the basis of the matter concerns two truths, and we are required by Scripture and Tradition to believe both at the same time.

Truth One

Men and women are equal. They are both made in the image of God and share equally in the glories of being created by God, redeemed by Christ, and filled by the Holy Spirit. They both share freely in the riches of God's grace, and will share equally in the glories of eternal life. Being made in the image of God, this human equality reflects the divine equality found within the Persons of the Trinity.

Truth Two

Men and women are different. They were created to have different and complementary roles. Their relationship is defined in terms of male headship and female submission. Being made in the image of God, this relationship reflects the divine headship of the Father and the divine submissiveness of the Son and the Spirit within the unity of the Trinity.

At first sight these two truths are irreconcilable. How can a woman at the same time be equal with a man and submissive to him? Submission in the human mind is so often associated with inferiority, *but it isn't in God's mind because it isn't in God's nature as revealed in the Trinity*.

If we accept only truth one, we are feminists. If we only agree to truth two we are sexists. When we affirm *both* we are traditionalists and proud of it. As traditionalists we follow the example of Jesus Christ, who dealt with and affirmed women equally with men, but appointed only a male apostolate to lead the Church after his departure. We follow in the footsteps of the apostles who affirmed the same two truths as Christ did, welcomed women to share in ministry with the men, but also maintained the truth that the man is the head of the woman, and the woman is submissive to the man, both in the Church and in the human family.

The divine order of these two truths is described by Sheldon Vanauken as

> inbuilt in what God has created. Christians if they are to remain in the Obedience must accept the New Testament teaching on male and female nature and roles. But that teaching is in harmony with the vision of other, non-Christian peoples . . . The subtle Yang and Yin. Animus and Anima. The deep difference. We deny it at our peril. We cannot make a world that is all warp and no woof without disaster.[5]

We must stand in agreement with over 60 generations of Church leaders, who, often at the cost of their lives, faithfully passed on the Scriptures and maintained in the face of many heresies, these two truths. Like Martin Luther, we are bound to say, 'Here I stand, I can do no other.'

Chapter 22

Epilogue:

Learning to be lonely

The strong must learn to be lonely.
    (Henrik Ibsen, last line of *An enemy of the people*)

The Norwegian dramatist Henrik Ibsen probably based the story of his play *An enemy of the people* on two separate incidents. The first was a true story about an Hungarian scientist, who discovered poisoned water in a town's water supply and was pilloried for his discovery, because it embarrassed the 'experts'. He was saying, in our analogy, that dogs have four legs, and everyone else was insisting that they have five. The second incident, which was personally painful to Ibsen, was when he was stoned off the stage after the presentation of another of his controversial plays.

A man called Dr Stockmann is the leading character in *An enemy of the people*. He also has found poison in the town water supply, and is in effect saying that dogs have four legs. Again the all-knowing majority of the people say they have five. He shouts to the crowd who are throwing stones through his windows, 'I am in revolt against the age old lie that *the majority is always right*.' Dr Stockmann goes on, 'Was the majority right when they stood by while Jesus was crucified?' (we are told in the script, 'The crowd is stunned into silence'). Then the last words of the play are interesting. As bricks sail through his windows, Dr Stockmann shouts, 'The strong must learn to be lonely.' So do minorities when faced with the confidence and rhetoric of majorities.

Arthur Miller, the famous American playwright, comments on Ibsen's play, 'it is about an individual in the hands of a majority, and the inviolability of objective truth'.[1] In other words, standing up for the truth that dogs have four legs, when the majority say they have five. We are concerned in this book with objective truth, revealed by God through the Scriptures, and through the faithful handing down of the Church's understanding of them through many generations. It is also about integrity and about swimming against popular streams of opinion, and being misunderstood for doing so.

Minorities are no more guaranteed to be right than majorities. They can sometimes be horribly wrong, as were the followers of the religious extremist David Koresh in Waco, Texas, most of whom lost their lives when their centre was burnt down in April 1993. We must remember that those demanding the ordination of women were once a minority, and some of us believe they were wrong then, as we believe they are still wrong, even with a majority. Kierkegaard once described the majority complex: 'The crowd is untruth.' Majorities can sometimes be right, and minorities sometimes wrong. But majorities are never right because they are majorities, neither are minorities wrong because they are minorities.

Truth and minorities

If you are beguiled into thinking that majorities are always right, ponder for a moment the famous words of Jerome: 'the whole world groaned, and was astonished to find itself Arian . . . the ship of the apostles was in peril, she was driven by the wind. Her sides beaten with the waves; no hope was now left.' Athanasius will be remembered as the man who with a minority of supporters took on the Christian world that had lapsed into the Arian heresy. Truth won in the end, as I am sure it will in this controversy.

We could also recall the Polish scientist Nicolaus Copernicus, who in 1543 expressed the view that the earth and planets move around the sun, and whose views were greeted with incredulity by the majority. The Roman Catholic Church forced Copernicus to renounce his views, and declare that the earth stands still and the sun revolves around it. Or there is the case of Galileo, the Italian who dropped metal objects from the top of the leaning tower of Pisa to show that objects with different masses fall at the same velocity. The minority was right, the majority wrong. The same can be said of Winston Churchill in his 'wilderness years', when he prophesied German aggression, and warned Britain and her allies of the imminent dangers of German rearming. At the time his words fell on deaf ears, and he was despised by the majority of his countrymen. Only a handful of people supported him. But he was later proved correct.

History abounds with further examples. Most of the great things that have been effected in this world have been done by minorities, of which the greatest example is Jesus Christ himself. One of the great fallacies of democracy is that majorities are always right. That is not true, *for they are nearly always wrong.*

Minorities that are right are always ultimately vindicated by history. Cardinal Suenens recalls a conversation he once had with Metropolitan Anthony Bloom. Bloom told the Cardinal he did not see much in a majority deciding over and against a minority. The Cardinal replied that in his view 'The most important opinion within a council is that of the holiest person.' Bloom replied that 'It is much the same in music – the one with the sharpest ear is better able to recognise the off-key note, although he may be the only one to do so.'[2]

What is the minority to do in its loneliness and pain? First, we must be clear that we are not the first to have had to walk this way. The issue was not decided on 11 November 1992. It was not the end of the argument, or the beginning of the end of it. Nor was it, to quote Winston Churchill's words, 'the end of the beginning'. We need faith in God that nothing in his hands is ever wasted. Earlier I said how thankful we should be for the feminists in Corinth; I can say the same for the feminists of our day, who have with great courage raised the gender issue. I believe they are wrong, but they challenge us to take the matter seriously.

We also need to strike the note of repentance. Most of us are guilty to some extent for what has happened. One of the most moving statements of penitence I have read comes from Clarence Haden, an American Episcopal bishop. He expressed his sadness in these words: 'many times I have felt the Church was wrong . . . but I largely remained silent, doing my job as I conceived it as a Bishop in the Church of God . . . *For too long I have remained silent in the face of the inroads made upon the wholeness of the Church by liberals . . .'* There are parts of my own pilgrimage that now shame me. I too have missed what God was saying, and remained silent, when I should have spoken out. This book I trust will be a part of the restitution I owe to the Body of Christ for my sins of omission.

A song and a dance

I want to end this book on a positive and hopeful note. The subject is a glorious one, even if men and women have often sullied it ever since Eden. Our sexuality is a gift of God, his most creative, and full of wonder. Perhaps that is why Satan focuses most frequently on it, and spoils the rest of God's creation through its abuse, and is now dividing the Body of Christ because we don't seem to be able to agree about it.

So let us end with 'a song and a dance' – two more of God's creative gifts which sweeten life for us, and help us to worship our Creator, and enjoy his creation. In the preface to his book *Man and Woman in Christ*,[3] Steve Clark shares about how a prayer group he was a member of used to sing songs which had separate parts for men and women. For a while they did not pay much attention to the two parts, and their music leaders instructed the group to ignore the differences and sing in unison. But then there were those who thought this was insufficient because it did not bring out the differences between men and women, their vocal ranges, tone qualities, and so on.

When they tried it the consensus was that something worthwhile had been added to the worship of God. 'In fact,' he writes, 'most people were enthusiastic about the new dimension of beauty and expression that had been added to our life together.'

Can this not be symbolic for us of the theme of this book? There is much in God's creation that men and women can do and enjoy together. There is a place for singing the songs of life in unison. But equally, there is a place for the *different* gifts of men and women to be experienced. If we understand this properly we shall find that it is not divisive, nor does it assume inferiority or superiority. In the recognition and joyful owning of the differences there are actually greater benefits.

A song often leads to a dance. For a man and a woman to dance together there needs to be the reciprocal appreciation of the music. The man leads, the woman follows his lead gladly, and the sight of the two moving in perfect harmony is a delight to the eyes. The great American dancer Fred Astaire once described his art as, 'I just put my feet in the air, and move them around.' The song and dance of life for men and women is to put our trust in God, and to let him move us around *his way*, not ours.

Appendix

Personally speaking

Like many others I have thought a lot about the ordination of women. Dr Johnson once said, 'When a man knows he is to be hanged in two weeks, it concentrates his mind wonderfully.' The thought for many as to whether they could remain members of a Church which ordains women has served to concentrate the mind.

My study of the subject began in 1976 when I wrote a book, which became a best-seller, *Let My People Grow*. It was about ministry and leadership in the Church. Obviously I had to face this matter, because it was relevant to the subject. So I devoted a whole chapter to the *ministry*, not the *ordination*, of women, and I called it 'All the best', after the words of General William Booth, 'All my best men are women.'

The chapter was a celebration of the enormous value and consequence of the ministry of women, and an endorsement of Booth's dictum. For over ten years, my wife and I had pioneered a new style of ministry, the partnership of men and women, we hope exemplified by our own, and the encouragement of women in charismatic ministry. We invited women to share at conferences, and found them particularly able in the field of healing and deliverance. It was they more than the men who opened up the whole area of 'healing of the memories'. Although today I regret some of the things I wrote in that chapter, and have had to revise them in the light of what God has shown me since, nevertheless, it was written with *ministry*, not *ordination*, in mind. In that respect women have always been partners with men in the priesthood of all believers. In that sense women have had a priestly ministry since the day of Pentecost, in some areas more effective than that of men, particularly those of intercession, healing, counselling and prophecy.

It is interesting to note that David Watson was going through a similar time of enquiry into this subject, and I remember discussing it with him. He raised the issue in a book published shortly after *Let My People Grow* called *I Believe in the Church*.[1] In the section on the ministry of women he paid me a great compliment when he called my book 'the best and most balanced view on this subject that I have read'. In his book David was fairly speculative, as I was, but did discuss the issue of ordination. He expressed the view rather tentatively that leadership in the Church was, according to the Word of God, male in terms of the minister or head of a church or diocese (that is, in the Anglican setting, the bishop or vicar) – a view that I have always held.

Memories can play tricks with one after sixteen years, but I can remember some of the background for the thoughts expressed in it. It has to be remembered that it was in 1975 that the General Synod agreed that there were 'no fundamental objections to the ordination of women to the priesthood'. The Church was then asked to study the question (a trifle peculiar after deciding there were no fundamental objections!). This 'study' period lasted for seventeen years, and produced many books and pamphlets for and against. My recollection is that the sheer openness of my chapter on this subject was deliberate in order to be part of the process of reflection, and I have continued to try to follow that attitude ever since.

Let My People Grow was an inadequate source for the subject of the ordination of women because it does not even discuss the two most important issues, 'headship' (*kephale* in the Greek) and the symbolism of a male presbyter or priest representing the male Christ at the Eucharist, which is the main Catholic argument. It was written to encourage the *ministry* of women in general, and their partnership with men in ministry, *not* to address head-on the contentious issue of whether a woman may teach, take authority over men in the Church, or celebrate the Eucharist.

I am ashamed to say that the period 1976–88 for me was one of comparative indifference, certainly not strong feelings on either side. I have never thought women should be ordained, but equally never until the last few years felt strongly they should not.

The change for me came in 1988 when a revised version of *Let My People Grow* was published, this time with a foreword by the then Bishop of Bath and Wells, who is now the Archbishop of Canterbury, George Carey. That marked the end of my period of uncertainty, and from then until April 1992 I became increasingly convinced that the ordination of women was contrary to God's laws of nature, to Scripture, and to Church Tradition. In the case of the Anglican Church, this is the view that has been consistently held from the planting of the Church in Britain long before Augustine came to Canterbury at the end of the sixth century, right up until 1992, when the doctrine was changed. In the case of both the Orthodox and Roman Catholic Churches traditions this view has prevailed for nearly 2,000 years. On 1 April 1992 I wrote to my bishop, the Bishop of Chichester: 'I now feel pretty sure that to go ahead would be wrong . . . and it will have most serious effects on the Church of England . . . my fears won't go away.'

On 11 November 1992 those fears were realised. At the time of writing this book my wife and I do not know what we shall do, whether we shall remain Anglicans or seek membership of another Church. Only God knows the answer to this question for us and all like-minded people.

Notes

Chapter 1

1. *Why Priests?* (Fontana, 1972), p. 72.
2. *Again* magazine, March 1993, p. 7.
3. op. cit., p. 21.
4. *First Things*, April 1993, p. 30.

Chapter 2

1. *Recovering Biblical Manhood and Womanhood* (Crossway Books, 1991), p. 205.
2. Manfred Hauke, *Women in the Priesthood?* (Ignatius Press, San Francisco, 1988); German original *Die Problematik um das Frauenpriestertum vor dem Hintergrund der Schopfungs und Erlösungsordnung* (Verlag Bonifatius-Druckerei, Paderborn, 1986), p. 185.
3. op. cit., p. 185.
4. Hodder & Stoughton, 1993.

Chapter 3

1. *Genesis* (Neukirchen and Vluyn, 1974), p. 316.
2. In Werner Neuer, *Man and Woman in Christian Perspective* (Hodder & Stoughton, 1990). Originally published as *Mann und Frau in Christlicher Sicht* (Giessen and Basle, Brunnen Verlag, 1988), translated by Gordon Wenham, p. 75.
3. Quoted by Werner Neuer, op. cit., p. 75.
4. ibid., p. 76.
5. Quoted by Werner Neuer, op. cit., p. 76.
6. op. cit., pp. 409–410.
7. Werner Neuer, op. cit., p. 80.
8. Op. cit., p. 202.
9. Quoted by Harry Blamires in *Where do we stand?* (Servant Books, 1980), p. 8.
10. Temple Smith, 1977.

11. 13/5/93. In another letter (7/9/93) Dr Fenwick shared about the beard: 'When I came back to Britain from a year in Greece I was forcibly struck how alien and unnatural clean-shaven clergy looked . . . I note that in *Screwtape Letters* (C. S. Lewis), it is Screwtape and the forces of hell which take credit for having persuaded western man to be beardless. This was all part of their plot to confuse sexuality in European society. It is interesting that Lewis, himself a clean-shaven academic, should have seen the force of the argument. Why are the splendidly bearded images of Abraham, Moses, and Father Christmas so powerful? I think there is a lot in there which will bear examination. I note that the new *International Dictionary of the Christian Church* (edited by J. D. Douglas) under its entry for "beards" states that the painter James Ward (1769–1859) wrote a book giving 18 scriptural reasons why man was bound to grow a beard. From a zoological standpoint, no animal would remove its secondary sexual characteristics (the mane of the lion, the horns of the bull, etc.), why do we?'
12. op. cit., pp. 26–27.
13. SPCK, 1984.

Chapter 4

1. op. cit., p. 239.
2. Donald Bloesch here quotes Paul Ricoeur. See *The Battle for the Trinity* (Vine Books, 1985), p. 37.
3. *Man, Woman, Priesthood* (SPCK, 1978), p. 93.
4. *Leadership is Male* (Highland Books, 1988), p. 29.
5. op. cit., p. 210.
6. ibid., p. 211.
7. ibid., p. 212.
8. ibid., p. 213.
9. op. cit., p. 83.
10. ibid., pp. 86–87.
11. *Das Weib im Alten Testament* (Germany, 1920), p. 82.
12. Goldberg, p. 32.
13. ibid., p. 44.
14. ibid., p. 20.
15. ibid., p. 22.
16. ibid., pp. 26–27.
17. ibid., p. 175.
18. ibid., p. 196.

Chapter 5

1. See Hauke, op. cit., p. 327.
2. Quoted by Werner Neuer, op. cit., p. 93.
3. SPCK, 1985, pp. 156, 158.
4. op. cit., p. 38.

5. *Das Amt, der Mann und die Frau im Neuen Testament* in *Signo Crucis*, 1963, pp. 7–24.
6. Servant Books, 1980, pp. 235f.; for subject of culture, see pp. 156–158.
7. Quoted by Hauke, p. 330.

Chapter 6

1. In *Man as male and female* (Eerdmans, 1975), p. 142.
2. March 1991, interview by Russell Twisk and David Moller.
3. *The Church and the Second Sex* (Geoffrey Chapman, 1968), p. 38.
4. op. cit., p. 134.
5. *The Epistle to the Galatians* (Eerdmans, 1982), p. 189.
6. *Latimer Comment*, an occasional paper from Latimer House, Oxford.
7. *Man, Woman, Priesthood* (SPCK, 1978).
8. op. cit., p. 359.
9. op. cit., p. 86.
10. From *Memories & Hopes* (Veritas, Dublin, 1992), p. 59.
11. op. cit., p. 58.
12. ibid., p. 86.
13. January/February 1993, p. 44.

Chapter 7

1. A summary by Paul Jewett (op. cit., p. 81), based on Karl Barth's *Kirchliche Domatik*, III/2, p. 353.
2. op. cit., pp. 180f.
3. Quoted by Paul Jewett, op. cit., p. 80.
4. op. cit., p. 381f., 474f., and summary of thesis, p. 479.
5. op. cit., p. 365.
6. *A Bible Commentary* (ed. C. J. Ellicott), p. 344.
7. *1 Corinthians* in the Tyndale New Testament Commentary series (Tyndale Press, 1958), p. 203.
8. Klaus Thraede, *Frau*, in RAC VIII (Stuttgart, 1972), p. 198.
9. *The Letters of C. S. Lewis to Arthur Greeves* (Collier Books, New York, 1979), p. 427.
10. *Surprised by Joy* (London, 1955), chapter 4.
11. Originally published in the magazine *Time and Tide*, 1948. Reprinted in a book of his essays, *Undeceptions* (London, 1971), p. 191, and published posthumously.
12. Eusebius, *Ecclesiastical History*, Vol. 1, III.28.6.

Chapter 8

1. Piper and Grudem, p. 101.
2. *The Epistle to the Ephesians* (Tyndale Press, 1963), p. 101.

3. *Let me be a woman* (Hodder & Stoughton, 1979), p. 142.
4. Fontana, 1952, p. 99.
5. In *Men and Women: Enjoying the difference* (Zondervan, 1991), p. 105.
6. op. cit., p. 143.
7. Hodder & Stoughton, 1985, p. 194f.
8. ibid., pp. 204f.

Chapter 9

1. Barth, *KD* III 4, p. 192.
2. Quoted from J. Vergote, *Religionspsychologie*, p. 212. See Hauke, p. 133.
3. *Gnosticism as a world religion* (Zurich, 1951), p. 46.
4. The title of an extract from Sheldon Vanauken's book *Under the Mercy*, published in *The Christian Activist*, Spring 1993.
5. *Man, Woman, Priesthood*, p. 21.
6. *Again* magazine, March 1993, pp. 10f.
7. ibid., p. 7.
8. ibid., p. 7.
9. *The Orthodox Church* magazine, September 1975, p. 4.
10. op. cit., p. 188.
11. op. cit., p. 192.
12. *L'Osservatore Romano*, 13 March 1993.
13. *Adversus haereses*, 3:22.
14. 'Epilogue: The Marian stamp of the Church' in *Devotion to Mary Today* (Freiburg, 1977), p. 276.
15. *Christlicher Stand* (Einsiedein: Johannes Verlag, 1967), p. 234.
16. *Frau*, p. 133, quoted in Hauke, op. cit., p. 325.

Chapter 10

1. In a letter to the author from Bishop Bertil Gartner (7/7/93).
2. *Women in the Theological Profession* (Munich, 1969), p. 89.
3. Reported in Mary Daly, *The Church and the Second Sex*, p. 111.
4. *Women in the priesthood?*, quoted by Hauke, op. cit., p. 22.
5. ibid., p. 81.
6. *Man, Woman, Priesthood* (SPCK, 1978), p. 75.
7. *KD* III/1, pp. 348–350.
8. op. cit., p. 417.
9. *The Synod Debate* (Church House Publishing, 1993), p. 23.
10. op. cit., p. 143.
11. *The Clergy Review*, April 1983, p. 127.
12. *Under the Mercy*, p. 178.

Chapter 11

1. op. cit., pp. 80–81.
2. See Hauke's reference to H. J. Vogels, p. 392.
3. *History of the Church in relation to the history of ideas* (Munster, 1962), p. 85.
4. See Hauke, op. cit., p. 405, footnote 5.
5. op. cit., p. 165.
6. *De praescriptione haereticorum*, 41.
7. *Pistis Sophia*, an ancient Gnostic writing.
8. *De virginibus velandis*.
9. *Adversus haereses*, I:13.
10. ibid., 49:2.
11. op. cit., 408.
12. *Diaskalia*, III, 9, 1.
13. *Adversus haereses*, 78:13.
14. *De sacerdotio*, 2, 2.
15. *Again* magazine, March 1993, p. 7.
16. *In Lucam* II, 28.
17. Said by Jerome, *Epistula* 127, 9–10.

Chapter 12

1. Part 2, Chapter 7, pp. 445–468.
2. Quoted by Hauke, op. cit., p. 447.
3. op. cit., p. 447.
4. Gisbert Kranz, *Challenged by their times: The lives of six women* (Regensburg, 1976), p. 33. Ignaz Dollinger also cited in Kranz, p. 33.
5. *The Subversive Family* (Jonathan Cape, 1982), pp. 224–225.
6. Quoted in Adrian Schenker's *Life of St. Catherine of Siena* (Dusseldorf, 1965), p. 99.
7. Quoted by Hauke, op. cit., p. 465.
8. ibid., p. 465.
9. *Again* magazine, March 1993, p. 10.
10. Werner Neuer, op. cit., p. 135.
11. ibid., p. 24.

Chapter 13

1. *The War against the Family* (Stoddart, Toronto, 1992), p. 51.
2. *The origin of the family, private property and the state* (Stuttgart, 1919), p. 62.
3. op. cit., p. 74.

Chapter 14

1. Published by the University Press of America (1989) and edited by Nicholas Davidson.

2. *Calgary Sun*, 22/1/93.
3. op. cit., p. 312.
4. Quoted in the same book, p. 313.
5. ibid., p. 321.
6. Sinclair-Stevenson, 1992.
7. Boxtree, 1993.
8. 4/8/93.
9. Quoted by William Gairdner, op. cit., p. 308.
10. op. cit., p. 308.
11. *Daily Mail*, 7/3/93.
12. Quoted by George Gilder in *Men and Marriage* (Gretna, Pelican Publishing, USA, 1986), p. 77.
13. op. cit., p. 118.
14. Quoted by Hauke, op. cit., p. 32.
15. 30/10/90.
16. Quoted by Hauke, op. cit., p. 38.
17. Mandala, 1991 (ed. Alix Pirani).
18. Women's Press, 1986, p. 96.
19. Ignatius Press, San Francisco, 1991.
20. 15/1/93.
21. 20/11/92.
22. Quoted by Hauke, op. cit., p. 42.
23. 13/11/92.
24. op. cit., p. 109.
25. op. cit., p. 330.
26. *Under the Mercy*, pp. 179f.
27. ibid., pp. 201f.

Chapter 15

1. From *William Temple*, by F. A. Iremonger (OUP, 1948), p. 108.
2. ibid., p. 488.
3. ibid., p. 452.
4. Quoted in a letter by Anthony Lane, *Church Times*, 26/2/93.
5. In a Foreword to *Where do we stand?* by Harry Blamires, op. cit., p. vii.
6. Quoted by William Gairdner, op. cit., p. 297.
7. ibid., pp. 297–298.
8. Quoted by Hauke, op. cit., p. 32.
9. Nils Johansson in *Women and the Church's Ministry* (Ottawa, 1972), p. 10.
10. See Hauke, op. cit., p. 474 and footnote 3.
11. *First Things*, April 1993, p. 27.
12. *Under the Mercy*, p. 178.
13. op. cit., p. 156.
14. Hauke, op. cit., p. 53.
15. ibid., p. 153.

16. ibid., p. 153.
17. *Women towards Priesthood* (CUP, 1991).
18. ibid., p. 233.
19. ibid., pp. 246–261, where the author gives a critique of the book.
20. *Man, Woman, Priesthood*, p. 15.
21. Mr Monty Francis, 21/7/93.
22. *The Ordination of Women: the Archbishop of Canterbury's Correspondence with the Vatican* (CIO, 1986), p. 8.

Chapter 16

1. *Sunday Telegraph*, 1/8/93.
2. *Man, Woman, Priesthood*, p. 11.
3. From Goldberg, op. cit., p. 35.
4. *Man, Woman, Priesthood*, p. 74.

Chapter 17

1. *Beyond God the Father* (Women's Press, 1986), p. 19.
2. *The Orthodox Church* (Penguin, 1963), p. 216.
3. ibid., p. 216.
4. ibid., p. 219.
5. ibid., p. 219.
6. *Man, Woman, Priesthood*, pp. 84–85.
7. op. cit., p. 185.
8. *Life Giving Spirit* (SPCK, 1989).
9. SCM, 1981.
10. ibid., p. 70.
11. *God does not only have strong sons: fundamentals of a feminist theology* (Gutersloh, 1980), p. 297.
12. op. cit., p. 33.
13. February 1993.
14. ibid.
15. 3/3/93.
16. Ignatius Press, 1991, p. 23.
17. 20/11/92.
18. *Church Times*, 4/12/93.

Chapter 18

1. 6/3/89. A letter of mine responding to this article was published in *The Times*. In it I wrote: 'History is not on the side of the bishops. It has shown that the State cannot possibly be an extended family. Many countries have tried it and failed. It leads inevitably to corruption, oppression, inefficiency

and the waste of resources. In the long term it has the opposite effect to that intended' (18/3/89).

2. Women's Press, 1979, p. 75.
3. Granada edn., 1971, p. 221.
4. Quoted by Ferdinand Mount in *The Subversive Family* (Jonathan Cape, 1982), p. 10.
5. ibid., p. 153.
6. op. cit., pp. 104–105.
7. ibid., p. 105.
8. 22/9/93.
9. 20/4/93.
10. SCM Press, 1963, p. 108.
11. 11/7/93.
12. 26/9/93.
13. *Again*, op. cit., 11.
14. 6/7/93.
15. IEA Health and Welfare Unit, 1992.
16. *Daily Telegraph*, 23/5/93.
17. op. cit., p. 117.
18. op. cit., p. 118.
19. *Credo*, 28/08/93.
20. ibid.
21. Kingsway, 1988.
22. *The Absent Father: Crisis and Creativity* (Arkana, 1989), pp. xi–xii.
23. ibid., p. 118.
24. *Male and female* (London, 1949), p. 184.
25. *Sexual Suicide* (London, 1974), p. 18.
26. Report in *The Times*, 3/11/93.

Chapter 19

1. op. cit., p. 147.
2. *Daily Mail*, 7/3/93.
3. 21/3/93.
4. Written 28/6/93, from the Human Rights Policy Department.
5. *New York Times*, 10/2/91.
6. *Child Neglect in Rich Nations* (UNICEF, 1993), reported in *The Times*, 27/9/93.
7. op. cit., p. 113.
8. The title of chapter 15 of William Gairdner's book. Op. cit., pp. 415–473.
9. February 1991.
10. Wendy Dreskin, quoted by William Gairdner, op. cit., p. 338.
11. *Hansard*, 23/6/93. Lady Maitland was moving the Young Offenders (Detention) Bill.
12. *The Times*, 4/11/93.
13. *The Times*, 27/9/93.

Chapter 20

1. p. 18, published privately, and quoted with permission.
2. HarperCollins, 1993.
3. *Concerning Women's Ordination* in Karl Lutge's *Sexuality, Theology, Priesthood* (San Gabriel), pp. 12–13.
4. *The Orthodox Church* magazine, November 1976, p. 5.
5. *Man, Woman, Priesthood*, p. 69.
6. Quoted by Hauke, op. cit., p. 50.
7. Quoted by Hauke, op. cit., p. 51, footnote 20.
8. Quoted in *Metropolitan Philip, his life and dreams* (Nelson, 1991), by Peter Gillquist, p. 165. The biography of Archbishop Philip Saliba, Metropolitan of the Archdiocese of North America, of the Antiochian Orthodox Church.
9. The Lambeth Conference 1988 (ACC, 1988), p. 287.

Chapter 21

1. *Fernseeds and Elephants* (Collins, 1975).
2. Hodder & Stoughton, 1979.
3. 16/7/93.
4. *First Things*, p. 25.
5. *Under the Mercy*, p. 205.

Chapter 22

1. An edition of the play edited and introduced by Arthur Miller, Nick Hen Books, 1989, p. 94.
2. *Memories and Hopes*, op. cit., p. 165.
3. op. cit., p. ix.

Appendix

1. Hodder & Stoughton, 1978, pp. 245f.

Bibliography

This is by no means a comprehensive list of books, but includes those which the author has relied on most fully. There are many books on the subjects covered by this book, so one is bound to be selective.

1. General books on the theology of sexual equality and order

Baumert, Norbert, *Frau und Mann bei Paulus*, Echter, 1991.*
Clark, Stephen, *Man and Woman in Christ*, Servant Books, 1980.
Daly, Mary, *The Church and the Second Sex*, Geoffrey Chapman, 1968.
Daly, Mary, *Beyond God the Father*, Women's Press, 1986.
Field-Bibb, Jacqueline, *Women towards priesthood*, CUP, 1991.
Hauke, Manfred, *Women in the priesthood?*, Ignatius Press, 1988.
Moore, Peter, ed., *Man, Woman, Priesthood*, SPCK, 1978.
Jewett, Paul, *Man as Male and Female*, Eerdmans, 1975.
Neuer, Werner, *Man and Woman in Christian Perspective*, Hodder & Stoughton, 1990.
Oddie, William, *What will happen to God?*, SPCK, 1984.
Ovey, M. & P. Walker, *Distinctive Roles for Men and Women*, published privately.
Pawson, David, *Leadership is Male*, Highland Books, 1988.
Piper, J. & W. Grudem, *Recovering Biblical Manhood and Womanhood*, Crossway, 1991.
Synod Debate, *Ordination of Women to the Priesthood*, Church House, 1993.
Wenham, Gordon, 'Ordination of women, why is it so divisive?', *Churchman*, Vol. 92/4, 1978.

*The English translation of this book was being prepared as I finished mine. Not being able to read German meant I was unable to make use of it. I am grateful to the author, a German Jesuit, for sending me the first few chapters of the English translation, but sadly they do not refer to the passages I have covered.

2. Feminism

Beauvoir, Simone de, *The Second Sex*, London, 1962.

Davidson, Nicholas, ed., *Gender Sanity*, University Press of America, 1989.

Firestone, Shulamith, *Dialectic of Sex*, Women's Press, 1979.

Friedan, Betty, *Feminine Mystique*, Gollancz, 1963.

Friedan, Betty, *The Second Stage*, Abacus, 1983.

Greenstein, Ben, *The Fragile Man*, Boxtree, 1993.

Greer, Germaine, *The Female Eunuch*, Grafton, 1970.

Greer, Germaine, *Sex and Destiny*, Picador, 1985.

Lyndon, Neil, *No more Sex War*, Sinclair-Stevenson, 1992.

Millett, Kate, *Sexual Politics*, London, 1972.

Scanzoni, Letha and Nancy Hardesty, *All we're Meant to be*, Word Books, 1974.

Steichen, Donna, *Ungodly Rage*, Ignatius Press, 1991.

Storkey, Elaine, *What's Right with Feminism*, SPCK, 1985.

3. General theology

Moltmann, Jürgen, *The Trinity and the Kingdom of God*, SCM, 1981.

Ware, Bishop Kallistos, *The Orthodox Church*, Penguin, 1963.

4. The family

Dennis, Norman and George Erdos, *Families without Fatherhood*, IEA, Health and Welfare Unit, 1992.

Gairdner, William, *The War on the Family*, Stoddart, 1992.

Goldberg, Steven, *The inevitability of Patriarchy*, Temple Smith, 1977.

Mount, Ferdinand, *The Subversive Family*, Jonathan Cape, 1982.

Pytches, Mary, *A Father's Place*, Hodder & Stoughton, 1993.

5. Human sexuality and marriage

Elliot, Elisabeth, *Let me be a Woman*, Hodder & Stoughton, 1979.
Gilder, George, *Men and Marriage*, Pelican, USA, 1986.
Gilder, George, *Sexual Suicide*, London, 1974.
Mead, Margaret, *Male and Female*, London, 1949.
Payne, Leanne, *Crisis in Masculinity*, Kingsway, 1988.
Pirani, Alix, *The Absent Father*, Arkana, 1989.
Pirani, Alix, *The Absent Mother*, Mandala, 1991.

6. Inclusive language

Bloesch, Donald G., *The Battle for the Trinity*, Servant Books, 1985.
Lewis, Alan, ed., *Motherhood of God*, St Andrew Press, 1984.
Marriage, A., *Life Giving Spirit*, SPCK, 1989.
Miller and Swift, *Handbook of Non-Sexist Writings*, Women's Press, 1981.

7. General

Blamires, Harry, *Where do we Stand?*, Servant Books, 1980.
Bloom, Allan, *Closing of the American Mind*, Simon & Schuster, 1987.
Green, David, *Equalising People*, IEA, 1990.
Hamilton-Dalrymple, W., *City of Djinns, a Year in Delhi*, Harper-Collins, 1993.
Iremonger, F. A., *William Temple*, OUP, 1948.
Lewis, C. S., *Undeceptions*, London, 1971.
Lewis, C. S., *Fernseeds and Elephants*, Collins, 1975.
Suenens, Cardinal, *Memories and Hopes*, Veritas, 1992.
Vanauken, Sheldon, *Under the Mercy*, Hodder & Stoughton, 1985 (especially chapter VIII).

Scripture index

Name index

Subject Index

The pages in italics are where the subject has a fuller treatment.

'I thought you'd killed my son,' Hec Ridgeway said.

'But I hadn't. So you go your way and I'll ride on with the only person I can trust.'

There were no goodbyes. The Red Hammer riders were the first to leave, Charlie Grisham leading the way on his palomino, cutting an easterly trail that would take them south of Fetterman's Pool and on to their own range land. A chastened Hec Ridgeway went south, leading the Broken Arrow crew, men with whom Jim had worked but who parted from him like strangers. Only young Dean Ridgeway, his head swathed in a fresh bandage, raised a hand as he passed the place where Jim and Waktaya stood.

'I've decided,' Jim said, picking his words with caution, unsure how the fiery Sioux woman would react to what he proposed, 'that when you go back to Pine Ridge I'll go with you. It'll be safer that way.'

'And if I choose not to return to the reservation?'

Jim looked at her questioningly. He wasn't sure where else she could go but a kind of serenity had settled on the girl and he was loath to destroy it. Even though he had no clear idea of what the future held for him he was aware that his life and Waktaya's were now inextricably linked.

'Then I'll take you wherever you feel most safe. Where you go, I'll go.'

The doubt she had once had for her grandfather's final words had long since disappeared. When Jim Braddock had pushed himself between her and the soldier's bayonet point, she had known that her future home would be with him.

'I feel safe with you,' she said. 'Where you stay, I will stay.'